Legend Who Died Young

Legend Who Died Young

By MAGNUS NYSTRÖM

First published in English in August 2006 by
Retro Speedway
Tel: 01708 734 502
www.retro-speedway.com

First published in Sweden by Sportforlaget in 2005 under the title of:
Utan bromsar – Tommy Jansson: legend som dog ung

Printed by Biddles Ltd, King's Lynn, Norfolk

Distributed by Retro Speedway
103 Douglas Road, Hornchurch, Essex, RM11 1AW, England
Email: editorial@retro-speedway.com

Set in Times Roman

ISBN 0-9551176-5-8

Cover photography by Mike Patrick & Alf Weedon/Retro Speedway

The views expressed in this book are those of Magnus Nystrom
and not necessarily those of the publisher.

To
Joel and Inga-Lill Jansson and to Bosse Jansson.

Above: A common sight in the early 70s – Tommy leading for Smederna at home against Getingarna in the Swedish League. This action shot was used on the front cover of the original *Utan Bromsar* book.
Below: Classic Tommy, powering out of the corner at Wimbledon, front wheel slightly off the ground.

Contents

Acknowledgements

Thanks must go to the following people, for many different reasons:

First and foremost to the Jansson family: Joel, Inga-Lill and Bosse. I'm proud to say that we have become great friends.

Then to my own family: Kristina and Frida.

Other people who played an important part by supporting me include:
My parents, Thomas Nilsson, Kjell Lovén, Peter Lindgren, Sven Gustavsson, Katrin Säfström, Anders Åberg and Ulf Claesson.

In Britain, I'm more than grateful to my editor, Tony McDonald. And to Shannon Ruane, Sandra and Dave Dixson, Mike Patrick and Ian Perkin.

Of course, without the great photos taken by Mike Patrick, Alf Weedon, Lennart Nyström, Sören Lindell, Lasse Widegren, Björn Zetterwall and Mikael Johnsson, this would have been a totally different book.

Many thanks to all of the following who gave interviews for this book, some of whom spent hours in my company answering hundreds of questions:
Joel Jansson, Inga-Lill Jansson, Bosse Jansson, Anders Michanek, Ole Olsen, Eva-Lotta Jonsson, Göte Nordin, Lennart Rytterström, Percy Lundkvist, Kenneth Swedin, Lars Jansson, Bengt Jansson, Olle Nygren, Sven-Olof Lindh, Bernt Persson, Scott Autrey, Gavin Elms, Shannon Ruane and Gunnar Arnold.

Thanks also to all the reporters at newspapers in Sweden and England who covered Tommy Jansson during his career. I spent countless hours reading articles and books from that time. Mainly Speedway Star and books by Ivan Mauger, Barry Briggs, Ole Olsen, Dave Lanning and Martin Rogers. But also many other publications, including magazines and programmes. Backtrack magazine and recently published books by Ian Perkin and John Berry have also been a great source of information.

And finally, thanks to Marios Flourentzou for designing the cover.

Introduction

Joel Jansson is a tough but very straightforward man. His philosophy is: 'Whatever you do in life, make sure to do it as well as you can, to the best of your ability.'

As the top rider and then as team manager at Swedish League team Smederna he treated everybody the same. and was never afraid to confront anybody who wasn't ready to do his best.

When his own son, Tommy Jansson, didn't listen to him during a practice session, and another rider had a flat tyre, Joel simply removed a wheel from Tommy's bike himself and gave it to the rider concerned.

When Tommy complained, Joel shut him up by saying: "I told you to take it easy. You didn't listen."

Another time Tommy and fellow Swedish superstar Bengt Jansson were riding together for Smederna, and Tommy forgot to team-ride, which cost Smederna important points. Back in the pits, a furious Joel told him. "That's not the way to ride if you're a professional."

Joel was never afraid to speak his mind.

Of all speedway riders, only a select few can become World Champion. But everyone on every level can do their absolute best to reach their own potential.

'If you aren't willing to give it your best shot, just give it up, don't bother, do something else' – that's the way Joel Jansson sees it.

I couldn't agree more.

But knowing this about the man, I was a little nervous when I knocked on Joel's door at home in Eskilstuna in the autumn of 2004. He opened the door, I introduced myself and told him why I was there.

"I want to write a book about your son, Tommy."

Later he admitted to me that he had been very sceptical at first. When Tommy was at his peak I was just a kid and I never actually saw him race.

So a book, about Tommy, 29 years after his tragic death?

Joel questioned me: "Is there really a market for a book like that?" And, more pertinently: "Can you do it?"

Our first meeting lasted three hours. After that he understood that I was going to do this book the Jansson way – as well as I possibly could.

I used my experience of almost 20 years in journalism to prepare my research and interview around 20 people close to Tommy, as well as reading hundreds of articles from Swedish and British publications. I was given unique access by the Jansson family to read Tommy's own diaries. I also watched TV and video footage of his races, travelled to England to meet his old friends and, finally, attended a speedway meeting at the historic Wimbledon Stadium, where Tommy was a superstar in the early 70s.

I was going to do all I could to make this book worthy of Tommy's memory.

The book was originally published in Sweden in the summer of 2005 – with the title of Utan Bromsar which, translated into English, means No Brakes – and the reception from fans and critics has been all positive.

But nothing was more satisfying for me than when Joel read the first chapters and said: "It's like you were there the whole time. You have done a fantastic job."

For me it was important. Tommy Jansson was a fantastic speedway rider and a great person.

He deserved a book all about him to be written the Jansson way.

The worst thing in life must be losing your own child.

As a proud parent of a wonderful daughter, I can't even try to imagine the horror and heartbreak that engulfed Joel and Inga-Lill Jansson on the night of Thursday, May 20, 1976.

That night their youngest of two sons, Tommy, went out on a speedway track full of hope and dreams of the future. He was a very good-looking 23-year-old with an excellent chance of becoming the best in world in his chosen profession.

Instead, everything changed forever that night, when Tommy died as a result of a crash in Stockholm.

I started writing his story 29 years after that fatal night and during the course of my work on this book, Joel, Inga-Lill and myself were going to spend numerous days in each other's company. Nothing in my professional life has made me more proud than their support for this book.

For them, this title is another way of perpetuating the memory of their deceased son forever.

But even though Tommy's life ended so tragically, they wanted it to be a positive story. They wanted it to include all the good times and all the great memories.

And that's exactly how I wanted it to be as well.

During one race in Eskilstuna last year, a man unknown to me approached me and said: "Magnus, I just want to thank you for doing the book about Tommy. You made me both laugh and cry."

Praise like that is, of course, rewarding after all the hard work involved in writing a book of this nature. The thrill of hearing people talk about it, and making comments about different aspects of the book, is always a joy.

But something even more amazing than that was when speedway fans from Britain bought the book – yes, the Swedish edition!

I received many emails from Brits thanking me for Utan Bromsar, telling me their own memories of Tommy and praising the book – even though they could barely understand a word of the story!

To Joel, a book about Tommy in Swedish was something that he hadn't imagined would happen.

For me, an English edition meant the same thing.

But all those fans who sent emails made me understand differently – and no-one more than Shannon Ruane. Her part in the book is significant, because it describes so well how important sports heroes can be to other people. And without Shannon, who gave up her time as well as the loan of a number of personal Tommy Jansson mementoes, the book would not have turned out the way it did. It's probably fair to say that without her, it would never have made it into English.

Without Shannon's support and encouragement I would never have contacted Tony McDonald at Retro Speedway. He loved the idea of a translated edition from the start and said his company wanted to publish the book in English before he'd even read the first chapter!

This UK edition has been edited to include more of Tommy's racing experiences during his all too brief time in Britain. It also contains many additional black and white photographs that didn't appear in the original hardback published in Sweden, plus the offbeat illustrations supplied by supporter Shannon Ruane from her scrapbooks of Tommy.

Like the Janssons, I'm from Eskilstuna myself, where I grew up close to the old track in my home-town and started attending meetings there the year after Tommy's accident. I know how important the sport and the Smederna team have been for Eskilstuna over the years. In this summer of 2006, Tommy also got received further recognition when, on the 30th anniversary of his death, the road leading from the highway to the new track in Eskilstuna was named Tommy Janssons väg (Tommy Jansson's Road).

I wrote this book because it was the book I wanted to read myself.

I did it because Tommy Jansson deserves it.

I also did it for the love of the sport and for the pride of my home-town and because it's always important to be reminded that you can be successful – even if you're just a small town kid from Eskilstuna, Sweden.

Great things can happen – if you only give it your best shot.

MAGNUS NYSTRÖM
Stockholm, July 2006

Joel and Inga-Lill Jansson with author
Magnus Nystrom at the launch of the
Swedish edition of *Utan Bromsar* in 2005.

Prologue
National hero

"If I'm going to win, I want to have a maximum. I want to show everybody that I'm the best and win all my races. That's the way you become a real champion."

Tommy Jansson, before the Swedish Championship Final in 1974

ANDERS Michanek was a little scared before the Swedish Championship and his mood was all thanks to Tommy Jansson. It was quite an achievement for a 21-year-old newcomer to evoke fear in a world champion.

In September 1974, Anders Michanek, nine years older than Tommy, had proved that he was the best speedway rider in the world by winning the individual World Final in front of 38,390 spectators at the Ullevi Stadium in Gothenburg.

Michanek had never ridden better.

Despite his brilliant form, he had been more confident of winning the World Championship than of triumphing in the Swedish national championship. When he prepared himself that morning at home in Stockholm, before the trip to Eskilstuna on Friday the 20th, it struck him how often a speedway rider is away from home.

In Eskilstuna nobody was interested in celebrating the new World Champion. There, everyone wanted Tommy – the kid who could attract close to 1,000 spectators when his Smederna team held their practice sessions – to win.

Anders Michanek had a different view of things. If there is something a champion is good at, it is recognising a future champion.

Michanek could intimidate many of his rivals. He could be totally ruthless on the track and even force his own team-mates towards or into the fence. Many gave way when Michanek came thundering underneath them, or turned off the gas and let him pass. Tommy Jansson did neither. Not even after having felt an unfriendly greeting in the form of Michanek's elbow in one of their early meetings.

Nothing scared the young talent, so wily, old Michanek had been impressed with him from the first moment.

He was certain that, one day, he would have to hand over his title of Swedish speedy king to this special lad from Eskilstuna.

Another quality the World Champion had discovered in Tommy was his impatience, a quality which characterises the best in most walks of life.

Tommy didn't want to wait long for success. He used to say that he saw himself racing for another 10 or 15 years, that a speedway rider usually reaches his peak in his thirties and that his time would come.

But this statement was not really true – it was simply his 'official' line. Tommy had learned how to say the right words, to be a good diplomatic. Deep inside, he was very eager. He wanted to win from Day One.

The day before the national final, he told reporters: "Anders Michanek will win the gold in the Swedish Championship."

Tommy lied.

He didn't think for one minute that the new world No.1 would repeat his success from Ullevi, where he won the title with a maximum, by becoming Swedish champion two weeks later.

Anders Michanek was the people`s favourite to win. There were many other world class riders in the Swedish final – Bengt Jansson, Christer Löfqvist and Tommy Johansson (all three had raced in the Gothenburg World Final), plus Bernt Persson and Hasse 'Manolito' Holmqvist. Many of them appreciated the long, fast track in Eskilstuna.

The advantage of racing at your home track is not as significant as one might believe when it comes to a national final. One single machine failure or tape exclusion inevitably means the end of your title dream.

Tommy was not only the least experienced rider in the line-up but also the youngest in the starting field. It was close to a month before his 22nd birthday, while most of the other riders were in their thirties. Many of them had enjoyed fine international careers and had spent a number of years racing as professionals in England behind them.

No-one could demand victory from Tommy Jansson.

Nobody did. With one exception – Tommy himself.

In his eyes, Anders Michanek would not become the indisputable King of Speedway in 1974. Tommy had decided to put an end the domination of the world's best speedway rider. Tommy would win. To him, nothing else mattered.

Given his great determination, he was feeling very energetic when he got out of bed on the morning of the meeting. Tommy left his room in his parents home – a three-roomed apartment at Törnerosgatan – and went down to his workshop in the garage of the apartment block to work on his bike.

The night before, Tommy had competed for Sweden in an international match against the Soviet Union at the Gubbängen track in Stockholm.

Always strikingly handsome, Tommy had a wry look on his face in the team picture taken right after that event.

There were two reasons for that facial expression. One was that his bike had not worked perfectly. The engine had kept going wrong and the only time he won a heat was when he borrowed a bike from Bengt Jansson. And despite a Swedish victory,

Tommy was dissatisfied because he had only scored eight points himself.

The other reason for his disappointment was his frequent visits to the toilet. Ever since a trip to Poland, his stomach had been upset. He was in pain and his health hadn't improved fast enough for his liking. So, because of that, he was not feeling hungry that morning either.

His mother, Inga-Lill, prepared breakfast but Tommy ate only a little. He did, however, accept the choal pills offered to him.

"This is probably the best thing for me right now, I'm not feeling well," he said.

"Choal pills are good, " said his mother convincingly.

"For the stomach, yes, but I wonder what will make the bike go better," Tommy muttered to himself.

"What are you going to do about it?" Tommy's father, Joel, wondered.

He had been together with Tommy in the garage the night before and seen the state of the engine.

"Kenneth will be here soon and we'll dismantle the whole bike into pieces. I have to do that, it's my only chance. I have to do it even though I won't have time to test the bike before the meeting tonight," added Tommy.

All three were feeling nervous before the rapidly approaching final. Tommy, because the bike was not in order. His dad Joel, because he wanted everything to be perfect. As the team leader of the local Smederna club, he was the one who had worked the hardest to bring the individual Swedish Championship final to Eskilstuna. He was the one in charge of the meeting and was responsible for the show.

Inga-Lill was always nervous before meetings. She had felt butterflies in her stomach during Joel's time as a rider and now she felt them again whenever her sons, Tommy and Bosse, competed on the track.

She was afraid that they would crash and hurt themselves.

At the same time she was, of course, proud of her sons and she didn't even dare to think how wonderful it would be to see Tommy become Swedish Champion at his home-town track. She tried to forget her nerves by nagging at Tommy and Joel about their clothes – the smart suits they should wear at the banquet to follow the speedway meeting later that evening.

"I have put your clothes out ready for you," she said.

Mechanic Kenneth Swedin gets ready for work...

The Jansson family always had a nice appearance and this was all thanks to Inga-Lill. She had worked at a clothes store for several years and always wanted her men to be stylish and well-dressed.

"You are famous in this town, so you can't dress sloppily," she had told them, and Tommy had several times heard her say: ". . . there are clothes to wear other than old jeans with oil patches."

Joel and Tommy promised to put on what she had chosen for them, even if Joel had his mind on the coming event and Tommy on his bike – and he needed to go to the toilet again.

At the same time, when mechanic, Kenneth Swedin, rang the door bell at the Jansson's residence, the local radio station broadcast the first message to people urging them not to take their car to the local track, Motorstadion. The host club Smederna were expecting 8,000 spectators, which would mean a new record attendance.

Kenneth was one of few who really thought that Tommy would become champion that day. He had worked with Tommy for three years and had seen the determination he had. When Kenneth looked at other riders' gear, he saw tools and engine parts in one big mess. Tommy demanded perfect preparation, everything should be in its correct place. Nothing could be left out of order.

"Tonight we win. Tonight you will be a Swedish champion," Kenneth said when they came down to the garage.

The room smelt of oil and lubricate, the walls were covered with posters advertising past meetings – many that Tommy had participated in and also a few from Joel's racing days. Laurel wreaths were put up and neatly arranged above the workbench. Some belonged to Joel, others to Tommy. There was plenty of room for more.

"This can be a good night, if we can just get this thing to work, " said Tommy with a resolute face.

They had been back in the garage only a few hours since they were last there, following the meeting in Stockholm the night before. Kenneth had been with Tommy at Gubbangen but they were back home in Eskilstuna at around eleven o'clock that night, starting to take the bike apart.

Kenneth could see that Tommy was nervous – he had learned to read the signs. When Tommy was quieter than usual, more concentrated and focused while working on the bike, Kenneth knew Tommy was ready for action, really up for it.

Even Kenneth was nervous and he tried to calm himself by giving his pep-talk to Tommy.

"You´ll win tonight. You're going for gold. You'll do it," he said over and over again during that day in the garage.

Tommy smiled.

"If I'm going to win, I want to score a 15-point maximum. Then I'll really have shown everyone that I'm the best. I want to win all my five heats, because that's when you can call yourself a real champion. That's when you really have beaten everybody else.

"But you can become a champion without a maximum," said Kenneth.

"Yes, but then you have to hope that somebody else is making mistakes. No, that's not how I wanna win. And if you haven't won all your races, it means somebody has beaten you, so you've not been the best."

Kenneth never stopped being impressed by his employer's burning desire to win. Tommy couldn't accept compromise.

During his years working with Tommy, Kenneth had seen the typical Swedish speedway rider – a young man from a small town whose first goal was not to become a champion, but simply to escape boring, everyday life. For them, racing was a very nice break from the daily seven-to-four routine.

Only a few riders wanted much more.

Tommy Jansson could be very egotistic and only think about himself. He could be brazen and ruthless.

On the track, that is.

The same demands he made on himself, he applied to others. Like during a meeting with Smederna, when Tommy noticed that a team-mate had problems with his bike. Tommy walked over to him in the pits and checked the bike.

"Adjust the throttle a little bit – like this, " he helpfully suggested.

In his next race, the team-mate rode as badly as he had before and a puzzled Tommy went over to him and checked his bike again. He wanted to help – but then he realised that his team-mate hadn't listened to any of his advice or made any adjustment to his throttle.

Tommy turned his back on his own team-mate and never spoke to him again.

Tommy's brother, Bosse, always listened to good advice.

But even he had to learn the hard way sometimes. Like when Smederna had a tough race against Bysarna at their track on the island of Gotland. Bosse had one of the best nights of his career and in the final race of the evening, the Jansson brothers were racing together against a pair from Bysarna.

Bosse had held the lead from the start until the final lap. Smederna had already won the match. It was Bosse's night – or at least that's what he thought. But just before the finish line, Tommy passed him and won the race instead.

Beaten by his little brother just seconds before the checkered flag. Bosse was furious and close to tears. He wasn't even a regular in the Smederna team, while Tommy was the big star. A victory like this was merely a nice ending to another good night for Tommy.

For Bosse it would have been a highlight in his career.

"Why couldn't you let me win?" an irate Bosse shouted at his brother.

"It looks better with only threes against your points tally," replied Tommy, referring to the five heat wins he'd accumulated on his way to completing a selfish maximum at his brother's expense.

Two hours before the Swedish Championship was about to begin Bosse arrived at Motorstadion. He was there to sell programmes. Joel was there, of course. Outside the gates there were already long queues of people waiting to get in. Most of the riders were already there as well but Tommy and Kenneth were still in the garage in the basement at Tornerosgatan.

Joel had a meeting with dignitaries and other officials working at the meeting. This was going to be a great event. Nothing could go wrong. The track was in great shape. Normally the surface consisted of sand and gravel transported from an old country road outside of town. Tonight it was topped with red brickflour, from a nearby brickyard. The wooden fence was scrubbed clean and shining white.

An hour-and-a-half before the first race thousands of fans packed together in the wooden stands and climbed up the natural grass bank around the track. The first bikes roared into life.

The track in Eskilstuna – known simply as Motorstadion – was in the centre of town, a goalkick away from the Tunavallen football stadium, a venue for one football match in the World Cup finals tournament of 1958. The neighbourhood was called Grangärdet and close by the track, the soccer stadium and the woods there was also a zoo. The track was built in a natural valley within the woodland.

Along the start there was a stand, with simple wooden benches. Over on the opposite side was a stand that Smederna had acquired from another stadium in town. Opposite the pits was the best place to watch the races – the hill beside the first bend, which provided a perfect view of the track. Sitting there in the shadows of the pinetrees, fans were packing up picnic baskets. Out came thermosflasks of coffee and beer.

Bosse was feeling hot coping with the great demand for programmes.

Joel's only thought was: 'Nothing can go wrong now, everything is in order.'

Inga-Lill spoke warmly with everybody she met, even if she just wanted to hide somewhere. That's how nervous she was about the racing.

The crowd just grew. After all, it wasn't every day you could have this much fun in Eskilstuna. The best football team in town – IFK Eskilstuna – was in the middle of the second division table and only 916 spectators turned up for their last game, a boring 1-1-draw against Sandviken.

A few days later Smederna's reserve speedway team rode a match in front of 500 people. The club's practice sessions drew around 1,000 fans to the track.

Eskilstuna was a speedway town, because, locally, there wasn't much else to rave about. At the end of the summer the escalating street crime was once again in focus and what people talked about most. When speedway rider Gote Nordin came to Smederna, he instantly described the city as an overgrown village and that was the case. Eskilstuna was a smaller version of, say, Sheffield, a rough and tough town of factories and blue collar jobs.

At the time, police were chasing a rapist who had attacked several women. He had raped one, threatening her with a knife, and he had attacked others – one girl had only managed to escape when her dog chased the fiend away.

To get away from reality for a while was an opportunity most people in town cherished.

At cinemas you could see some of the most talked about films of the year: Magnum Force, with Clint Eastwood, and The Sting, starring Robert Redford and

Paul Newman. It was also possible to go to cinemas in town and watch porno movies. One of the most popular in the genre was a Danish movie called The Sign of the Bull. According to the advertising, it was "a porno-party with loads of delicious ladies".

Porn still had a big place in Swedish society. It was considered normal to go and see these adult films and the local newspapers even reviewed them. The Sign of the Bull received the following write-up in the Folket newspaper: "...if anything positive is to be said about this movie, it's that the actors do their work in a good mood and they seem to have fun. And some of that happiness transmits itself to the viewers."

No wonder people in town longed for some fun. It was great that Eskilstuna had Smederna and that Tommy Jansson was a boy from town. He gave them someone and something to be proud of.

In 1973, Smederna had won the Swedish League Championship for the first time. Now it was Tommy's turn to become a champion in his own right.

"I think we'll get more than 8,000 spectators in here tonight," some of the fans told Joel, realising that it was an extremely good number for a speedway meeting in Sweden. Joel just nodded his head, knowing a record crowd would turn out. But he wasn't totally relaxed. He knew it wouldn't take much for something to go wrong. He was a perfectionist, who demanded the best of everybody and everything.

In the past the crew working the track were dressed in a variety of clothes. This time Joel wanted them all to be dressed the same way, in new white overalls. The only thing he wasn't worried about was Tommy. Joel was optimistic, he believed his son was going to win. Like Kenneth, Joel had also heard Tommy's desire to win with nothing less than the maximum 15 points. "Fourteen points is not a proper championship success," Tommy had said to his father.

Joel had witnessed at first hand his son's total dedication. When Tommy had his 15th birthday he didn't want a 50cc road motorcycle (which kids reaching that age were allowed to ride in Sweden), as most of his friends did. Instead, Tommy wanted a speedway bike, and to become a star just like his father. Three years later, in 1971, he rode in his first individual World Final. But on that occasion he was in Gothenburg just to watch and learn. Now he was ready to step up to the top of the podium and become a champion.

Joel was sure that Tommy had a great future as an international rider. He also knew that Tommy could be egotistical, that he had the single-minded approach it took to be a winner in an individual sport like speedway. To win you had to think about yourself above everybody else.

If there was anything Joel and his son disagreed on it was Tommy's style of riding the Eskilstuna track. Tommy rode at full speed into every turn and lent his bike over slightly later than the others did – so late that the space between his back wheel and the fence was minimal. Many times Joel just expected to see the wheel hit the fence and result in a fall. "We're going to be forced to come and pick you up soon," he warned.

"Don't worry, I have everything under control," Tommy tried to reassure his father.

At home in Eskilstuna, Tommy really did have everything under control.

He knew his home track, inside-out, and by going faster than all the others into the turns, he maintained speed. Even if he was behind, by the time he left the bend and entered the next straight, there was usually nobody in front of him.

An hour before the first race Kenneth and Tommy arrived at the track.

By then, Bosse had no programmes left to sell.

Something very few people knew at the time was that Tommy had one more driving force within him that night. He always wanted to win. For himself. He knew that if he was riding as good as he could, he always had a great chance of victory. But this time it was a little different. He wasn't only thinking about himself, he was thinking about Joel as well. He wanted to win for his father.

Joel was the reason Tommy was racing in the first place. It was Joel who introduced him to speedway. Father and son had spent numerous hours together in the workshop and on the road. Joel deserved to see his son win. What a reward for all the time Joel had spent helping Tommy to get his bikes in top shape and driving to and from tracks all over Sweden. Tommy had said it to Kenneth in the garage the same day: "My father would be so happy if I won, so I want to win it for him."

Less than an hour before the first heat, all the bikes in the pits roared into life. The turnstiles were still moving fast and there was no longer any doubt about it – the all-time attendance record would be shattered.

Bosse went to the pits just before heat one. His eyes almost popped out of his head when he saw the shining, white fence, the red track with its brilliant white inside line – and all the fans. There were 12,245 fans around a small track in a small town.

Bosse Jansson had lived a rough life, a strong kid from a tough town. Suddenly he stood there and was moved. His only thought was how beautiful it was. Like a perfect painting, he thought.

During the pre-meeting parade of the riders, Joel Jansson received a medal from SVEMO, the Swedish speedway federation, for his dedicated work with Smederna and the crowd gave Jansson senior well deserved applause. Tommy smiled and thought that this was just the beginning – it was going to be the Janssons' night from start to finish.

But neither him nor Kenneth knew if Tommy's bike was good enough. This was the point of no return. This was it . . . it was showtime.

Tommy's first start wasn't until the third heat and the wait was painful.

Anders Michanek won his first race. Easily.

Returning to the pits, he looked over at Tommy. Anders liked racing in Eskilstuna, where he always felt good about the track. His fear had definitely gone now, the competition had started. He was there to win and no longer cared at all about the fans or about Tommy's ability. He didn't care either that he liked Tommy as a person and that he thought he would succeed him as the Swedish number one some day.

Michanek was the World Champion. And he was going to show it. He was going to teach young Tommy a lesson. If it meant putting Tommy out in the shiny, white fence, so be it.

Anders' only thoughts were for himself and his determined to win.

Another Swedish superstar who wanted to steal the show was Bernt Persson, another home-town boy from Eskilstuna. But after a bitter dispute over compensation and money with Joel Jansson, Bernt decided to leave Smederna's team and race instead for Indianerna in Kumla.

He had a silver medal from the 1972 individual World Championship to his credit and he was always a threat to his opponents, despite having had a tough time after a bad crash during the Swedish Championship at Gothenburg in 1973. On that occasion he'd passed one of his best friends, who then deliberately crashed into Bernt and broke his arm.

The 'friend's' name? Anders Michanek.

Even though a year had passed since the incident, and despite a tearful Anders having said he was sorry on the night of the crash, Bernt was still mad at his old friend. He rejected all apologies and even found it a major effort managing to say 'hello' to Anders when their pathes crossed in the pits.

Bernt wanted to beat Anders on the track. He also wanted to show Joel Jansson's kid just who really was the best speedway rider from Eskilstuna.

Bernt was a smart rider. He always had a good feeling for where everybody else was on the track, he had quick reactions and was brazen – if he spotted an opening, he went for it without hesitation.

Like Bernt, fellow superstar Bengt Jansson had a silver medal from an individual World Championship final (1967), plus a third place (1971), and when he was at his best he could beat anybody.

Even Anders Michanek, who usually didn't care one bit about who was after him, disliked being chased by Bengt Jansson. Few riders in the world could pass the way 'Benga' could.

Bengt was a team-mate of Tommy's at Smederna – but not tonight.

Benga still lacked an individual Swedish Championship and he thought it was about time for him to win it.

In the second race of the night, Bengt Larsson crashed on the first turn. The fans closest to the fence were astonished.

"Did you see that? His handlebars broke in half!" they yelled to each other.

Larsson escaped the crash unharmed. Tommy Jansson didn't even notice the drama. He had watched the first race, like he always did, to assess the condition of the track, but then he returned to his spot in the pits, just focusing on what he was about to do. He was in his own world.

Time for race number three: Tommy Jansson, Bernt Persson, Stefan Salomonsson and Lars Jansson.

The bikes was pushed out onto the track as usual, then started up and Tommy's engine sounded good. Tommy slowly went up to the gate, he felt the throttle. It felt good, it sounded good and he also felt happy within himself. He looked at the crowd. He knew most of the fans were there to see him win.

But gating was never his strength and he usually had to chase his opponents and pass them. Joel had even joked about this with him and said that Tommy's bad gating was the reason why he was so popular with the fans.

Joel was right. Everybody wanted to see thrilling overtaking. But most of all they wanted to see victories.

When the tapes rose, Tommy got a flier.

Bernt Persson was close for one lap but pretty soon he realised that the race was over. Tommy was too fast for him, his bike worked perfectly and everything was in sync. It gave him such a thrill and a surge of elation went through his veins when he finished the race and heard the noise from the crowd.

This was the reason he loved the sport, from the first moment he sat on a speedway bike. To feel the speed and experience the feeling of being chased by three others who were ready to do anything to pass him. The feeling of leaving them all behind, to get away like bank robbers in the wild west, with a posse trailing somewhere in the dust behind them.

'This is going to go my way,' Tommy thought.

'There is no doubt any more . . . he will be the Swedish Champion,' Kenneth told himself.

In the fourth race, Bengt Jansson came in third. That was it for him. That's how tough this Swedish Championship was. A potential Swedish Champion can't afford a third place and Bengt was left shaking his head. Then he thought to himself: 'Now I hope Tommy is going to win.'

In the sixth heat it was time for Tommy again. Against Anders Michanek.

Even in the pits everything came to a standstill and most of the riders walked over to the fence to watch the next race. The crowd went silent. Nobody walked away to buy hot dogs or souvenirs – everybody wanted to witness the big duel. Once again Bosse Jansson was amazed by the crowd. He couldn't understand how so many people could be so silent at the same time.

Tommy Jansson against Anders Michanek.

Eskilstuna held its breath.

Tommy was in gate two, with Michanek next to him in the third grid.

The other riders in the vital race were Bernt Johansson and Eddie Davidsson. But like two extras in a movie, nobody noticed them.

Anders had a plan, the same plan that he always had. He was about to control the start. Nobody in the world did it better than him. He did it by rolling in to the tape and staying there as long as possible. By doing so, he knew the referee would be very eager to get the race going, that the exact moment Anders moved, the tapes would go up.

It was a plan that almost always worked and made other riders furious. Many of them accused Anders of cheating.

This time, however, Anders never got the chance to start fooling around at the gate. The tapes went up so fast that 'Mich' was caught by surprise and Tommy got away first. They went in to the first turn first and second, with the 'extras' left trailing.

It was a tough race but Tommy felt the engine respond to him just like he wanted it to, enabling him to choose exactly where he wanted to go on the track while keepingAnders behind him.

After the first turn the roar from the crowd was louder than the speedway bikes. Michanek stayed close to Tommy for two laps before the World Champion was forced to realise that he was a loser. No matter what he did, there was no way he was going to pass.

Back in the pits with Kenneth, Tommy said: "What a gate, it was like a dream. It was the most perfect start I've ever made."

The roar from the crowd amazed Bosse once again. He had thought no noise could ever beat the sound of rock 'n' roll when, many years earlier, he'd attended a concert in Eskilstuna given by a then little known band called The Beatles.

But this noise was even louder.

It was a thunder and lightning of happiness – it was more rock 'n' roll than The Beatles.

And all because of his little brother Tommy.

In heat 12 it was Tommy's turn again, this time against Hasse Holmqvist, Bengt Jansson and Kjell Haage. It was the best race of the night. Holmqvist was fastest from the gate, with Tommy right behind him. On the second lap he passed Holmqvist on the inside and the roar from the crowd probably startled the animals at the nearby zoo.

In heat 15 Tommy knew he had the whole night in a firm grip and the threat from Tommy Johansson never materialised. Jansson led from start to finish. Bernt Persson couldn't help smiling in the pits. Even though he was beaten, he felt pleased for Tommy.

Race 17 was Tommy's last of the night and, once again, he was first from start to finish. For the first time during the night, his mother Inga-Lill forced herself to at least see the end of the meeting. Normally she would always cover her face when her son was racing. Inga-Lill was so happy, she cried. Bosse cried as well. And so did Kenneth Swedin.

Joel walked over to his son, gave him his right hand, they shook hands and Joel said: "Good work, kid."

Joel and Tommy were men of their respective generations. They were men in an overgrown village. Those men didn't hug each other.

By contrast, Inga-Lill threw her arms around her son's neck and hugged him.

"Stop it. Don't make a fool of yourself," said an embarrassed Tommy.

He couldn't understand why everybody now wanted to make a fuss of him. As always, he wanted to keep a low profile, so that no-one would think him cocky. 'Show class at all times,' he thought, just like his father had taught him.

Even opponents like Benga Jansson and Bernt Persson felt pleased for Tommy.

Bernt couldn't help thinking how it must have felt for Tommy at that moment. To win in front of your home-town fans in this way. Bernt was all smiles. Bengt Jansson also. Not even Anders Michanek could help but feel pleased for Tommy and be impressed by how the large crowd paid tribute to their huge favourite. Even though Anders was thinking the same he always did when he took part in the traditional hoisting of the winner: "I just want to take a step back and see the winner crash to the ground."

Above left : Tommy is given the victory bumps after winning the Swedish Championship at Eskilstuna.
Above right: Anders Michanek and Bernt Persson salute the winner.
Below: Runners-up Anders Michanek and Tommy Johansson join the new national champion on the rostrum.

Anders stayed put. Tommy didn't land on the ground. He landed on top of the rostrum instead.

A 15-point maximum. He was the undisputed best. A real champion.

In Eskilstuna, fans celebrated throughout the rest of the night. Around the town square, supporters drove around in cars honking their horns for hours afterwards. At the banquet held at the best hotel in town, riders and everybody else connected to the meeting partied.

Anders Michanek also had fun. He wasn't mad or sad. Not at all. Normally he hated losing and, indeed, even this time he had stood there during the crowning of the champion and thought about walking away. But at the same time Anders loved his sport and if there was anything speedway really needed, it was new stars. New, young riders willing to take risks, not afraid to take hits in order to win. Riders who had the guts to maintain the same speed even when old Michanek came thundering underneath them at high speed. The sport needed Tommy Jansson. So when people at the banquet asked Mich how he felt, he was totally honest when he smiled and said: "I'm happy with my silver medal. A second place is nothing to be ashamed of. Not if you lose against Tommy Jansson."

The Swedish Champion is crowned . . . a very proud young man in his home town.

1
The murder capital of Sweden

"Eskilstuna is a city one hour's drive west of Stockholm. It's a blue collar, industrial town. Eskilstuna is also known as the murder capital of Sweden. If you don't know anybody there, stay away."

From a tourist handbook published in the USA.

It was not by mere chance that The Beatles' concert in Eskilstuna in 1963 received bad reviews in the local newspapers. According to the writer, who later became a TV celebrity in Sweden, The Beatles were "not that different, too hyped-up, well paid – but not worth the admission."

One of the most popular singers in the country, a lady called Lill Babs, was also 'killed' in the local papers, who savaged her by writing: "Too bad that this once upon a time natural singer seems to have gotten herself into a menopause and all that comes with it in the form of sleazy, sexual fixation and shallow, below-the-belt humour".

Later, a local rock band were destroyed with the lines: "For some strange reason this band had a group of fans in front of the stage, but it only awoke suspicions of a mass escape from an asylum".

Eskilstuna was a city very affected by what in Sweden is called the Law of Jante, meaning 'nobody is supposed to think he or she is somebody special'. That attitude held the people of the town in a tight grip – nobody was supposed to believe that they were anything special at all. Nobody should be cocky. The atmosphere demanded straight lines – stick with the group and keep quiet.

It was not by chance that Joakim Berg, singer with one of the most popular bands in Swedish rock history, wrote lyrics about his home-town on the band's first album and, from two different songs, included the following lines: "Some know that they are stronger than others, some love to knock in a row of teeth".

And: "He caught the kick with his head, he had been thinking all his thoughts anyway".

Eskilstuna had always been a violent place, even during Tommy Jansson's younger years. Like a midsummer (it's a Swedish tradition to party like crazy one Friday late

Joel in his racing days as the No.1 at Smederna.

in June and celebrate the summer) at the end of the 1960s.

Parties all over town ended in ugly violence and the local papers had massive headlines describing the mayhem caused by people tumbling up and down after drinking neat liquor straight from the bottle. The police could only arrest a certain number of people and just had to let others go, hoping they were not going to kill themselves or somebody else.

A pregnant woman was kicked in the stomach. At another place, a man armed with an axe threatened innocent bystanders.

In Torshalla, a suburb of Eskilstuna, a little bit like the city's cocky little brother, Finnish immigrants arranged a party and the local paper reported on the scenes of horror: "The Finnish colony had a hot tempered get-together with fun and games, music – and fights with knives, flashing in the hot night".

The biggest employers in Eskilstuna were truck makers Volvo, Assa Stenman, a key manufacturer, and steel manufacturers Nyby Bruk.

Many of the inhabitants were characterised by a philosophy that you work hard all week, then partied hard during the weekend. In those moments they chased away the demons and everything became lighter and more beautiful. Men became braver. If anybody said the things sober that they said during weekends spent intoxicated by vodka, they would have been regarded as total idiots. You could keep on dreaming until you were woken up by the alarm clock on Monday morning. Then it was back to work . . . fight the hangover . . . look forward to the next weekend.

Tommy Jansson was just 16-years-old when he understood that there was another way out of this pre-determined, everyday life. He didn't want to become a regular guy, working seven-to-four and then drink himself senseless during the weekend. He knew he could do it differently.

His way was faster. And so much more fun.

He wanted to be a speedway rider, like his father Joel. That way, Tommy could enjoy another life. A better life. He could get out of town, travel to foreign countries.

He just had to let go of the throttle and wave Eskilstuna goodbye – well, at least for short periods of time. If his father could get to a World Championship final, as he did at Wembley in 1958, then so too could Tommy.

Tommy was addicted to the speed. As a kid he had loved watching Joel race. He was just nine-years-old when his old man stopped racing but Tommy had lasting memories of exciting races. And the speed – he loved watching the races as close to the fence as possible. The closer he got, the more he understood how difficult it was to manoeuvre those bikes at full speed into tight corners.

When Tommy and some of his friends got together one winter's day in February 1969, to ride a speedway bike on the ice in a bay outside of Eskilstuna, they weren't there acting out dreams of leaving town and returning with glory and trophies and exciting tales of life abroad.

Sure, those thoughts were always there in the back of their minds. But the main reason they confronted the icy winds and huffed and puffed to get the bike out on the ice was plain and simple. They just wanted to race.

It was so much fun just to get astride a motorcycle. During the winter the team Smederna had arranged a few practice sessions on a nearby lake. Under very strict and controlled order, Tommy had left many veterans behind and he just wanted to race some more. The bike they had with them had metal screws fitted in the tyres to provide the grip the bike needed to remain upright on the ice.

"This will be great," said Percy Lundkvist, as he started the bike by getting towed behind a car – and the bike started with a bang.

"I wonder what people in the neighbourhood will think about this noise?" Tommy shouted to another team-mate, Sven-Olof Lindh, who smiled, moving his feet like crazy just to stay warm.

"Oh, don't worry about them," said Sven-Olof, dismissively.

Tommy didn't care about the people in the neighbourhood either. At the same time he and the others were sure that most of the buildings they could see on land were empty summer houses. The police had better things to do than bother some motorcycle riders. Nobody was going to bother them.

Startled birds flew over the ice when Percy rode round and round on an imaginary speedway track.

Tommy was just getting ready for his first season with Smederna Speedway. A few years earlier, as a 14-year-old, he got the chance to try a speedway bike for the first time and after that he told his father that he didn't want a regular motorcycle. He wanted a speedway bike – and his wish came true.

Smederna rider, Bengt Andersson, sold his JAP for 900 Swedish kronor and later the same year Tommy was able to practice on it with the big boys.

After Percy had finished his few laps on the ice, it was Tommy's turn. He felt comfortable already, had no problem going full speed and never hesitated to slide the bike low into the corners. It was bumpy and the bike pulled in all directions on the ice but the speed took over and Tommy felt in control.

"I'm impressed by Tommy. What a technique he's got in the corners and look how well he's maintaining speed," Percy said through clenched teeth, desperately trying to combat the effect of the cold winds.

"Tommy's going to be very good," Sven-Olof added.

Then the cops showed up. A black and white patrol car stopped by the bay and two officers walked towards the group performing on the ice.

"So typical. Now we're going to get fined," commented one of the guys.

"And what the hell do you think you're doing?" asked one of the police officers.

Tommy stepped back a little from the others and couldn't help smiling. He knew what was going to happen. Percy was going to talk – he did that a lot. Never afraid of anybody, always eager to say whatever he wanted to.

"We're racing with this motorcycle," he told the policeman.

"You're bothering people in the neighbourhood," came the reply.

"That was not our intention," Percy pointed out.

The police officers were still unsure about what kind of bike the friends were riding. They seemed to believe it was a regular motorcycle that just made a lot more noise than usual.

"We need to check this one out," an officer said.

"Sure, go right ahead," Percy responded.

One of the officers grabbed the handlebars and looked at the bike. He looked very serious.

"How about the brakes?"

"The brakes," Percy said.

"Are the brakes working properly on this thing?" the policeman demanded to know.

"There are no brakes."

"No brakes!"

"No."

"Of course you must have brakes on a motorcycle."

"It's a speedway bike. There are no brakes," explained Percy.

Tommy smiled again but the police officers weren't amused. They radioed in to the sergeant at the station and eventually they were all issued with tickets and fined for riding an unregistered motorcycle in a public place. The officers cursed them.

"Who do you think you are?"

When they were gone Tommy couldn't help showing his enthusiasm for the race he had finished before.

"Just wait until we go out onto a real track. Then we're going to race for real," he said.

And that's exactly what was going to happen – although so much faster than anybody could have expected.

★★★★★★

Two rounds into the 1969 season and Smederna were bottom of the second division. Manager Joel Jansson was under fire from local reporters before the third meeting and the club's first at home.

"Are you really this bad?" Folkets speedway reporter Ulf Claesson asked Joel.

"Absolutely not. There is an explanation for this. Even though we're in the middle of May, we haven't been able to practice once at our home track. Of course, that makes the riders a little uncertain on their bikes," he explained.

Joel did not want to say something special about his own son, preferring instead to talk more about the other riders in his team. Smederna had 18 riders, many of them young kids, but none of them had as much talent as Tommy. But Joel didn't want to talk about it – he wanted the fans to find that out for themselves.

Tommy couldn't wait for his first home meeting. He had trouble sleeping the night before, which showed just how anxious he was. His first practice ride at Motorstadion was on a borrowed JAP in the spring of 1968 – Joel had taken some pictures of Tommy and later Tommy joked with his father about how difficult it was for Joel to catch his son in focus.

A year later and real photographers would be following Tommy – and it was time for the crowd to get to see the much talked and written about son of Joel Jansson. It was time to prove that 'the son of the manager', as one paper had called him, could do it on his own.

Tommy was mostly concerned about what Joel had told him about technique and style. "Few riders can get by being too one-dimensional. Sure, Ove Fundin was an extreme inside line rider. He held on tight to the inside line and he won the World Championship five times. Myself? I preferred the outside and liked to gain speed going out of the corners," Joel said.

"But the best thing you can do is try to be as versatile as possible. You also have to remember that Ove Fundin was almost always first out of the gate. That's most important of all. If you are in the lead, you can always choose where to go on the track, which gives you the best chance of winning."

Tommy really wanted to show everybody what he was made of – and he did, sooner rather later.

Smederna won their home opener, creating a big sensation. Tommy was faster than established stars like Soren Sjosten and Hans Holmqvist and the local papers wrote that a new star was born: "And who would it be, if not Joel and Inga-Lill Jansson's – the speedway family's – own son ‚Tommy," the Folket newspaper reported on its front page.

Right from the beginning fans started to speculate whether Tommy was going to become better than his father and if he would also reach a World Final one day. Joel was in the 1958 final at Wembley but failed to score a single point.

When assessing Tommy's long-term potential, many fans took the view: "One point is enough to be the best in the family. Of course you can do it."

Tommy laughed the first time he heard that comparison with Joel but he soon grew tired of such talk. He really hated it and decided that he had to end it. Fast.

★★★★★★

"You're going too fast! You don't have control of the bike. Take it easy," said an anxious Joel Jansson.

Tommy ignored his father's advice and kept riding the same way during practice with Smederna. When one of the other regulars in the team had a flat tyre, Joel walked over to Tommy's bike, unscrewed the back wheel and gave it to the rider in need. Tommy became furious at this charitable act and on the way home after practice he complained to his father: "Why did you do that?"

"I told you to take it easy but you didn't listen."

When they arrived home, Inga-Lill knew immediately that father and son were not on the same wavelength.

"He's stupid," Tommy said.

"Who?"

"My father, of course."

The anger disappeared fast, though. Joel was Tommy's idol. He had grown up watching his father race and had witnessed, up close, how Joel prepared himself and methodically worked on his bike before every meeting. He had inherited the willingness to do his best on the track and the love for working in the garage. Tommy had been very helpful in maintaining Bosse's road bike and took care of anything that went wrong with it. And Bosse's bike had a habit of breaking down.

Joel's good advice was also something Tommy took on board. Like the time when it became obvious that he'd win a place in Smederna's team and Joel explained to him about the responsibilities that came with it.

He said: "You must have your equipment in order. The bike, all your tools . . . everything. There are riders who don't even care about washing their bikes. Who comes to a meeting wearing dirty leathers and with a dirty bike?"

"What does that matter?" Tommy asked.

"You should never forget that you perform in front of an audience. Fans pay money to see you. You are an artist, just like an actor, so you have to present yourself with class. You have to be nice and clean and have all your things in order. Nobody would walk up onto a theatre stage looking sloppy and untidy."

Because Tommy looked up to his father, and because the young man had already realised that, as a famous speedway rider, his dad attracted attention, he listened carefully to this lecture. Inga-Lill had to sew his leathers so that they fitted him better and he always cleaned them very carefully as soon as he got even just a little speck of dirt on him. Later, he designed his own racewear.

The fans came because they wanted to see a star.

So a star was exactly what they were going to get.

★★★★★★

On May 25, 1969, Indianerna and Getingarna met in a first division match on the Sannahed track in Kumla. Joel was supposed to be there as meeting referee and the day before the match, the manager of Indianerna called him and asked Joel if he could bring along his youngest son. The rumour about young Tommy's talent had obviously spread.

"We have an open spot in a race for juniors and it would be nice if Tommy could make it," explained the Indianerna team boss.

Inga-Lill didn't like it, she didn't welcome her son's commitment to speedway at all. Not when it interfered with school work. The year before, Tommy had finished ninth grade and he was meant to progress to a new college in town, where he was supposed to study natural science at St Eskil's gymnasium. The school year started and Tommy would wake up early each morning, have breakfast with his mother and then leave. He'd return in the afternoon and tell her all about his day in school.

After a week, a teacher called the Jansson family home and asked Inga-Lill why Tommy hadn't been to school at all. Inga-Lill confronted her son.

"How was school today?"

"Well, fine."

"A teacher called and said you haven't been there the whole week."

"No . . . and I'm not going to go there either!"

Tommy just refused. Later he got a place at another school for mechanics, at the Rekarne gymnasium. In that educational programme he was allowed to work with engines, day in and day out. 'The second best thing to do in life,' he thought. 'The only thing better was speedway racing.'

The only consolation to Inga-Lill, and what made her feel good about the situation, was that Tommy did at least take what he was doing seriously. Tommy had been pretty wild as a young child and ran away from home a couple of times. One time, at a very young age, he staggered all the way to his father's work place a few blocks from home. Another time, he went home to his grandmother and brought along a dog he had found tied up outside a store along the way.

As a teenager he had calmed down. All he wanted to do was work in the garage and race his speedway bike.

With Bosse, it was the total opposite. Calm and pleasant as a young child, he became a true rebel as a teenager. In fact, his parents had been forced to place Bosse at a foster home, with a family in the southern part of Sweden, for a few years during his teens. A change of scenery was a must for Bosse, to stop him getting totally out of control.

Bosse's problems also made Tommy more dedicated to what he was doing. He liked Bosse – of course – and he thought that Bosse's wrong turns in life were going to turn out much better for him, but during the tough years Tommy really didn't want to disappoint his parents by misbehaving.

Joel quickly understood that Tommy was serious with his commitment to the sport – and that's what Mr. Jansson stressed to his wife.

"Tommy is learning more and more and he's got control over what he is doing. You don't have to be afraid watching him race any more. Nobody practices harder than him – he's not taking any shortcuts. He doesn't take anything for granted."

Inga-Lill had followed her husband's career and learned what separated the riders that had that little bit extra in them. She had also had to lecture father and son after they had come home all gloomy after bad meetings.

"You can't be that moody, not when you are back home. You must be able to take victories and defeats in the same way," she told them.

The men of the house felt ashamed. They knew she was right.

In Kumla, old memories resurfaced in Joel's mind. It was here he'd made his debut as a rider, when Griparna and Indianerna raced against each other in 1949, and it was here that Joel had ridden for Indianerna for two years, between 1955-56. Joel had always liked this track and in many ways Sannahed symbolised his own journey out into the world.

Joel Jansson was born on a farm in the countryside, 40 kilometres from Eskilstuna, in July 1924. Now, some 45 years later, he was standing behind the fence at a speedway track in Kumla and his son was about to follow in his footsteps. He felt very proud.

Joel had difficulty explaining his love for the sport. And, as mentioned earlier, he was a man of his generation – those men never talked about their true inner-feelings. But deep down inside, he knew it was a love affair.

He would never forget the first time he experienced a racing competition, up a hill in a city called Arboga. It was in the summer of 1939, when Joel and his best friend, Kare Norberg, had read about the competition in a local paper. The boys were still teenagers and knew their parents would never allow a trip to Arboga. Without asking permission, Joel and Kare rode their bicycles 30kms one way. The trip back was the easiest ever on a bicycle for Joel, because he was so thrilled by what he'd just witnessed.

"Some time in my life, I'm going to have a motor bike. Just imagine being able to ride that fast," Joel said to Kare.

Joel's father, Per Otto Jansson, had been a farm worker but he died when Joel was only nine-years-old, leaving his wife, Anna Olivia, to raise Joel and his brother Josef. For six years Joel was in school, during the summer he walked back and forth and in winter time he travelled the two kilometres each way on skis. He liked to play football but broke a window at school and was forced to pay for it. At home on the farm, he had seen the mailmen and the milk transport coming along in motor vehicles – and the cars sparked a lot of interest in him. He was curious about engines and on the farm there were a few tractors to arouse further interest.

Joel was a quiet, young man who enjoyed life and very seldom showed a hot temper, except on occasions when he felt somebody was treated unjustly. When the school teacher, Mr Dahlin, went too far in how he treated the kids, Joel wanted to get back at him. He and a few friends went to Mr Dahlin's outhouse, to hide the teacher's chopping block in his wood pile. Mr Dahlin was furious, of course, but Joel made all his friends promise not to say a word.

"Nobody is going to blab about this. Mr Dahlin has gotten what he deserves. Nobody should treat us the way he has," Joel insisted.

Mr Dahlin screamed at the poor kids, he threatened them and tried to force them to tell the truth. Nobody gave in. It was two months before the chopping block was found.

The only thing that scared Joel in his childhood was when a young girl at his school died of polio. She was just 13-years-old and Joel thought it was so unfair. All the hours in a children's group in church had not helped. A human being created his own destiny, Joel thought, and you have to go your own way in life.

Because of that Joel refused to let go of the dream about a life far away from the farm, a long way from home. Even if he could get a job in his home town, just like his father, Joel wasn't interested. He wanted to leave, to find something else in life.

In September 1939, German tanks crossed the border into Poland and that was the start of the second World War. Joel was 15-years-old and applied to join the Air Force. He wanted to become a fighter pilot but was forced to go home when doctors discovered that he was almost colour-blind.

Instead of joining the Air Force, he went to Eskilstuna.

An uncle lived in the city and he had promised to house Joel and had helped him get a job at a car repair shop. Joel had written a letter to them and although his own family didn't have a phone, the uncle sent a positive response back by mail. Joel was more than welcome there, so off he went.

He put all his stuff on the back of his bicycle to travel the 40kms to town. Out by the main country road, a neighbour said: "Well, well Joel. Here we go. Good luck, boy."

Joel was 18-years-old. His boss at the repair shop allowed him to test-drive cars in the backyard. Joel started flying with lightweight aeroplanes, just so he could experience the feeling of travelling soundless – and fast – through the air. Gradually he moved on and gained a licence to drive a car and, using the inheritance money from his father, he planned to buy a motorcycle.

But the war loomed large and rationing affected the mood of the people, many of whom were afraid. Would the war come to Sweden? Joel received sad news from the shocking reality across the border. His friend, Kare Norberg, who had followed Joel to the racing competition in Arboga, had been killed. Kare had been recruited to work at sea and his cargo ship had been bombed by German fighter pilots and sank to the bottom of the Nordic Sea.

In November 1944 Joel was drafted. After basic training at an air force base in Nykoping, he ended up in Kristianstad, in the southern part of Sweden and frighteningly close to the war. During his first night at the base a British bomber had to perform an emergency landing there. A week later an American B17, partly damaged by enemy fire, went down at the same base. Joel and the other Swedish soldiers were forbidden to talk to the foreign crews but their presence instilled some positive feelings among the men at the base. The war was coming closer to the end – Hitler was on his knees.

Thankfully, next year peace was restored and the Swedish soldiers went home dreaming of a better life. Joel returned to Eskilstuna, got an apartment of his own and continued his work at the repair shop, where he was now a car electrician about to get his first chance to test-ride a motorcycle. Imported bikes like Harley Davidson, BSA, Triumph, Norton and AJS were increasingly visible on the streets, even in Eskilstuna. Talk about great symbols for peace and freedom.

Joel became more anxious and made his first bargain in . . . oh, yes, Kumla.

Standing in the tower as a referee, looking out over the track awaiting his son's junior heat, he remembered that Sunday night in 1947 like it was yesterday.

Joel went to Kumla with his inheritance – 3500 Swedish kronor – in his pocket. He was about to leave Kumla on a motorcycle – a Royal Engfield.

The best race of the evening was exciting but the walk in the car park afterwards was even better. When Joel had found the motorcycle he wanted, he and his friends waited for the owner. When the man arrived, things moved fast and Joel paid him in cash. That's when it really started for him, Joel recalled, at the same time as Tommy and three other young riders emerged on to the track and mechanics pushed them towards the start.

Joel felt a tingling feeling run through his body. He loved the straight exhaust pipes and belonged to the group who, in later years, complained when the authorities enforced the use of silencers on bikes. Joel liked to hear the banging in the pipes, the loud roar of the speedway engines, how they made it sound like the bikes went faster than they actually did. At the same time it was easy to say: "Is it really going this fast?" That was what people asked if they had never experienced the thrill of sitting on a bike, going flat out into a tight corner, side by side with three other riders who were ready to do anything to get ahead of you. To do that and then, in a few moments, feel that you were in total control.

According to Joel, that was the soul of the sport, its true essence.

And then there was the smell. Joel took a deep breath when Tommy and his three opponents took their positions by the gate. Methanol is without any odour whatsoever. What creates the special, unique speedway smell is the vegetable oil in the engines. And what tickled in the nose was, in Joel's mind, a scent as beautiful as the most wonderful perfume ever.

Above: Inga-Lill, Joel and their two lovely boys, Bosse and Tommy.
Below: The brothers strike a pose for the studio photographer.

The start is always a critical part of a race. Four men, side by side, all of them with the willpower to be the first one into the first corner approximately 60 metres ahead of them. When the gate went up, speed, balance and throttle control were the only things that mattered, and then the aspect of being in total control.

Without gears, it was how quick you let go of the clutch, used the throttle and how you shifted your weight on the bike that were the most important factors. Together with knowledge of the track surface, so you didn't wind the throttle on too fast, because then you wouldn't get the traction needed between the back tyre and the surface.

If you were too eager to get away, the result was often an unintentional wheelie, which handed an advantage to your opponents. And that was also something for the fans to laugh about, especially if a rider ended up flat on his back. In Sweden they called it a 'cavalier start'.

Tommy had always had problems at the gate. If there was anything in speedway that looked so much easier than it really was, it was getting it all right at the start of a race. But this time he made the perfect start.

He knew how proud his father was going to become if his son won the heat. He was also hoping that many of the stars from the two teams, Indianerna and Getingarna, riders like Anders Michanek and Bengt Jansson, Bengt's brother Lars and Bernt Persson from Eskilstuna, were watching him.

Tommy wanted to show everybody that he was more than just 'Joel's kid'. He wanted to show them all that he was who he was – Tommy Jansson. He wanted everybody to understand that he knew what he was doing.

He was way ahead of the others going into the third lap. But then, all of a sudden, he lost control of his bike and slowly slipped to the ground.

But he refused to give up.

The other riders passed him one by one before Tommy jumped up on his feet, got back in the saddle and chased after them. There was less than a lap to go.

He passed the rider immediately in front of him, then the next and in the last corner, he finally overtook the race leader. Tommy was the first rider over the finish line and his achievement even impressed some of the veterans looking on from the pits. It also impressed the crowd and, of course, Joel.

On the way back home to Eskilstuna, Joel told his sons in the car about his original trip to Kumla and about that first motorcycle.

"It was a grand piece of machinery – a 1939 model and totally chromed. I paid 2,200 Swedish kronor, pulled my garage overalls over my nice clothes and drove home to Eskilstuna."

Tommy and Bosse sat in the car, listening to their father and smiling at each other. They had heard the story before, but they wanted to hear it again.

"By Kvarntorp, right between Kumla and Eskilstuna, on a great straight, I felt it was time to test how fast I could go with this thing. I got up to 120 km/h and then a piston got stuck in the cylinder. I thought I had wasted all my money. It was terrible. But I let the bike cool down and then it was all right again. I had that bike for years. It was on that bike that I learned to ride a motorcycle," he told them.

Later Joel bought a Norton and that was the first time he unscrewed the front light and also removed the back light, silencer, licence plate, and front and rear mudguards and participated in his first speedway races with standard motorcycles on a track in Eskilstuna, where he later put up an unbeatable track record. Pretty soon he was faster than everybody else and his love of speedway had begun.

Now he was sitting in his car, with his youngest son, who had come to the same conclusion.

"What should I do about the ice hockey – am I going to have the time to keep on playing it?" Tommy asked.

For many years Tommy had played ice hockey for a local team. He played as a forward and was a pretty good goalscorer, even if he was small and thin and not very good in the corners or in front of the net.

"At least continue to practice hockey," Joel urged him. "Speedway and ice hockey are a good combination. In hockey you need to be tough, have a strong will and temperament – qualities that are necessary if you want to be successful in speedway as well. A period in a hockey game – where you need to be extremely explosive for a short time – is like a heat in a speedway meeting," reasoned Jansson senior as he looked back at his sons in the rear-view mirror.

"If you want to succeed at anything, you have to do whatever you can to be as good as possible. You have to always do your best. Otherwise there is no point in participating. If you don't want to give it your best shot, you should stick to doing something else."

Joel suspected that Tommy already had understood all of this. Bosse was sitting in the car thinking that Tommy was better than even he thought he was.

In his own mind Tommy was thinking that he was going to give speedway his absolute best shot. School, girls, friends – everything was going to come second to his main goal and nothing was going to get as much of his attention as speedway. The speed had captured him like a drug . . . and his instant success in Kumla only made him hungrier for more.

What nobody in the Janssons' car that day could have foreseen was what that kid – who the year before had said no to a motorcycle to request a speedway bike instead – was about to do pretty soon.

Tommy Jansson was just two years away from his first World Final.

2
Tommy's mother closed her eyes

"I was scared every time Joel raced speedway, I was scared every time Tommy and Bosse raced too. I closed my eyes during every heat. There is probably nobody else in the whole world who's been to as many meetings as me, without actually seeing what happens on the track!"

Inga-Lill Jansson

In August 1969 Tommy won the qualifying meeting in the Swedish Junior Championship at the Motorstadion, scoring a maximum. After this victory he received a wreath from his mother and later that very evening his father hung it up among all the other prizes on the walls of the workshop back home at Tornerosgatan.

It was Tommy's first winners' wreath and he was very proud of it.

Despite the fact that Smederna had not had a great season, he continued riding well and, above all, had learned the value of always striving to become even better and to improve details which could gain him an extra advantage on the track. His mother cut out and kept everything that was written about him in the local press and when his parents were not around, Tommy enjoyed reading the articles once more. He didn't want to show them how much he enjoyed all the attention, though.

Tommy was especially interested to read the words of Arne 'Vargfar' Bergstrom, the legendary team manager of Vargarna and the man who had introduced speedway to Sweden. Bergstrom, who had been the referee in the qualifying round, said: "Tommy Jansson is very promising and must be recognised as a great talent. If he learns to show more control at the gate and how to sit still on the bike, you can count on an interesting future for this rider."

Tommy liked the praise but not the Swedish speedway supremo's critical observations of his gating technique.

"What does he mean, sit still on the bike?" Tommy asked Joel later.

"Never mind, don't think too much about that, people like to spot your weak points," his father replied.

Tommy took his dad's advice and enjoyed only the praise from the widely respected speedway chief. Inga-Lill saw the joy and the pride in her son. She had seen it before. Everything was so familiar, because Tommy was so much like his father – the Joel she had met in the summer of 1948, when he'd just decided to become a speedway rider and began riding competitively.

Father and son had the same cool and calm attitude on the outside but, under the surface, there was exactly the same stubborn will to win.

When Inga-Lill met Joel she was only 16. For her Eskilstuna was nothing new and exciting, it was simply her home, the place she had lived all her life. After school, which she'd not enjoyed very much and wanted to leave as soon as possible, she had started working as an apprentice in a store that sold men's and women's wear. This she had found much more fun compared to a dull life sat at a school desk. She wanted to get out into the real world, make money of her own and have the feeling of independence.

At an even younger age she had worked as a hostess at the Centrum cinema and shown people to their seats. The dress-code was very proper. She had to wear nice dresses and while she was under-aged she couldn't work when the cinema showed X-rated movies.

When Joel first met Inga-Lill he started their relationship by scaring her. She was on her way home from a dance night at the amusement park in town, when Joel and a friend came thundering along on a motor bike with a sidecar. They stopped right next to her – two tough-looking guys dressed in leather. According to the older generation, it was guys like these that she should have stayed away from. Inga-Lill was curious. Joel, who sat in the sidecar, smiled at her and said: "Hey, where are you going?"

Two years later, in 1950, they were married.

The same year Bosse was born. Two years later, on October 2, 1952, his younger brother, Tommy, came into the world. Getting married, having babies and building your own little nest . . . that made most people calm down. But for Joel the difference was not that great. Other women didn't interest him and neither did late nights at the local clubs and bars. Speedway was what held him in his grip. His passion for the sport had actually formed during his first job, in the repair shop.

During lunch breaks Joel and his work-mates competed against each other, to see who could ride the furthest on the back wheel of their self-made bicycles. The employees of nearby factories stood at windows and in the streets, where the exhibitionists came cycling by.

Joel and his friends stood for the daily entertainment, which helped to brighten the grey everyday life of the factory workers. Already at that time, Joel felt the burning sensation of having an audience cheering and admiring his talent. He wanted to perform. He wanted to show off. No matter how relaxed and cool he seemed on the outside, he did enjoy the attention very much. And he wanted more.

Family life did interfere with long coffee breaks at his favourite hangouts – Strandbaren, in Rådhuset square, and Mjölkbaren, at Kungsgatan.

Inga-Lill wasn't too impressed when he and his friend Henry 'August' Tornblom crashed with the sidecar on their way to the city of Gnesta. Both of them were wearing only hats, not helmets. Joel lost control of the vehicle on a sharp turn and they flew off into the woods. August ended up still sitting in the sidecar, under a big pine tree. The others had to look for him under the branches. Joel urinated blood and was taken to the hospital, where the doctor said he had injured one of his kidneys.

A senior physician had disciplined him. Not because of his reckless driving, but because the doctor had found out that Joel and his friends had found the combination of echoes – created by the roar of their bikes, without silencers, between the hospital buildings – fascinating. Patients and staff were not so amused by the din they caused.

Despite a ticking off from the doctor and his injured kidney, when Joel was alone he couldn't help but smile at the memory of speed before the accident and then by the thought of the noise outside the hospital.

Inga-Lill realised it was no use scolding Joel. The attitude of this cheeky, fun-loving young man was part of the reason she liked him so much.

He made his debut in the regular races the year after they had met. Then he rode for Griparna in Nykoping – as a stand-in when the team were missing a rider. He did well and became a team member.

Joel rode speedway for 14 seasons. Firstly for Griparna, who changed their name to Smederna, where he spent four years before the club closed. He continued with Indianerna and Vargarna, where he won the Swedish league championship twice and finished runners-up in two other years.

Joel's career ended with a crash in 1962, when his Vargarna team rode away against Dackarna. Joel was the team captain and Vargarna were pushing to win the heat, which was going to be his last. He rode too hard, the bike reared and and Joel vaulted.

He damaged his spleen and, at 38-years-old, he'd had enough and said goodbye to the sport as a rider.

Tommy had followed his father's career for a few years – and now it was his turn. He liked Joel's reference to him being an 'actor' on stage. Just like his father, he could be a bit shy away from speedway. But on the track, he wanted to win, show the audience what he could do. He wanted to make them all cheer him loudly.

'I am a big boy now – stop nagging me about when I'm going to ride in the World Final,' he thought as he put the scrapbook together.

Then his mother distracted him with a memory from his childhood.

"I remember when you were little and watched your father race. You were more wild than tame and you were always so dirty from the gravel at the track. You were as black as charcoal. I was always dressed nicely and I had to scrub you clean before we left Motorstadion. Every time you screamed – people must have wondered if I'd tortured you!"

★★★★★★

In Inga-Lill's eyes Tommy would always be her son, her little boy. She felt happy about his accomplishments but by treating him like she did, she made sure he kept his feet firmly on the ground.

The apartment on Tornerosgatan had been the Jansson family's home since 1957, when the building opened up for the tenants. It was from here that Tommy ran away from home. Not because he didn't like his parents – far from it. The reason was that he was curious and wanted to explore the world. He was only six-years-old when he took off to the park, Stadsparken, and found a little lake. A woman who passed by heard the little kid who was sitting in the water singing a song. She stopped to check him out out because he was singing so beautifully.

These days a lot more people stopped in their tracks to check out this kid.

He made the headlines in the papers more and more often. He was 16-years-old and celebrated by the legendary Arne Bergstrom. Everybody who witnessed Tommy's riding was impressed.

Except Inga-Lill.

Sure, in one way she was impressed, but she never allowed herself to watch her son race. She didn't have the guts to do it, preferring to hide her face in her hands, or just turn her back to the track. Otherwise, not many things could scare this lady who was brave enough to demand independence and to live her life as she wanted to from an early age.

Besides tributes to 'the new Ove Fundin', people in Eskilstuna could pick up the local newspaper and read the following: 'The latest fashion in the underworld is the use of torture equipment' – after a brutal attack on a 47-year-old man who was assaulted by someone armed with a chain. The only motive for the attack was that the innocent man had answered 'no' to the question: 'Do you have some liquor?'.

The paper continued: 'The other day we told of the young man who used a chain with a piece of metal welded tight in one end. The ways of being armed is becoming more and more life-threatening.'

Another shocking report in the papers concerned the birth of children and the claim that 'many fathers can't handle childbirth'. A self-appointed 'expert' in Stockholm said: 'There is a risk that a father attending the birth of his own child can be so shocked by the experience that he will remember the details for a long time afterwards. Memories like those can cause the man trouble in the future when it comes to being intimate with his wife.'

However, men had no problems checking out the pin-up photos in the local papers, where half-naked women posed willingly for the titilation of readers. The same year a promoter arranged a competition called Miss Naked at a stadium in town. Hundreds of men conquered the ice cold winds to stare at seven completely nude women who walked back and forth over the stage before Brittmarie Engstrom, from Stockholm, won the first prize. All the contestants were shown completely naked in a photo splashed across the front page of a local paper.

No woman from Eskilstuna had wanted to take part in the competition. If somebody had even considered it, they flatly refused when thinking about the gossip it would have provoked in town afterwards.

Yet to go to events like Miss Naked as a spectator was a totally different thing.

Inga-Lill wasn't scared by the violence in the city. She wasn't afraid of the brutal male-dominated society, where woman were expected to show their breasts in the papers or stand in the freezing cold totally naked . . . while at the same time they were expected to give birth, preferably on their own without their men by their side, and then, of course, to take take care of home and family.

Inga-Lill wasn't happy sitting quietly in a corner somewhere. No way. She had her own job at the store for men and women's wear. She lived the life she wanted to live and enjoyed doing so.

In that respect, Inga-Lill was also an inspiration for Tommy.

His mother couldn't care less for convention. She had a razor-sharp tongue and never hesitated to say whatever she wanted to. When the men of the house complained too much after losses, she could silence them. It wasn't to make her happy that they would shut up. It was because they knew she was right.

The only thing that could worry her was the thought of an accident on the track. Joel had retired after a crash – but he had been lucky. Others had died on the track. Speedway was a dangerous sport.

She was reminded of the dangers when the Swedish government launched an aggressive campaign against drink-driving. Naturally it is a totally different thing to racing speedway bikes – and something that should be condemned at all times. Giant posters were put up all over the country showing scary photos, one of them of a completely smashed car accompanied by a caption that referred to a happy song that Swedes liked to sing when they were pouring down their favourite shots of vodka.

Another picture was taken by a photographer while lying on his back on an operating table in hospital. The effect was again stunning. The image showed doctors and nurses looking down into the camera lens, with the accompanying caption: 'Cheers . . . and welcome.'

The horror propaganda proved very effective. Many people then realised that it was best to leave the car after a few drinks. And the message that life could suddenly end tragically, really struck a chord with people.

In an instance, totally without warning . . . your life could be changed forever.

Exactly the same thing could be said about speedway.

A great day . . . beautiful weather . . . a perfect engine . . . shouts of 'let's go' and 'come on' from the terraces – and then, bang! It didn't take much. An engine failure could cause a crash, or two riders slightly coming together, or somebody who just went for it a little too hard, or perhaps a fallen rider hit by others who are unable to avoid him . . .

Anything can happen in speedway.

Inga-Lill was not worried that Tommy would get into trouble on the streets. She was scared that he was going to get hurt doing what he loved most of all in life. When he rode speedway, that's when things really got dangerous.

Inga-Lill went to all the home meetings in Eskilstuna. But when she was there she kept out of the way, trying to think about anything but the racing. She'd talk to friends about anything except speedway until the meeting was over. Then she would be all smiles again, happy and proud on the way to the next meeting, where she'd start worrying all over again.

Sweden was still a prosperous country and the city of Eskilstuna had high ambitions. The local zoo expanded with Disneyland as its model, and the success of Jungle Book at the cinema led the zoo to stage a grand exhibition. An old pub on the premises was rebuilt like a 'shining dance palace, Chinese-style.' The venture had a price tag of around a cool Swedish million kronor and included giant posters at downtown Stockholm, advertising famous performers appearing on stage in Eskilstuna.

The community also pushed hard to try to attract tourists to town and had a huge market and exhibition in the city centre during spring, with a TV celebrity as the main attraction. Fifteen thousand people showed up.

Luckily, the people had things other than speedway to interest them at the time – because the team was still not doing too well. In 1969, Smederna finished second from last in the second division. The best rider was Jan Strid, while Tommy collected 22 points in six races for an average of 3.7.

He was not happy with himself, knowing he could do so much better. That was also the main reason he really wanted to end the '69 season in style at the Swedish Junior Championships, held on his home track.

It was open for riders up to the age of 24, so Tommy – at 16 – was by far the youngest in the field. There were an amazing 1,622 spectators at the track just for a junior meeting – and that was mainly because of him. Realising his appeal, he felt added pressure to perform very well.

Inga-Lill just covered her eyes.

In his first race Tommy finished third. Angry and disappointed, he returned to the pits believing that he'd let down those who had come to see him victorious.

Before his last race, he still had a chance to win the meeting. He was in second place, having won three straight races, so his only thought was to give it everything he had.

"Take it easy," Joel said.

But Tommy didn't listen. The only thing on his mind was first place and on the third lap, while chasing Karl-Erik Claesson from Ornarna, he tried too hard, crashed and hit the fence.

The ambulance crew on the centre green ran over to him – it was not the first crash in the meeting, but it was the most serious looking. Tommy had lost consciousness and was immediately rushed to hospital.

Inga-Lill felt sick. She had wanted to present Tommy with the winner's laurel wreath and now she was by his side at the hospital instead. But Tommy quickly came round, suffering no broken bones or lasting damage, only bruising.

"You wanted it too much," Joel said.

Tommy was ashamed. He knew the accident was his own fault and that he'd been too eager. 'I have to take it easy, my time will come,' he thought.

He didn't concern himself much about what happened in the world around him at this time, the final year of the 60s decade. Sure, he followed the stories about how Olof Palme had replaced Tage Erlander as the prime minister of Sweden, the horror stories about the drugs and rock 'n' roll at the festival in Woodstock, and of course he had paid some attention to the landing on the moon and Neil Armstrong's famous words: "That's one small step for man, one giant leap for mankind."

Talk about fulfilling your dreams.

But Olof Palme, Neil Armstrong and the others were in a totally different world compared to Tommy. In his world only one person had reached his ultimate dream that year. A star who was bigger than everybody else. One person who could be happier then everybody else and totally satisfied with himself.

His name was Ivan Mauger – and he was speedway World Champion again.

★★★★★★

For many years Smederna started their season with a training camp in Esbjerg on the west coast of Denmark. It was the place for talented, young riders to show what they were made of – on and off the track.

The riders from Eskilstuna had a tough attitude and this came to the surface not only during meetings, but also when they were together socially in Denmark, where they would frequent the all-night bars in Copenhagen and get into scrapes with the local trouble-makers.

On the other hand, the Swedes always rode well the day after their drinking excesses and during the years they went to Denmark, Smederna won almost all of their tour matches.

And when it was showtime, Joel Jansson didn't want to hear excuses from his riders. Everybody had to be serious and do their best out on the track. When a meeting started, that was the end of fun and games. That's when Smederna meant business.

The pranks also had another effect on the riders. It showed that they had courage – or a taste for craziness, depending on how you preferred to look at it – and that was looked upon as a good quality to have. It also proved that the guys liked to have fun together. Above all, they stood up for each other when the going got tough.

Even if the bar fights in Nyhavn (Copenhagen) were not what they had been looking for and not something they had wanted to happen, when all hell broke loose, nobody backed down.

By expressing that same attitude of unity on the speedway track, this team had a bright future.

Tommy liked this attitude, but he stayed at home while the others went out boozing. Not because he didn't enjoy the others' company – he did – but because he felt if he wanted to become a star in his sport he had to take care of himself in every situation. He knew the others riders made a little fun of him for being 'the manager's kid' and a little boring, but Tommy felt that was a price worth paying. He also knew the others were impressed by him and what he did on the track and anticipated that it wouldn't be long before he was no longer going to be talked about as 'Joel's kid'. Soon, people were only going to know him as Tommy Jansson.

★★★★★★

Before the 1970 season began the local papers published stories claiming that Smederna would be happy if they managed to simply avoid relegation. The reason for their pessimism was that Joel managed a very young team. Many of the veterans had retired, so it was time for the next generation to take over. Joel himself talked down Smederna chances of doing well and agreed that his team would be pleased if they could finish one spot above the relegation zone.

But, deep down, he was pretty optimistic.

Left: Christer Lofqvist joined Olle Nygren at West Ham in 1970. Right: The spectacular Torbjorn Harrysson was expected back after suffering a badly broken leg in the 1969 World Final at Wembley.

He knew that Tommy was going to get better and better and it was no secret that Joel preferred young, hungry riders over veterans who'd already had enough of success. He didn't hesitate to use a promising, young rider instead of a veteran, even if the older rider was still faster, because in the long run he believed it was always wiser to go with the youngsters.

Joel was also sure that very few riders in the league would be faster than Tommy – provided his son could just stay on his bike. Tommy himself heard all the stories about the tough competition Smederna faced from Masarna superstars like Hans Holmqvist and Soren Sjosten. Tommy Johansson and Anders Michanek's brother, Lennart, were riding for Dackarna. Bysarna, the team based on the island of Gotland, had a line-up spearheaded by West Ham thrill merchant Christer Lofqvist and expected former Newport favourite Torbjorn Harrysson to make his comeback after badly breaking his leg in a crash at the 1969 Wembley World Final. Taxarna's big star was Yngve Nilsson.

'I'm not impressed by any of these guys,' Tommy thought before the season opened at the Gubbangen track in Stockholm – a circuit he'd never visited before.

Tommy, then 17-years-old, unloaded his bike at Gubbangen, looked around and thought: 'Hey, what's the problem, this is a track around a football field – just like home. It means it's a fast track and I can go flat out all the way round.'

Up against Smederna were three teams, Bysarna, Dackarna and Taxarna, but only 600 fans were at Gubbangen. Speedway fans in Stockholm were still upset over their team's enforced move from the classic Kanalplan track, in the suburbs of Stockholm. The local residents didn't enjoy the loud noise from the engines either and showed very little interest in supporting their new local team.

When the opening match was over nobody was happier than Joel Jansson. Tommy had put on a brilliant show and ended the night with maximum points.

"Well, I guess he's better then I expected," Joel said to reporters.

The only person not surprised by the events was Tommy himself.

And when he was picked for the national team for the first time, he just felt it was a natural course of events for him. During 1970 he was allowed to go with the Young Swedes to race in Poland and England, which was another ambition fulfilled.

Joel had told him all his old tales about travelling to other countries, like when he and his Griparna team went to Turkku, Finland, in the summer of 1949. Finland was a country damaged by the war and the Finns had just started to live again. Now they wanted to ride faster than the Swedes – and drink them under the table. None of the hosts succeeded with their intentions but, oh, yeah, they all had a lot of fun.

★★★★★★

Remembering his father's stories, Tommy walked aboard a ferry in Gothenburg bound for England. Now it was his turn to explore the world beyond Sweden. Many of his fellow passengers became sea-sick on the stormy North Sea crossing but Tommy felt fine and looked forward to his first meeting in the UK.

He longed for new adventures abroad. Back home, a travel agent had started operating charter flights to Spain – direct from an airport in Eskilstuna to Mallorca, eight days at a hotel, sun and nightclubs, all for a very good price.

Fun? Sure.

But nothing like blasting away out in the big, wide world on a 500cc speedway machine without brakes!

On Young Sweden's tour of England in 1971.

Tommy was amazed by England from the first moment he set foot on land and talked about the great, red double-deckers buses in central London. He had never seen buses like those. He was also astonished by the fact that the English drove on the left side of the street – Swedes had changed from left to right after a referendum in 1967.

And all those people. In London, there were people everywhere! Talk about being far away from a small place called Eskilstuna, up in the cold, white north. Tommy laughed to himself about how he'd always regarded the capital Stockholm as a really big city.

Tommy enjoyed success at the start of the tour in England. In the first meeting of the tour, which England won 68-38 at Middlesbrough, Tommy salvaged some of the team's pride by scoring 10 points and proving by far the best Swede.

Young Sweden line up before the tour match at Eastbourne in June 1971. Tommy, who top-scored with 12 points in the 64-43 defeat, is pictured standing to the left of team manager Christer Bergstrom. Other riders in the shot are: Hakan Karlsson, Lars Ake-Andersson, Stefan Salomonsson, Tommy Bergkvist, Karl-Erik Claesson and Christer Sjosten. The English second division team won the series 3-2.

After the first match on Teesside, the tour continued the next night at Workington, but at Derwent Park Tommy crashed, hurt himself and didn't score a point. Although he was disappointed and disheartened, on the other hand he wasn't that impressed by his opponents chosen from English second division clubs. Sweden, with Tommy Johansson outstanding, managed to draw the third Test at Berwick, but they lost the remaining two matches, at Reading and Ipswich, without the injured Jansson.

During the trip home, when some of his team-mates became sea-sick again, Tommy kept thinking about the riders in England and said to himself: 'England has the best speedway riders in the world and the best league in the world, so I'll have to go back there soon.'

And that's exactly what happened, even faster than Tommy had expected.

★★★★★

In 1970, more than 100,000 Swedes in Stockholm joined a demonstration against the Vietnam war. Out in Europe, Palestinian and Arabic terrorists created fear after attacks on international air travellers.

This was also the year when the mini-skirt became fashionable and colour television was introduced in Sweden. And a 14-year-old named Ingemar Stenmark won the World Junior Championship in downhill skiing – he would later become one of the greatest Swedish athletes of all-time.

Brazil won their third World Cup in football and Pele, who had been in all three of their cup-winning teams, was acclaimed the greatest footballer ever.

Eskilstuna, with 92,247 inhabitants and the 11th biggest city in Sweden, was where police started to get really tired about escalating street crime and demanded that the authorities installed better lighting in its central park.

The local media blasted out in big, black headlines that Eskilstuna had its own ghetto for immigrants. Imported workers from Finland were forced to live in inhuman conditions when the Volvo factory rented an abandoned building to house its workers – sometimes three men shared a one-room apartment, and in one case there were seven people crammed together in a three-room apartment. In those buildings nothing worked properly – the toilets were broken, the garbage collection didn't exist and the buildings were a disgrace to the city. Children of the immigrants suffered and one paper interviewed a family from northern Finland, who had sold their farm in search of a brighter future in the neighbouring country, but gave up and moved back home when none of the promises from Volvo were fullfilled.

Optimism about the future wasn't high at the time, so Tommy naturally sought refuge by seeking inspiration from the biggest stars in the sports world. He followed football like a fan and, of course, ice hockey. Like his fellow countrymen, he was impressed by the Big Red Machine, the Russian hockey team that came to Stockholm and the World Championships. Even though the hosts played well, the players with CCCP on their chest was just in a different class.

What impressed Tommy the most was how the best always reached their best when everything was on the line.

When Brazil faced Italy in the World Cup Final, most observers expected a tough game, but the ever-stylish Brazilians won 4-1 and played to their brilliant best at just the right time, when it was most needed. Tommy was deeply impressed by their flair and ability.

His big goal for the year was to win the Swedish Junior Championship.

During a qualifying round on his home track, he got over the finish line after re-passing a rider in the same race. Around 1,000 spectators witnessed the race, Smederna having opened the gates for free in order to attract more supporters.

The club championship – when Tommy won a race even though he had a flat tyre – also attracted a good crowd to the track. The city of Eskilstuna started to become a speedway city.

By the time the junior final was staged in Avesta. Tommy had learned his lesson. His toughest opponent was Christer Sjosten, younger brother of Soren who had finished third in the previous season's World Final and raced professionally in England for Belle Vue. Tommy was still at the school for mechanics, but he regarded his work there as just something he did before fulfilling his dreams.

'If Bernt Persson from Eskilstuna could become a professional in his younger years, so can I,' Tommy thought. He even said as much to his family at home – even though his mother didn't like to hear about his ambitious plans to become an international speedway star. She felt a decent job, combined with racing for his home-town team, was more than enough for her son.

But even Inga-Lill understood that Tommy was made for more than a regular job when she witnessed him in action at the Junior Final.

The meeting was at Christer Sjosten's home track, where he was the big favourite to win. 'Now I'm going to be smart,' Tommy thought, before the first race of the meeting in which the big two faced each other.

"It's his home track. He is the favourite to win. He is terribly nervous. That's very good for me," Tommy remarked to his father as he left the pits and headed round to the starting gate area.

Christer was so eager to make the perfect start, though, that when the tapes went up, his front wheel lifted. In contrast, Tommy moved off the start-line smoothly, led to the first corner and never looked back.

With four more emphatic wins to complete a maximum, Tommy became the Swedish Junior Champion. As well as Sjosten, he also beat fancied challengers Stefan Salomonsson and Borje Klingberg.

"I hadn't expected this at all," Tommy lied to reporters afterwards.

"Now playing hockey comes second to me," he added truthfully.

He continued, and this is what impressed his father the most: "Of course I wanted my revenge after my failure in the Junior Final last year. I was never nervous. Sometimes I'm a little shaky before a race but not today. It all went perfectly."

Joel was so happy, he couldn't find words to describe his feelings. Inga-Lill was as thrilled as her husband. She looked at Tommy's happy face after the event and how he enjoyed standing on top of the rostrum. She was also happy that the meeting was over and done with, so she could relax again.

The slippery surface in Avesta had caused a few crashes and Soren Rydensjo, also from Smederna, had cracked his kneecap in a fall. Still, he was at least fit enough to travel home with the others.

It was only a crack in the kneecap. He'd been lucky.

All eyes on young Tommy as he starts to make his way in the sport with Smederna.

3
For 100 Swedish kronor
you could 'buy' a race

"Of course riders helped each other in qualifying meetings, once you were through yourself. A rider who really needed to win could ensure that he did so by putting up a hundred or two, so that the others took it easier and everybody was happy."

Anders Michanek

A summer's day in 1971 the Expressen newspaper wanted to do a story about the Jansson speedway family. Team manager Joel, the star Tommy – and the newcomer, Bosse. Yes, Tommy now had company in the team in the form of his big brother but the main focus of the story still centred around Tommy and the headline read: 'Coached by his father, sparred by his brother.'

A photographer had the brothers put on their racejackets, even though Bosse was not yet ready for the senior team, and then the three of them posed for the camera in the pits. Then it was time for regular practice.

If anybody had been excited about the visit from the newspaper's snapper, it was Tommy's sparring partner Bosse, who was determined to show what he was made of. In his first 'race' he was up against Tommy and two younger riders – he borrowed a bike from Stefan Salomonsson.

Soren Pettersson was fastest from the gate but Bosse still felt good. 'I have a lot of speed and can keep up with Pettersson without a problem. I know how to do this,' he told himself.

Then Pettersson went down. Tommy was experienced enough to read the situation immediately and he deliberately laid his machine down to avoid a collision. But Bosse panicked and couldn't think straight. He tried desperately to steer clear of the fallen rider but lost control of his bike, went one way and then the other and finally crashed into and over the wooden fence. He landed on the other side with a broken cheekbone and a dislocated shoulder.

When Joel and Tommy picked him up at the hospital after practice, Bosse was fuming and remarked: "If that God-damned Pettersson hadn't gone all over the place, I would've won the race."

Joel thought that Bosse had a lot to learn, although Tommy believed that his elder brother could become a decent speedway rider – eventually. His view was that Bosse just needed to have a little patience and avoid crashes, then everything would work out all right for him.

For Bosse, the story about the Jansson speedway family in the newspaper was a huge victory in itself. He was, without doubt, the black sheep of the family.

While Tommy grew up with dreams of becoming a speedway rider, Bosse didn't care much about anything and ended up in bad company. He partied hard, smoked weed, tried other drugs and ended up in fights now and then. He was not the one who started any trouble – but he never backed down if anybody wanted to fight him. And he ended up in trouble a lot.

Bosse sometimes joked that his little brother didn't smoke, didn't drink and didn't hang out with girls – so he did all those things for both of them!

As a teenager he wasn't that good looking and he hung out with older mates. So his only way to get recognised by girls and win respect from his friends was to be wild and crazy. That was his way of bringing attention to himself. He succeeded and after a few arrests and some bad episodes, he ended up at a foster home far away from his family.

A few years later came the turnaround. Many of his friends had ended up in really bad shape after too much drugs and booze. Some of them died young.

After one late night Bosse woke up behind a train stationed at the local marshalling yard in Eskilstuna. He crawled up on his feet and thought to himself: 'What the hell is this? I can't continue this way, I've got long, dirty hair, I look like s**t. No, this has to end – now.'

It was a promise to himself he was going to keep. And before he even started

Tommy welcomes 'black sheep' Bosse to Smederna.

racing speedway he had an offer from the Indianerna team in Kumla.

Bosse and Tommy had never really talked about big brother's previous wild behaviour and all the bad things he had been through. Joel hadn't said much about it either. Bosse knew that his father was a tough man – but if Bosse said that he was going to shape up and then do his best by working on the bikes and racing, Joel was going to take him at his word and help him.

Tommy, who had helped Bosse with his motorcycle before, so that his brother could impress girls in the streets – now started to work on Bosse's speedway bike as well as his own.

Bosse was surprised by how serious Tommy approached everything and now understood what a great deal of respect all the riders in Smederna had for Joel. And after an incident at practice, Bosse realised too that he wasn't going to be able to do whatever he wanted to – even around his own family.

One rider had a bike that wasn't working properly and Joel said to him: "If you come here with a bike that doesn't go better than this, don't show up here at all. Go home, fix your problems and then you can come back."

Inga-Lill wasn't happy that Bosse had also started racing – and it didn't make her feel any better when he crashed and flew over the fence. There were people who thought Bosse should do something else, that speedway was not for him, but Bosse had the opposite opinion and his driving force was simple – he wanted to beat his little brother at speedway. When Bosse complained that he was in pain after crashing in practice, Joel replied: "One thing you have to know now, young man, is that if the head isn't screwed on right, two things suffer: the body and the wallet."

Bosse felt pain all over his body and he also had to pay Stefan Salomonsson for the damage done to his bike. Inge-Lill's concern was not unexpected expenses. She was worried for Bosse's safety: "I don't like what you're doing, I'm worried that you're going to crash. It was the same when Joel was racing," she complained.

Jansson senior added: "If you think right on the track, you can avoid most situations by putting your bike down."

"And by the way, mum, we all race the same way, you know?" Bosse continued.

"But the speed scares me," she said.

Tommy interrupted: "That's what's fun about speedway. To be first out of the gate and before everybody else in the corners. Or trick somebody and pass him, at such high speed. That's just such a great feeling."

Tommy's mother had to give up voicing her fears and just keep hoping that nobody was going to get hurt.

She still kept her eyes closed during races. At the same time she was proud of her boys and the story about the Jansson speedway family, published in Expressen, was carefully soon cut out and added to her ever-growing, red scrapbook.

★★★★★

Tommy received his first offers to ride in the British League in 1971, his first year as a senior grade rider. The junior champion of Sweden had sparked some interest in Britain and many promoters started to wonder if he was an unpolished diamond.

At 18-years-old and still in school, Tommy didn't have to worry about the growing number of unemployed and the bleak outlook facing many of his friends who'd soon be searching for a job. When Volvo in Eskilstuna cut staff by 500, it was considered a major crisis.

Some rock 'n' roll gigs at the town's amusement park did nothing to raise spirits. Depression was lurking in the background and many inhabitants of Eskilstuna feared for the future.

Not Tommy. He had a future in England.

He had to say 'no' to Belle Vue when they wanted to sign him, because he couldn't get a work permit. But then, finally, he was given a four-week contract to race for Wembley Lions.

While some of his friends worried about getting a job at all, Tommy took some time off school, boarded a ferry to go back to England and was surprised at being offered a chance to ride in the British League so soon.

Double World Champion and former Wembley Lions hero Freddie Williams was the manager who collected the young Swede on arrival. Tommy stayed at Fred's home just outside of London, where he lived with the Williams family and received all the help he needed to become comfortable in his new home.

This was the second year back in the first division for Wembley Lions, since millionaire promoter Bernard Cottrell reintroduced the team. He wanted to recreate the good, old times when the Lions raced in front of 50,000 fans at the magnificent Empire Stadium beneath the famous Twin Towers.

Tommy was so impressed – what a home track to ride at.

But even if the Lions were supported by well-known BBC radio celebrities like Ed 'Stewpot' Stewart and David 'Diddy' Hamilton, and launched a spectacular advertisement campaign with a team mascot in the form of a real lion, patrolling the centre green during some meetings, the fans didn't show up in as many numbers as hoped.

The year before Tommy's arrival, fellow Swede Ove Fundin had ridden 14 official matches for the Lions, but nothing helped improve crowds to the level Bernard Cottrell had hoped. The Wembley Lion was not a roaring lion – they were just an ordinary, middle-of-the-table team and after some bad results, panic was around the corner.

It wasn't a great atmosphere to be in for a young rookie from Sweden

Joel gives Tommy a friendly nudge towards Britain and his first taste of league action with Wembley.

Above: The re-opening of Wembley Lions in 1970, Reidar Eide leads out the home team, alongside Hackney and Swedish star Bengt Jansson. They are followed by Allan Emmett and Des Lukehurst, while Ove Fundin is next to Freddie Williams and in front of Bert Harkins on the Wembley side.
Right: How the front cover of the Lions' programme looked during Tommy's brief time with the club in 1971.
Below: Three legends – Ronnie Moore (Wimbledon) greets Ove Fundin (Wembley) with Freddie Williams in between.

who could hardly speak English. Before his debut, Tommy had hoped to be so successful that he could quit school altogether and start racing full-time.

But just four matches and 11 rides later, he was forced to pack his bags and return to Sweden – without a guarantee of a contract in the near future.

"Was it really that tough?" Joel asked Tommy when he came back home.

"Five points in the first match against Wolverhampton, two against Belle Vue, only one point in the next meeting, also against Belle Vue . . . oh, there's a big difference between racing in Sweden and racing in England. They really go fast when they let go over there. I need more experience," Tommy replied.

"Are you disappointed?" Joel asked.

"Not at all. It was great to get a chance to experience such tough competition."

Inga-Lill was fascinated by Tommy's apparent well-being and appearance.

"Fred and his family live on a farm outside of town. They fed me all the time, every day. I even gained some weight," Tommy laughed.

One thing that had been a major disappointment for Tommy was the fact that the Lions hadn't raced at home once during his brief time in London. He still hadn't actually ridden at Wembley.

Some qualifying rounds for the World Championship were about to take place in Sweden: three meetings involving the same 16 riders and in the end the six best riders overall would qualify for a place in the World Final at Ullevi Stadium in Gothenburg in September.

Of course, Tommy dreamt about winning a place in the final, about being one of the 16 in Gothenburg and put an end, once and for all, to all the talk about Joel's one-off appearance in the 1958 World Final. But not even Tommy, with his big ambitions, believed he was ready to take that giant step in his career – at least not yet and Joel even said it officially: "No, Tommy will not be in the World Championship Final. Not this year."

He meant what he said and neither of them felt any more optimistic after Tommy's first appearance for the Swedish national team, scoring only one point in a match against Norway at Kumla.

But before the first World Championship qualifier in Eskilstuna in May, Tommy-fever started for real in his home town.

The local Folket newspaper ran a big story about Tommy's greatest supporter, his 63-year-old grandmother Maja, who was quoted as saying that "speedway is great." At the same time she admitted that she never actually attended meetings

With grandmother Maja, his biggest fan.

Tommy during his short, but not so sweet, spell with Wembley Lions in 1971.

herself but waited instead for a phone call from Inga-Lill right after each one.

The paper continued to tell its readers about how young Tommy, with his stylish long hair and pop star looks, had gained the attention of girls. Tommy himself said: "Sure, it's fun to have a lot of fans but I won't have a chance in this competition – Gote Nordin and Soren Sjosten will be on the rostrum and I'm just glad to be in their company. If I can score five points in the first round at my home track, I'll be happy."

Maybe the most important thing to happen that night was when Joel Jansson went over to the superstar Gote Nordin, who raced for the Kaparna team in Gothenburg, in the pits before the meeting and said: "Gote, I have a suggestion for you. Since you race for Kaparna and you're going to be relegated this season, and I'm the manager of Smederna, who will move up into the first division, don't you think it would be a great idea if you joined us next season? How about agreeing on that here and now?"

Gote knew Joel from many years back, they had raced against each other during Jansson senior's days as a rider.

"What are you talking about? Us going down, Smederna going up?"

"That's what's going to happen, so let's get back together again after the season," Joel said.

"Yeah, right," Gote muttered.

Almost 4,000 spectators attended the Eskilstuna qualifier. It was a lovely, warm summer's evening and Tommy ended up with 10 points – a sensational performance by the youngster.

"I had counted on scoring five but I got twice as much," he said, "so I can't be anything other than extremely happy with my result tonight. I have never felt this happy after a race. I'm not going to make it to Ullevi but nobody can demand that of me either. I'm just here to watch and learn."

One of the most satisfying aspects of the night for Tommy was how, in one race, he tricked Olle Nygren and passed the legend in a stylish way that certainly got the fans up on their feet. Tommy felt that he could race with the best of them but, like he said himself, he was very impressed by Anders Michanek.

"The most experienced riders are extremely good – my God, are they tough! Michanek is just fantastic – and he is really tough, as hard as a rock if you get close to him," Tommy's added.

The only thing that made Tommy angry at himself was that he still wasn't good enough at the gate – not once during the evening had he been the first from the start. On the other hand, that just made his 10 points score even more commendable. Both Tommy and Joel were surprised by the result and felt justified about the time Tommy had been practicing in secret at the track in Norrkoping, the scene for the next qualifying round.

"It's good to practice at different tracks," Joel had told him.

No-one was brave or presumptuous enough, however, to admit it could also hold the key to him reaching Gothenburg.

When the meeting in Norrkoping was over, Tommy had scored 10 points again, which really put him in the hunt for a spot in the World Championship Final.

The last round was about to take place at Gubbangen in Stockholm – the scene of something that people were going to talk about for quite a while afterwards. Because when Tommy was about to go out on the track for the last time that night, in the penultimate race of the competition, he needed two points to qualify for Gothenburg. Everybody in the pits could see how nervous Tommy was. Everybody knew what a sensation it would be if an 18-year-old could reach the final and what a great thing it would be for the sport as a whole.

Joel was nervous. Arne Bergstrom felt edgy too – he wanted to see Tommy in the final. A large man from Norrkoping, Bergstrom was the manager of Vargarna, who liked the kid from their biggest rivals who had surprised a lot of people during the second round held in Norrkoping.

"You're terrible at the gate. You'll have to come over here and I'll teach you how to make perfect starts, so you'll be ready for the final at Ullevi," Arne had shouted during one practice session.

After that he'd talked to reporters and told them: "An 18-year-old in the World Final – that sounds great to me. I don't know who Tommy reminds me of, or who you can compare him with. Dan Forsberg had a great career from a young age but Tommy is better than Dan was. You'll have to go back to Ronnie Moore and remember that Tommy rides the turns like Bjorn Knutsson."

Bjorn Knutsson was in the pits at Gubbangen. One of the greatest Swedish riders of all-time, the only reason Knutsson never won the World Championship more than once was probably down to his own decision to quit racing way before his time as a world class rider was up.

Knutsson, the 1965 World Champion, had the same opinion as Bergstrom regarding Tommy's possible appearance in the final. Before Tommy's last race, Knutsson walked around in the pits and talked to the three other riders in the heat about how great it would be to have an 18-year-old at Ullevi Stadium. He explained what the fans wanted to see and what they should do about it. Talk about putting pressure on them.

Joel and Tommy didn't know anything about what was going on in the background and afterwards Tommy felt hurt by false accusations that he'd 'bought' his way into the 1971 World Final. However, it was not that uncommon to see some riders who, having already booked their own ticket to the next round, were ready and willing to do a favour for a friend or team-mate who desperately needed an extra point or two at the end of the night.

Many years later Anders Michanek admitted to the unwritten rule about giving way to riders in return for a small fee. For a Swedish 100-kronor bill or maybe two, somebody would ease up at the end of a race to do help another rider.

"That's how it worked at the time, everybody knew it," said Michanek. "I remember another qualification meeting for the World Championship. We were at Gotland and I desperately needed points in my last race and Gote Nordin came over in the pits and said: 'I haven't heard anything from you – can I see a 100 or what?' Then, at other times, you'd help people for free – if you liked them."

Anders Michanek and Gote Nordin were never the best of friends – they didn't like each other at all. And it showed in this particular meeting as well. Because besides Tommy's desperate fight to get his two points in his last race, something else was at stake in his final heat of the night. Anders Michanek had already won the round and he was up against Nordin and Soren Sjosten, who both needed points to advance to the World Final. Going into the final lap, Anders was at the front, followed by Soren and Gote in third place. If the race had ended that way, Soren and Gote would finish with the same amount of points and would face a run-off against each other to decide who went through to Ullevi.

Anders knew this and since he disliked Gote, he slowed down and let Soren pass him before the finish line. Soren got a free ticket to Gothenburg and Gote missed out on the big night, qualifying only as a reserve.

Things like this happened regularly in important World Championship rounds.

Ove Fundin allegedly slowed down during the World Final at Malmo in 1961, in order for Sweden to get their top three riders on the rostrum. Barry Briggs ended up in fourth place on the night and he was the one who suffered for Ove's friendliness towards his fellow Swedes, Knutsson and, ironically, Nordin.

Briggo himself stirred controversies on another occasion. In 1968, Swedish newspapers accused Briggs of 'buying' his way to the final in Gothenburg but nothing could be proved and Barry threatened to sue Swedish reporters. In the pits at the World Final, all hell was about to break loose when Briggs almost drove straight into Arne Bergstrom. The four times World Champion was upset after overhearing Bergstrom talking about him being "a cheater."

Another rider in the field, Swede Torbjorn Harrysson, tried to get in between Bergstrom and Briggs. But since Harrysson had tried to crash into Briggs out on the track earlier that evening, his attempt to make peace just further angered Briggs who told Harrysson to "go to hell." For many years after that Briggs refused to race at all in Sweden and he missed out on major matches for the Great Britain national team, World Pairs and individual events.

One thing was for certain, results of meetings were not always settled on the track. Sometimes things were taken care of in a dark corner of the pits, way before the tapes went up. Most riders did their 'deals' discreetly though.

Speedway in Sweden didn't regain popularity until the 60s – thanks, to a large degree, to a guy from Tranas, Sweden. Ove Fundin was the superstar the sport needed then and his skills helped move speedway onto a new level. Other riders could sometimes be described as rough characters on the track, but nice guys off it. Not Ove. He was the same all the time – and never Mr Nice Guy.

The main reason for that was his ruthless will to win. This hot-tempered redhead from the south of Sweden was never interested in winning new friends, and he didn't care much either for working on his bike. Ove cared about one thing and one thing only – winning.

Ove Fundin was king of the speedway world five times. He won the World Final in 1956, 1960, 1961, 1963 and 1967 and he also won three silver and three bronze medals. Many of his former opponents still call him the greatest speedway rider of all time. And the worst loser too.

When he lost he felt pain, physically.

Barry Briggs once said that people could talk all they wanted to about tough guys like Anders Michanek and Nigel Boocock.

"Sure, they were hard guys on the track but running in to Ove was like running in to a brick wall," said Briggo.

For the World Final at Wembley in 1963, Ove appeared at the stadium on crutches and his fellow riders tried to get him excluded, because they felt an injured rider would be a danger to all of them.

"Baloney," Ove said. Two hours later he was on top of the rostrum.

At Malmo in 1961, Ove forced fellow countryman Bjorn Knutsson out towards the fence and the Swedish fans booed Fundin loudly. Ove could also fire up fans to the extreme and in Norwich, where he was a God for many years, some supporters bombarded riders in the opposition teams with apple cores and other missiles.

Speedway was introduced in Sweden slowly during the 1920s and 30s with dirt-track races on track and field arenas and at horse racing tracks. It became known as speedway after Arne Bergstrom had been to England on a business trip. He attended a meeting at Wembley and said: "We have to import this to Sweden."

Three years after the end of the second world war, organised league races started in Sweden, although England had staged racing like this since 1929. But Sweden wanted to catch up and used the same type of bikes, without gears and brakes and with an emergency stop button on the handlebars. The first Swedish champions were Filbyterna.

Smederna, formed in 1951, were originally a team from Nykoping called Griparna, who moved the whole operation to Eskilstuna. The name Smederna – 'Blacksmiths' – came from Eskilstuna's past dating back to the 17th century.

After Tommy's triumph in the last qualifying round in Stockholm, a reporter from the Eskilstuna-Kuriren newspaper met the Jansson family in the pits, where the reporter had never seen the normally subdued Janssons so happy and animated. A delighted Joel said: "This is the happiest moment of my life. Not even my own World Final appearance in 1958 can compare to what I feel right now."

Tommy still had problems mastering his gating technique and too often left the start-line with his front wheel in the air. That was something he had to eradicate.

"It's all about details, about coordinating my right hand and my left hand and being able to control the clutch better. I'll get there," Tommy said.

He admitted that the pressure in the end had been enormous.

"I have never been as nervous as I was before the last race. I knew it was enough to finish in second place but – phew – was that a tough race," Tommy said.

"Oh, yes. It was terrible, the toughest minute I've ever gone through. I was as nervous as Tommy," Joel admitted.

★★★★★★

The 1971 season became a big success for Smederna as the team fulfilled Joel's ambitions and won the second division championship. They had 20 registered riders, the most since the 50s, which was pretty impressive considering that the club had reformed only eight years earlier. Smederna left Eskilstuna in 1955 but made a comeback as a third division side in 1963, after Arne Bergstrom decided that Eskilstuna needed a team and he persuaded Joel to take over the management of it.

"We've been fooling around in the second division long enough now," Joel had told his riders at the start of that season. After beating the top teams from the beginning and with Tommy racing better than the great Bernt Persson, Smederna finished the year in brilliant form, winning a knockout match against Dackarna in front of a large crowd in Eskilstuna. This was the victory that sealed their promotion to the first division.

In addition to Tommy, who finished top of their averages, Smederna had great riders like tough Ake Dovhed, the veteran Lars Eriksson and youngster Stefan Salomonsson. Sven-Olof Lindh also started to show why he was going to become a perfect partner for Tommy.

★★★★★★

Ullevi Stadium, Gothenburg.

'Not exactly like the Motorstadion back home,' Tommy thought, sitting in the pits before the 1971 World Final. He tried to get to grips with reality, the fact that he was really there – one of the 16 best riders in the world.

Young men his age back home had trouble getting a job. The level of unemployment was growing every day but Tommy had left it all behind. He laughed just thinking back over his glorious year. At just 18, he'd been travelling to the Netherlands and East Germany. In Amsterdam he won the prestigious Dutch Golden Helmet in front of 20,000 fans.

He had been back to England with the Young Swedes and Speedway Star interviewed him for the first time. He brought the magazine home with him and showed it to family and friends. "Look, a story about me . . in an English magazine."

The Young Swedes had six Test matches against an English team made up of the top second division riders and it was hairy stuff at times. Terje Henriksson crashed and broke his collarbone, Christer Sjosten suffered bad concussion, another rider broke a toe and Tommy himself crashed right through the chicken wire around one circuit and ended up on the outside of the track.

Tommy felt embarrassed to be the victim of a stunt like that. It couldn't have happened in Sweden, where all tracks had solid, wooden fences. But in England, many speedway tracks were situated inside a greyhound track. Even so, the Swedish youngsters did much better than they had on the previous year's tour, winning the matches at Rayleigh and Middlesbrough but losing the series due to defeats at Ipswich, Eastbourne and Crewe.

Apart from his trip through the wire meshing, the tour was a success for Tommy, who, after being second top scorer behind Tommy Bergqvist in the opening Test at Ipswich, was the highest scoring Swede in all of the other four matches.

Tommy was in a new world now. The competition was so much tougher on that side of the North Sea. It was also more dangerous, but he loved it and tried to reassure his worried mother.

"I'd rather let go and slow down than take stupid risks. I put my health and well-being before anything else. That's the most important thing," Tommy told her.

His first adventure as a professional in England with Wembley had ended abruptly, but Tommy was sure about getting another chance, and hopefully as soon as possible. He was flattered by the article in Speedway Star and on hearing all the positive remarks about his skills from those feared and respected Englishmen. The fans followed him closely and he felt delighted every time somebody in England – the spiritual home of speedway – asked for his autograph, or when anybody just wanted to chat with him.

And here he was, at Ullevi Stadium. Fans filled the stands and 32,215 tickets were sold – one of the biggest-ever speedway attendances in the country.

Tommy studied the programme and loved to see his own name in print alongside great riders like Ray Wilson and the Boocock brothers, Nigel and Eric, from England, the Russian Vladimir Gordeev, Ole Olsen, Anders Michanek, Bengt Jansson, Bernt Persson, Soren Sjosten . . .

'I don't have a chance of winning against this opposition, but I'm gonna give it my best shot and hope to learn something on the way,' he thought . . . and then he was just stunned again.

He read a name in the programme: Ronnie Moore from New Zealand.

'Unbelievable!' Tommy thought, 'Moore is a legend, he raced against my father in the 50s.' Tommy realised that when Ronnie won the World Final in 1954, he was just two-years-old.

Now those two guys were in the same meeting.

Tommy had everything in order around him in the pits. It was nice and neat, showed he was a perfectionist. But suddenly there was somebody else in the pits like him. Somebody who took even better care of his machinery and equipment. Somebody who was even more of a perfectionist. His name was Ivan Mauger.

He never let anything slip out of his control, neither on the track nor off it. Nothing was left to chance by the reigning World Champion who had completed a hat-trick of World Championship wins in Poland a year earlier.

He was extremely talented, quick from the gate, brazen, smart and had a will to win that overpowered everybody else most of the time. Tommy put on his new leathers he had designed himself especially for this final, and which had cost him around £40.

"They were expensive and although I'm going to get dirty behind riders during the races, I still want to look good," he explained to his father, who just laughed and said: "During my time as a rider, It wasn't like this at all. If anybody showed up to a meeting dressed in red, for example, he would be seen as a complete fool, but I like the style of the more colourful outfits worn by today's riders."

Another rider who looked as smart as Tommy, but who rarely had to worry about getting covered in dirt behind the front-runners, was, of course, Mauger. With three World Final victories under his belt, he was the huge favourite to win again. Even Tommy thought Belle Vue captain Ivan was going to end up on top of the rostrum in Gothenburg again.

The Dane Ole Olsen wasn't among the favourites at all, even though he'd had a great season with Wolverhampton.

Before the meeting Ole had a surprise visit in the pits from Ove Fundin, the Swede who had retired before this season after his five World Final victories. Ove wanted to give Ole good advice about how to approach the slick Ullevi track. Ole was astonished that a Swede would want to help a Dane – in Sweden!

But he listened to Ove and discovered the best lines and other do's and don'ts. Ove didn't care about their different nationalities or the fact that there were six Swedish riders in the final – Leif Enecrona completing the home contingent. Fundin said many times that he only cared about character and the will to win – and he believed that the 24-year-old Dane had all the qualities needed to win.

One of the most nervous of all at Ullevi was Joel Jansson. Both he and Tommy were sick and tired of all the talk about who was the best rider and 'king of the Jansson house'. Joel just wanted his son to collect some points and end all of that nonsense. Joel knew how tough it was to ride in a World Final and he also knew how devastated Tommy would be if he ended the night with a big fat zero after his name, just as he had at Wembley in 1958.

Tommy was more calm and knew there were around 500 fans from Eskilstuna in the stands, including family and friends, team-mates from Smederna and former class-mates from school.

They all wanted that Jansson zero to disappear forever.

In heat four, Tommy was at the gate alongside Ole Olsen, Bengt Jansson and the Polish rider Jerzy Szczakiel. It was a moment of real speedway history, since this was the first time a son of a former World Finalist had appeared in the Final – an achievement that wasn't repeated for many years.

But even better than that piece of history . . . four laps later and that zero had disappeared in the wind.

Tommy scored one point when he came in third behind Ole and Bengt. Now he was the best-ever rider in the family – and Joel himself couldn't have been happier. Inga-Lill, who had fought against her natural instincts to turn away from the action, had peeked through her fingers to see the final lap – and now she was celebrating with other fans. Big brother Bosse yelled at the top of his voice while Tommy's school friends held up their huge banner in his name.

At the same time he was a little upset – he had wanted that second place behind the unstoppable Olsen. Tommy had been behind the Great Dane when he was tricked by Bengt Jansson and passed by the smart veteran who starred for Hackney in the British League.

The rest of the night was nothing else for Tommy but a case of look and learn. In his following four heats he ended up last every time. He had been close to a point in his last race but the Czech, Jiri Stancl, got past him.

"I think my father felt a little stupid when I got that point in my first heat," Tommy laughed afterwards. "To be honest, I didn't expect to score a single point tonight. It was best to approach it that way, as I knew this competition was a little too tough for me. I'm just glad I could finish in front of at least one rider. This is valuable experience for me. Remember, I usually race in the second division in Sweden and this is a completely different thing," he added.

Above: Another great night for Smederna, who made it up into the first division in 1971.
Below: Happy days for Stefan Salomonsson, Tommy and Sven-Olof Lindh.

Deep down inside he also knew that he lacked toughness. During this meeting he'd backed down in tough situations on the track, instead of just going faster and not caring about pushing other riders around.

Tommy understood that it was necessary for him to gain a new contract with a club in England as soon as possible.

The last man of all in Gothenburg on World Final night in 1971 was Jerzy Szczakiel of Poland, with no points.

Joel couldn't help but feel sorry for the Pole. He knew, better than anybody else, exactly how despondent Jerzy must have felt that night.

What nobody knew at the time, however, was what Jerzy Szczakiel would go on to achieve just two years later. Nobody knew either that Vladimir Gordeev had the banned nitro fuel additive in his tank and was going to be disqualified afterwards, which resulted in Tommy being upgraded to 14th place in the standings at his first World Final.

Ole Olsen was king on this night and he was celebrated by the fans when he stepped up on top of the rostrum alongside No.2 Ivan Mauger and third place man Bengt Jansson. The final had been covered by only two reporters from Denmark and when Swedish television representatives called their colleagues in Denmark and asked how many heats Danish TV wanted to receive, they just laughed at the Swedes and said: "Not a single heat. Why would we want anything from this meeting?"

"Because a Dane won it!"

"What?"

"Ole Olsen is the new World Champion."

The elegant, smooth Olsen would later become one of the most popular Danish sports personalities of all-time. And later on he would find a favourite of his own among the younger riders, in the same fashion Ove Fundin was keen to assist Olsen.

Ole Olsen's favourite among the emerging kids was a fellow by the name of Tommy Jansson.

In Eskilstuna the sporting year of 1971 ended with angry complaints from people about how the local government sponsored a poor football team, IFK Eskilstuna, who were almost relegated to the third division. "If they get relegated, I might as well leave town," complained one irate fan. "It's a scandal that tax money isn't put to better use," added another angry local resident.

Nobody could complain at Smederna's efforts during the year. The 'Blacksmiths' were promoted to the top division, their star rider Tommy reached his first World Final and, of course, he was also through to the final of the Swedish Championship.

But when that last big meeting of the year took place at the classic Stockholm stadium on Tommy's 19th birthday, the young man didn't have any gas left in his tank. The demands of the year had taken their toll on him and the result in Stockholm was nothing to shout about – just three points and a 13th place finish. He couldn't muster any more good results that year. The tiring Tommy had a job just holding on to the bike for four laps.

Gote Nordin became the 1971 Swedish Champion after a lot of trouble.

The final came down to a race-off between Gote and his arch rival, Anders

Michanek. After the gate, Gote stopped on the first straight when, according to him, he saw a red light and thought the race had been halted for some reason. But the light came from a tractor outside the track.

Anders continued for four laps on his own and was named the champion.

Nordin went crazy, ran up to the referee's box and demanded a restart, claiming the light from the tractor ruined the run-off for him.

"That's bullshit!" Anders said.

"Honestly, I thought the race had been stopped," Gote still claims to this day.

Bizarrely, the referee changed his mind and ordered a rerun.

Now Michanek was as mad as hell and refused to go to the gate.

When Nordin collected the title unchallenged, 'Mich' was in the dressing room fuming. This was just another chapter in the ongoing feud between these two Swedish greats. And more was to come, but in a new environment, because it was time for Gote to move on. When the season was over, Joel Jansson called the new Swedish Champion, whose team had been relegated, and reminded him about their conversation earlier that year. Joel had told Nordin: "Smederna are going to move up a division and Kaparna will be relegated – you should come over to us."

At the end of the '71 season, Joel said: "As a new team in the first division, of course, it would be great to have a rider with your experience. I think we can reach a deal for a contract."

Gote was impressed by Joel's ambitious style, the manager's hunger for success, and how seriously Joel worked with his team. Gote could also sense that Tommy had the same qualities as his father and when the Swedish Champion had the chance to ride together with the exciting young talent, he didn't hesitate.

Joel got the signature he wanted and believed that with Nordin at Smederna, his team would not be weak newcomers to the top division. In fact, he reckoned that with Gote and Tommy in the team, they could become Swedish League champions in their first year in the top flight.

4
Olle Nygren didn't like Eskilstuna

"I have never liked Eskilstuna. The lads in Smederna have always been too boring and serious. We, in Vargarna, like to have fun."

The legendary Olle Nygren of Vargarna 'Wolves', where he was so successful that he was given the nickname 'Varg-Olle.'

It was a mild and pleasant spring evening in May 1972. Over 2,000 fans had come for the match between Smederna and Vargarna at Motorstadion in Eskilstuna. It was the fourth round of the season. Over the the public address system, the announcer suddenly said: "We have a correction to the programme. Regarding Vargarna's team, instead of Thomas Pettersson it will be Olle Nygren."

When Tommy raced briefly for Wembley Lions he realised that Mr Nygren was not only popular in Sweden. Many British fans had asked Tommy about Olle and he heard a lot of people talk about the Swedish veteran, saying what a great guy he was with his infectious smile in the pits and, of course, at the pub late at night.

Everybody seemed to like Olle Nygren.

All the other riders respected him for his skills and most of the Swedish riders regarded Olle as their big idol while growing up. With his speedway schools in England, Olle had also trained and inspired a couple of generations of British riders.

Few riders in the world seemed so connected with the bike as Olle – and not only in speedway. He raced successfully in numerous forms of motorcycle competition – moto-cross, enduro, ice racing and road racing. He even participated in some car races.

If someone had invented a totally new motorcycle sport, even something as weird as racing down a ski slope, you can bet that Olle would have been there immediately – and would probably have been one of the most adept at it. That's how talented he was. He had racing in his blood like nobody else.

What he lacked, though, was a strong will to win at all costs. For him, winning was not the most important aspect. It was mainly about having fun.

That's why he never won the World Championship, or even finished better than third in one of his five finals over a career spanning 30 years. Many people believed he should have had more to show for his ability and time in the sport.

But Olle himself never complained. On the contrary, he was more than pleased about not having to do much more than race for a living. He had raced since the 40s and ridden in England since the 50s. He'd represented around 10 different teams and made good friends all over the world.

His memoirs were published in Sweden in 1955 and in that book Olle gave the readers an insight into his adventurous trip to Africa, when he rode a motorcycle across the continent. At one stage he had to kill a black mama with his rifle! He wrote: "I have been in many tough situations on tracks but I've never been afraid. This time I was, because there was something really scary about that black snake and I don't feel ashamed to admit it."

Over the years Olle was the main character in some scandals as well. He had a long, ongoing feud with the speedway federation in Sweden. He once blamed sickness for his absence from one competition in his homeland but when SVEMO found out that he'd raced in England and got a maximum there instead, he was heavily fine.

It wasn't the first or last time they imposed a fine on the head-strong superstar.

In Eskilstuna, in the pits at Motorstadion, he unloaded his bike. As usual, it was never a pretty sight, for Olle Nygren was infamous for not taking care of his machinery. Loose bits would hang from everywhere and he'd make all sorts of emergency solutions just to hold his bike together. And it was always dirty. As John Berry, Nygren's former promoter at Ipswich, dryly observed in Confessions of a Speedway Promoter: "The closest Olle came to cleaning his bike is when he left it out in the rain!"

Whenever Nygren was in the pits, the other riders studied and listened to him, because the man with the dirty bike was always full of stories. He liked the attention from the others and he usually delivered. Vargarna's team consisted of Olle, Hans Holmqvist, P-O Soderman and some youngsters. When Olle saw Joel on the other side of the fence separating the two teams, he said to his team-mates: "Joel Jansson was never a nice guy on the track. He was in a lot of international meetings in his time and I raced against him. He was a smart, daring rider and he could be nasty out there."

The others looked at Joel, as he studied the programme. Nygren

The old maestro Olle Nygren passing on some advice.

continued: "I've never liked Eskilstuna. The lads in Smederna have always been too boring and serious. Look at them – it's always been like this."

Tommy Jansson, Gote Nordin and the others were totally absorbed in looking after their bikes, while the kids around Olle laughed and wanted to hear more.

"We in Vargarna have never got on well with them. They have always been a little moody, while we've always just wanted to have fun. But we've had a lot of tough matches against them – the likes of Joel and Olle Segerstrom, two moody, old farts. But hey, they could ride with the best."

Immediately before the first race, Olle said to all his team-mates: "Okay, let's do our absolute best tonight. Because if there's one team in the whole world that I really wanna beat, it's those goddamned Smederna boys."

One man who liked listening to Nygren's pep-talks was the legendary manager Arne Bergstrom, in charge of the Vargarna team. As always, he was in the pits wearing his trademark cap.

What nobody knew at the time was that this was going to be a disastrous season for his team and that Vargarna would end up bottom of the league table. But not even that embarrassment could threaten Bergstrom's powerful position as the figurehead of the sport in his country. He lobbied for an expansion of the league for the next season, so even though his team was supposed to be relegated, he saved them and Vargarna continued to race in the top division.

That's how much power Bergstrom wielded at the time.

The big man liked to be in charge and get things done. He was tall and powerful in appearance, and he talked with a forceful, booming voice.

In his youth he sold motorcycles and cars in Norrkoping, while also managing teams in handball, ice hockey and football. Then he discovered speedway during a trip to England and introduced the 'dirt-track' sport to Sweden.

He started the team in Norrkoping, recruiting a young kid from Stockholm by the name of Olle Nygren and he named the team after a big sponsor in the town.

But it was a process that took some time, because the original team name was Svenska Motorklubbens Östgötaavdelning. Try getting a newspaperman to squeeze that mouthful into a headline! It sounded stupid even to Swedish people.

Another suggestion was 'The Rooster', after another sponsor, but Nygren complained: "Arne, do you wanna be called The Rooster? And do you think we wanna be called chickens?"

Thus Vargarna – 'The Wolves' – were born.

Bergstrom was as tough as nails, afraid of nobody. As manager of the Swedish national team, a position he held for many years, he even had a confrontation with Ove Fundin during a tour of England. Ove was late for the team bus on the way to the next city, so Arne ordered the driver to leave without him – and the other riders couldn't believe their eyes.

Fundin was furious at the manager. The only man who kept his cool was the man in the cap, Arne Bergstrom, who later had a one-on-one meeting with his top rider, where he explained to a shocked World Champion that rules would be obeyed by everybody in the team.

Olle flanked by Ipswich team-mates Tony Davey (left) and John Louis in 1973.

In the end, Ove Fundin apologised for being late for the bus.

On another occasion the local authorities in Gothenburg wanted to close Ullevi Stadium to speedway. Arne Bergstrom, who was a personal friend of many politicians, including the Swedish Minister of Finance Gunnar Strang, knew how to negotiate with people in power and Ullevi duly remained Sweden's premier speedway venue for many years to come.

Nygren only had good things to say about his mentor and during his early years in Norrkoping he and many other young Vargarna riders had day jobs working at one of Bergstrom's car dealerships.

"Arne Bergstrom pushed us harder than a sergeant-major in the army and he could really give us a rollocking when it was needed. But he made motorcycle riders of all of us," Olle said.

There was nothing Arne Bergstrom loved more than moments like this. A speedway meeting with his beloved Vargarna, especially in Eskilstuna – against Joel Jansson, the man Arne had assigned to take care of Smederna and kick-start the sport in Eskilstuna again, nine years earlier. Now Smederna were back were they belonged – in the top division.

Bergstrom was proud of Joel, a man he still considered one of 'his boys.' During his time as an active rider, Joel had raced for Vargarna for a few years and they won the Swedish League championship twice.

The result was 10-8 in Vargarna's favour after three heats, which was a little bit surprising considering that Smederna were the home team and in third place in the league table, one ahead of the visiting Wolves. In heat four, Tommy Jansson was up against Olle Nygren for the first time. At the gate, Tommy had Sven-Olof Lindh for company while Nygren's race partner was Peter Smith.

But this was really a race between Tommy and Olle.

The Vargarna pair were fastest out of the gate and looking to win the heat, 5-1, until Tommy passed his team-mate and then sneaked by both opponents in a very daring surge between them. The home fans gave Tommy a standing ovation after the 19- year-old had beaten the seasoned veteran of 43 years.

Vargarna should have been fuming after throwing away a great chance of victory in Eskilstuna, but both Nygren and Bergstrom couldn't help thinking the same thing – Tommy is exactly what this sport needs.

★★★★★★

Tommy had a new bike bought from prize-money he'd earned from racing in East Germany and Holland. His finances was not in the best state and with his schooldays about to come to an end, a contract with a team in England was his only chance of continuing his climb to the top.

During the winter he had worked out like never before – playing ice hockey, skiing and gymnastics. He was ready to take on the tough challenge a full campaign of British League racing would provide.

For the 1972 season he also had a tough, new opponent – the Swedish Army, who wanted Tommy to do his compulsory military service for 10 months. If he got the call from England and a club willing to take the chance and sign him, he hoped to be able to postpone his obligations to the army. Most of all, he hoped he wasn't going to have to dress in army uniform at all. But, in Sweden, every man is required to do his duty for his native country, even though Sweden had not been to war for hundreds of years and was hardly heading for any kind of military combat in the foreseeable future.

Tommy had no plans to try and bluff himself out of this commitment. As an international sportsman, it obviously wouldn't be easy for him to try to talk his way out of national service on medical grounds.

When Tommy passed Olle Nygren on the track, he felt the adrenalin rush he always did in those situations. He also knew how all his hard work during the winter had started to pay off. Tommy had the strength to be hard on the track, against the toughest opponents possible, with his stamina and conditioning. He never felt like he was hanging on to the bike, as he had in younger years. Now he felt completely in control of the bike, the track – everything.

Around him he also had a team to be proud of. His father had assembled a great group and he pushed them all to reach their full potential. Joel never demanded maximum points from all his riders – but he did insist that each and every one of them tried his very best.

Before the match against Vargarna, Smederna had won two out of three meetings and a major reason for that great start by the senior league's newest team was Gote Nordin. Tommy often studied Gote – the way he prepared his bikes and engines, how he found the right lines on the track and the manner in which he prepared himself at all times.

Nordin, who had also ridden briefly for Wembley Lions in 1971, had so much experience, he even raced against Tommy's father many years earlier. Tommy appreciated that Gote has been around for a while and, of course, he could learn a lot from the 37-year-old.

On the way down? Hell, no. In his second match for Smederna, Nordin broke Bernt Persson's five-year-old track record. Gote had been racing since the 50s, when he moved to Stockholm from his home town Avesta. He became an instant hit with the fans at old Kanalplan in downtown Stockholm. Female fans loved his beautiful smile and style and it was there that he earned his nickname 'Gentleman Gote'. The main reason for his impressive record – including a bronze medal in the 1961 World Final and many years spent as a professional racer in England – was his total lack of fear out on the track.

Another 'old man' of Smederna was Ake Dovhed, a 34-year-old who had never raced professionally but pretended that was the case whenever he flirted with some female fans. Ake was a regular steel fixer and lived in an even smaller, less glamourous town than Eskilstuna. Dovhed was a slugger on the track, loved by his team-mates but feared by opponents. His tough attitude and total lack of fear and respect for other riders sometimes caused big confrontations in the pits afterwards, but they were characteristics that inspired his team-mates.

Tommy liked to have Ake in his team. Away from the track, Ake was always smiling and up for a laugh, so he had a calming effect on everybody else.

Newcomer Christer Sjosten, who had lost the Swedish Junior Final to Tommy, had trouble following in the tyre tracks of his famous brother Soren and was never able to fulfil his potential. Sadly, he was killed while racing at Brisbane, Australia at the end of 1979.

Stefan Salomonsson, who joined Wimbledon in 1976, was a young man from the small town of Koping who worked as a plumber, but he was in his late teens when he finally decided to quit other sports and fully commit himself to speedway. He had

Gote Nordin (left) with a young Dave Jessup at Wembley in 1971.

finished third in the 1971 Swedish Junior Championship.

He was the kind of guy, not too unusual in the sport, who loved to work on the mechanical aspects of his bikes a little too much for his own good. In his quest for perfection he lost speed and was never able to reach the highs many people expected of him.

Two other riders in the team who, like everybody else, had full-time jobs outside speedway, were factory worker Sven-Olof Lindh and truck driver Stig Broman, who learned how to ride a speedway bike when he attended Olle Nygren's school in England one summer.

Bernt Persson was a kid from Eskilstuna and many supporters wanted to see him ride for his home-town team. After all, he was still a world class rider and a professional in England, who raced for Swedish second division side Indianerna after a fall-out with Joel.

Joel still considered that Persson had let his club down. When Bernt left Smederna at the end of the 60s, he was offered a lot more money to ride elsewhere and justified his decision to move by saying: "I make a living racing speedway and I have to earn enough to keep going."

In England nobody questioned his demands and he was one of the best paid riders during his long and successful career with Cradley Heath, where he also was a huge fan-favourite.

Tommy would be angry with himself if he felt he'd let the fans down every time he didn't race as well as he could. He knew when the fans were a little disappointed in his performance and, for him, it was a tremendous honour to represent his home-town team and to prolong the Jansson family name. When he suddenly became the idol of fans who wanted his autograph and girls who wanted much more than that, he dismissed it as part of being a speedway rider. But, secretly, he enjoyed being in the spotlight and he was flattered by all the attention. And who could blame him?

On the other side of the coin, the pressure on him was enormous. Nobody else in the team came even close to bearing the expectations that Tommy had to live up to.

Many times he complained to his father about reactions from outsiders – "the fans ask too much of me sometimes," said Tommy, who disliked having to almost explain any point he dropped. It was no easy task for a 19-year-old.

The fans in Eskilstuna were knowledgeable, among the best in the country. In good times they were great for the riders to have behind them. In bad times, they could be a nightmare.

But when Tommy raced well, he got so much extra energy and pleasure from the crowd and just the thought of hearing the roar and seeing them all stand up and applaud him would make him try even harder on track. These were the moments that he lived for.

During his long career Gote Nordin had heard demanding fans criticise their own favourites many times. But not even Gote had experienced a place where so much expectation was riding on the shoulders of one individual as it did with Tommy in Eskilstuna. Nordin had seen stars crumble under much less pressure than that which Tommy faced every time he set a wheel on the track but the youngster just seemed to thrive on it.

Gote couldn't detect anything that bothered his young team-mate. Tommy smiled at all the fans, politely answering their questions and requests. He never looked for cheap excuses. During their time together Gote never heard Tommy complain about anything. Instead, Tommy made his veteran team-mate very proud to be a member of Smederna.

Before the season started, Tommy had said: "I look forward to facing the toughest riders in the best league in Sweden. I know fans demand more and more from me but you can never be happy if you don't give supporters the show they deserve when they pay money to see us race. We always have to do our best. And if somebody tries to push me around on the track, and nudge my left leg, I'm not gonna back down. Because in those situations you can tell the difference between the really great riders and the mere good ones."

The match with Vargarna turned out to be another triumph for Joel's team. When Tommy's engine didn't work perfectly, and Gote had similar trouble, others emerged from the shadows and carried the load, especially Stefan Salomonsson who collected nine points. The strength of any team is when the riders who are usually at or near the bottom of the scale can occasionally step up and make the difference – and it was this ability which had Joel dreaming about league championship glory.

When the meeting was over, the floodlights had been turned on and the riders had packed up their gear, Olle Nygren was impressed. Not by Stefan Salomonsson – anybody could have a great night occasionally, but by Tommy Jansson's continuing development as a rider. Despite his unfriendly feelings toward the Smederna team, Nygren had found a new favourite rider. During the trip back to Norrkoping he couldn't stop talking about Tommy: "I've seen hundreds of talented, young speedway riders over the years but most of them have lacked that little extra you need to reach the absolute top. Tommy has somebody to take after in his father Joel, who always rode a bike with style.

"But having a successful father can also be a drawback – because of all the expectations or laziness if the rider in question expects to get a lot for free. Tommy is not like that at all. He knows what he wants and this kid is going to become a big star in the near future . . ."

Tommy and Olle would go on to meet a lot of times on the track, both in Sweden as well as in England, and the canny Nygren's good impression of the youngster was only going to increase. This, despite the fact that in Norrkoping one day, Tommy wanted victory too badly and crashed into Olle, causing them both to fall.

Olle reacted to getting hit like that instinctively – he was furious. If anybody gave him a cheap shot, he paid them back dearly. One time in Sweden, a rider named Pelle Sjoholm acted disrespectfully and dangerously by clattering into other riders and Mr Nygren decided to teach him a lesson. He deliberately crashed in to Pelle Sjoholm, causing the kid to go flying over the fence.

Back in Norrkoping, Olle wanted to have some serious words with the 'maniac' who had just crashed into him, even though he still didn't know who it was. Back up on his feet, he was ready to scream in the face of the crazy bastard who'd been racing out of control. Then, when Olle realised it was Tommy, he looked at the kid, smiled, patted him on the shoulder and just said: "Oh, it was you!"

★★★★★★

Before lunch one sunny day at home in Eskilstuna, Tommy decided to kick-start his bike in the garage at home at Tornerosgatan. By then, no police officers were going to issue him with a ticket for riding an unlicensed bike, not even if he went for a little spin on it between the apartment buildings in the middle of town. If ever a patrol car passed by, the officers would just smile at him and wish him good luck in the next meeting.

No neighbours complained either, because they were all proud of living near Tommy Jansson. Many of the local kids loved hearing him start his bike and watch him fly down the street on his back wheel, to send birds rushing from the trees.

He loved to put on a little show, just as he did on this particular day.

"Look out, here he comes."

A senior female member of staff at a school for kids with special needs looked out of the window and pointed at the speedway star racing by.

"Look, it's Tommy Jansson!" she said. "That's a boy with some flair to him."

She turned around.

"Don't you think so?" she asked.

"Well . . . maybe," Eva-Lotta Lindh answered. She was 18-years-old and worked at the school as an intern.

"And he's good looking, right?"

"I don't know if I ever want to be with somebody who races motorcycles."

"Why not?"

"Well . . . hmm . . . I don't know."

Eva-Lotta wanted to change the subject, because she found her supervisor a little too pushy. Sure, Tommy was kind of cute. After all, he was the young man the whole town talked about, but she was not impressed by celebrities. She had attended a few speedway meetings, mostly because, if you lived in Eskilstuna, that's where the action was. And besides, it was just fun being there watching with all the other local people.

During her time at the school, Tommy came thundering along outside a few times and the supervisor continued to ask Eva-Lotta if Tommy wasn't the cutest and she always insisted "No, he means nothing to me."

At the same time, Tommy believed that racing was all he wanted to do. There wasn't room for anything – or anybody – else in his life.

Both Tommy and Eva-Lotta both lied to themselves . . . but they didn't know that until the day they met.

A friendly moment between two of Sweden's toughest competitors –
Gote Nordin and Anders Michanek on league duty here for Smederna and Getingarna.

5
With life on the line

"It was a race against Russia, in Malilla. I tried too hard, got up on my back wheel and crashed down to the ground so hard that my heart stopped. Doctors had to give me an injection straight into my heart, right there on the track. But it all ended well when they got my heart going again."

Gote Nordin

Norrkoping had a speedway track that wasn't easy to handle, not even for the best riders in the world. The turns were different in length and width compared to all others circuits in Sweden. As the saying about Norrkoping went, 'if you could make it there, you could make it anywhere'.

Some riders hated going there and usually left town after scoring an embarrassingly low number of points.

On June 7, 1972 it was the venue for the Nordic Final of the World Championship. Of the 16 riders in the field, the top eight would qualify for the European Final, and from there the top 11 would progress to the World Final at Wembley.

One rider who disliked the tricky track at Norrkoping, and even protested against the decision to allocate such an important meeting there, was reigning World Champion Ole Olsen, who said: "This isn't a good track and it's wrong to hold a big meeting like a Nordic Final at a place like this. Why not Gubbangen in Stockholm, or Gislaved in Smaland?"

In Norrkoping it didn't matter too much if you made the gate, because it wasn't as big a factor there as it was at many other tracks. Fastest out of the gate never did guarantee victory, of course, but many races were settled after the first few seconds – except at the track Olsen disliked so much.

Riders who favoured racing there were the most technically skilled ones, like Bengt Jansson, who loved to come from behind with smart manoeuvres.

"This is a great track. It demands that you really must use your head, you can't win by just flying away from the start – you have to be really smart," Bengt said.

Joel Jansson walked around the pits, proud as a peacock about Smederna's two riders in the meeting – his son Tommy and namesake Benga Jansson.

Both of them fancied their chances of advancing to the next stage of the competition and both had a great chance of winning the Scandinavian qualifier.

In the starting line-up alongside Smederna's two Janssons and Danish No.1 Olsen were Swedish stars Bernt Persson, Hans Holmqvist, Christer Lofqvist, Jan Simensen, Anders Michanek, Soren Sjosten, plus the top Norwegian Dag Lovaas.

Most of them had crashed very badly at least once during their careers and they all knew the risks involved in the sport, that they raced with their life on the line.

Lofqvist, from Gotland, had been only five-years-old when his father, Fritz, died in a crash during a 1,000-metre meeting at the Solvalla horseracing sand track in Stockholm. Fritz had been an extremely talented motorcyclist and earlier in the same year of his fatal crash he'd ended up fourth place in speedway's Swedish Final, just three points behind the winner Olle Nygren and well ahead of Joel Jansson, in 12th place.

At Solvalla, Fritz was extremely unlucky when dirt from the track jammed his throttle open and his bike continued to gain speed. After crossing the finish line, he tried to lay his machine down but didn't stand a chance as he crashed into the fence and died instantly.

Obviously Christer's mother had wanted her son to do something else other than race – and she did in fact manage to talk him into quitting speedway for a few years in his early teens. But he couldn't handle being on the outside any longer, he was in love with the sport and all he wanted to do was race. Christer's mother had to live like Inga-Lill Jansson – with her eyes closed whenever her son was racing.

In the pits at Norrkoping before the Nordic Final, Christer wasn't thinking about the dangers involved or anything like that, he was only concerned about getting his machines in order. Christer was a star – the year before he had won the Swedish Pairs and Team Championships, as well as being No.1 for Poole Pirates in the British League.

Alongside Tommy in the pits, his mechanic Kenneth Swedin was doing his job. He and Tommy had talked about the development of the sport over the years and how the speed of bikes had increased. Tommy had also confided in Kenneth that there were certain riders who really made him watch his back, riders who really didn't have enough control over either their machines or themselves.

Tommy had also told Kenneth about Poland and the long, fast tracks and the Polish riders who knew no other way of riding other than to go for it as fast as they could without thinking of the possible consequences, and with no respect whatsoever for their opponents.

Kenneth admired the way Tommy always raced with his head, how he looked for openings, almost always found the right lines. He never took stupid risks and wasn't all over the place, like some of his fellow riders.

Anders Michanek sometimes had to fight with himself in order to get rid of thoughts about what could happen if something went wrong during a race. He often said to himself: 'I can't think about how dangerous this is, I just can't.' He was never going to forget a race with his Swedish team, Getingarna, when they travelled to the southern part of Sweden to face Lejonen. Before the first heat, Getingarna's manager Bengt Nilsson, the father of Swedish star Tommy Nilsson, said: "Okay, boys. The fence is really hard here in Gislaved and Terje Henriksson in the home team loves to bang in to every opponent out there."

"Cut it out, we don't want to hear talk like that," Anders told him.

One rider who forced many others to think about safety issues was Bengt Jansson who, together with his friend, engine tuner and European trials champion Don Smith, presented a prototype for a folding footrest. Until then, all riders had used rigid metal footrests that didn't yield on contact with safety fences. They were what Bengt called "murder weapons" when things went bad.

When Tommy talked to Hackney Hawks skipper Bengt about a career in England, Benga also stressed safety issues with his young friend. He warned Tommy to beware of the solid, steel fences to be found at one or two tracks in England.

"Stick to the inside as much as you can, avoid the wide turns and ideas about trying to pass recklessly on the outside," Bengt advised him.

But right before a race, like this one in Norrkoping, Bengt didn't spend time thinking about stuff like that. He was only concentrating on going as fast as he could, of course. During races everybody had to stop thinking about everything else other than what was at stake. A rider thinking the wrong thoughts in the middle of a race could never be successful. And riders who got scared in the heat of the moment on the track never reached the highest level of racing either.

Around 4,000 fans packed the stands around the track and applauded when Christer Lofqvist won the first race of the night, after a daring pass of Hans Holmqvist who was riding at his home track. More great passing moves and thrilling moments followed.

Before the 12th heat Gote Nordin was in an almost hopeless situation, needing

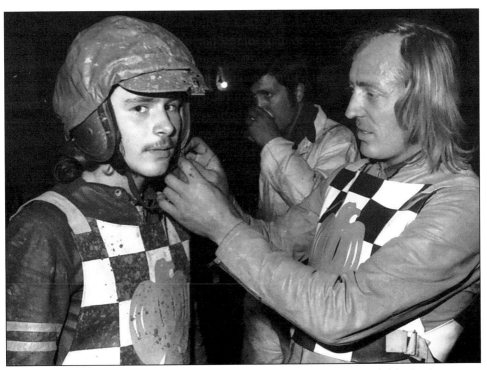

Benga Jansson gives his Hackney and Swedish team-mate, Tommy Nilsson, a helping hand.

points to qualify for the next round after falling in his first race and then collecting only two points in his following two races. The only thing that could save his night was a win in the next heat.

He was desperate and when he flexed his muscles before getting away his whole body hurt. After 20 years of racing speedway, Nordin had long since lost count of how many times he'd broken a collarbone or a rib, or sustained some other injury. This was simply the price a top rider had to pay.

He was brave but that was a quality that could be dangerous as well. In September of 1967, he almost lost his life during a Test match between Sweden and the Soviet Union in Malilla, in front of 8,500 fans. A couple of weeks before that meeting Gote had been a member of Sweden's World Team Cup-winning squad, the outstanding rider of the final with 11 points. In Malilla, Gote wanted to show everybody who the biggest star really was but it could easily have ended fatally for him.

In the middle of a race, after he had impressed the crowd with some daring rides, he suddenly lost control of his bike, reared up on his back wheel and slammed into the ground so hard that his heart stopped. The medical team rushed out and gave him an injection straight into his heart. That saved his life.

Five years later, he was in Norrkoping, getting ready to do what he always did – give it his absolute best, not thinking about anything other than the checkered flag. He was the reigning Swedish Champion, still a world class rider, but, as I say, he was desperate.

And in moments like this, an already dangerous sport can become even more hazardous.

At the gate, Gote was side by side with Bernt Persson, Jan Simensen and Soren Sjosten. It was a scary race from the outset, with four world class riders competing hard, changing positions, finding openings, giving it all they had. Into the last lap they were still a tight group and going into the last straight, nobody could predict the winner.

That's when it happened.

Gote Nordin wanted it too much, his bike just reared upwards. He had no chance to regain control and crashed with the bike on top of him. Bang! – it happened in less than a second.

It wasn't only the fans who held their breath. The crash sent reverberations through the pits, too. Many years after leaving speedway Kenneth Swedin would remember those moments when everything came to a standstill. All activity in the pits just stopped, the mood turned sombre.

Speedway riders wanted to know all the details at once, immediately after every crash, whatever the outcome. Even if the rider got up instantly, walked away and was fit for the re-start – all the others wanted to know why he had fallen.

Something wrong with his bike?

Had the rider himself done something stupid?

Anything wrong with the track – too slippery, too bumpy, anything unexpected due to how the track had been prepared?

Riders wanted all the information in order to avoid possibly making the same mistakes themselves.

This time Nordin was quickly up on his feet and he could even push his bike over the finish line to collect a vital point because Sjosten had suffered an engine failure.

Everything in the pits returned to normality. Kenneth smiled when he saw the reactions. It was always the same. Afterwards it was back to the usual routines and all thoughts about crashes were gone.

For the moment, at least.

Another way of calming nerves was to joke about the dangers and recount stories about tough speedway riders and their various ways of handling pain. Barry Briggs was once knocked off during a 1000-metre race in Hamburg, where he was catapulted into the air and hurt his knee very badly. He also broke a collar bone and a couple of ribs but, on his way in to the ambulance, and while lying on a stretcher, Briggo laughed and said to the other riders nearby: "I don't care about the re-start. I'm gonna do Hamburg tonight!"

Briggs, famous for his cursing and joking, always wanted to help people get into a good mood and would rather talk funny stuff. But in the middle of all the jokes he once reflected poignantly on the ever-lurking threat of danger and said: "A rider who thinks 'it won't happen to me' is a fool. Everybody in speedway has to realise it can happen to them. The most famous riders and the lesser lights at the bottom of the food chain . . . we all live with the same risks."

Bengt Jansson won the Nordic Final in Norrkoping and the riders who also made it with him to the next stage, the European Final in Poland, were: Anders Michanek, Ole Olsen, Hasse Holmqvist, Bernt Persson, Christer Lofqvist, Jan Simensen and Reidar Eide from Norway

Tommy Jansson finished in ninth place, qualifying only as a reserve. Gote Nordin wasn't even close to that, so it was a miserable night for the two star riders from Smederna.

'Patience, I need patience,' Tommy said to himself when he scrubbed his dirty race jacket and leathers afterwards.

Bengt Jansson looked as clean and tidy as he did at the start of the evening when he stepped up on the podium as the winner, while Tommy worked furiously with his scrubbing brush. "My time will come," he muttered.

He was disappointed. He had so much wanted to accompany the others to Poland. He wanted to go to England, to Wembley, to race with the best.

And now he had missed his chance, he thought.

But he was wrong.

Christer Lofqvist flying in Poole Pirates' colours.

6

A strange Swede ordered orange juice at the pub

"This kid is not going to disappoint you."

Anders Michanek to Wimbledon manager Cyril Maidment

Cyril Maidment was nervous when he walked back and forth in the terminal at Tilbury Docks. The ferry from Gothenburg had just arrived – but was it carrying the saviour of Wimbledon Speedway?

Maidment knew much was at stake for his club which, despite its rich history, was suffering a downturn in fortunes. The team wasn't good enough and some riders who normally scored a respectable amount of points were suffering from various injuries.

No, the 1972 season hadn't started well for the Dons from south-west London and even if speedway was becoming more popular after some lean years in the early 60s, at the same time fans lacked patience. They wanted to see winners, not a losing team like Wimbledon.

Cyril Maidment had received numerous calls regarding Tommy Jansson. One of his biggest backers was none other than Anders Michanek, who had raced very successfully in England for many years, with Long Eaton, Leicester, Newcastle and now Reading. He wasn't exactly famous for speaking very highly of other riders – on the contrary. So when Cyril asked Anders about Tommy, the fellow Swede just told 'Maido' to go for it:

"This kid is not going to disappoint you," Anders enthused.

When the gangways opened and passengers started to disembark to the terminal building at the Essex port, Cyril recalled his first conversation with Tommy, on the telephone – and the manager smiled just thinking about it.

On that occasion he had asked: "I have two simple questions for you: Do you want to come to Wimbledon and help us, and when can you be here?"

"Yes and now!" answered Tommy.

A few days later, very early in the morning, Cyril tried to find Tommy among all the passengers emerging through the gates at Tilbury Docks and when they discovered each other, Cyril just became more nervous.

'He is so thin, almost fragile in his appearance, and he looks so young. Oh lord, is this really a future champion?' Cyril muttered to himself.

Tommy pulled his hair back with his hands and took a deep breath.

Back in England. Back where he belonged.

Not even his closest family or friends back home knew what a burning desire he had to succeed this time. He had never in his whole life felt so determined to make an impression.

Tommy didn't believe in any nonsense talk like 'third time lucky'. This was his second chance to break into the best league in the world and this was his last chance. It was now or never, he was sure of that.

This time he was going to show the British that he had what it took to reach the top, he was not going to fail. He had come to England to stay, not to go back to Eskilstuna as a loser one more time and to stand in line to get a job as a mechanic somewhere. 'No way, no f*****g way,' he told himself.

"Welcome to England. You had a good trip? Cyril enquired.

"Yes, no problem," Tommy replied.

Tommy didn't talk much, he was shy in normal circumstances, and even more quiet when, on top of everything else, he had to try and speak English. All the years learning English in school still hadn't made him feel comfortable enough for that first meeting with his new English team manager.

At the same time he wanted to make an impression, not seem aloof or lost. He told Cyril about his bikes and the latest matches he'd had for Smederna and how he and Gote Nordin had recently won the Swedish Pairs Championships.

"Gote Nordin is still keeping up with the others?" asked Cyril, a little susprised by the enduring form of the former Poole, Newport, Wimbledon and Wembley stylist.

"Oh, yes, Gote has been great since he came to Smederna," Tommy said, and then he wanted to point out how well he and Gote had done in the national pairs final.

"We won the final with 17 points, one better than Anders Michanek and Lars Jansson. I had eleven, Gote six," Tommy added.

"Great, sounds great," Cyril smiled.

He told Tommy about Wimbledon's next meeting, due 48 hours later, at home against Ole Olsen's Wolverhampton. "I'm ready," Tommy assured him.

Cyril drove to his home, where Tommy was going to stay to begin with, and soon Tommy was introduced to Cyril's good friend, the reporter Darrell Mason. The Maidment family had arranged for Darrell and Tommy to have dinner at their home but Tommy was tired and went to bed early.

He loved being back in England, and London, with all the double-deckers buses and the cool looking black cabs and lots and lots of people everywhere. He even started to get used to the fact that the British were driving on the wrong side of the street.

But most of all, Tommy looked forward to seeing Plough Lane, the famous home of Wimbledon Dons. The following day he saw the floodlit Wimbledon Stadium, with its plush restaurant enclosed behind glass in the main grandstand that overlooked the start/finish straight. He noted that the track, situated inside the greyhound and stock car circuits, was shorter than the Motorstadion where he'd virtually grown up back home.

Cyril told Tommy that he had been in one World Final himself, at Malmo, Sweden, in 1961. Cyril remembered the freezing cold weather and how the 22,000 spectators had jumped up and down, chanting and screaming – just to stay warm – before they could celebrate the champion Ove Fundin. Cyril had collected three points and only three riders finished behind him when it was over.

Cyril was keen to make Tommy feel welcome so after the newcomer had been introduced to some of his team-mates, it was time for a night out. Cyril took Tommy and Darrell Mason to a pub in Colliers Wood, where they were in for some shock treatment. Cyril ordered drinks – pints of lager, of course – but at the same time the young Swede gave the barman a serious look and said: "I'd like to have a glass of orange juice, thank you."

Cyril liked Tommy immediately – the newcomer did whatever he wanted to do and didn't order a pint of beer to try and impress anybody. Young and innocent-looking in his appearance but at the same time so determined, Tommy had made a very good first impressions on Cyril, who couldn't wait until the following night and the Swede's first meeting against Wolves.

Tommy told Cyril and Darrell about Smederna, about the team's recent results, old Gote Nordin and his impressive racing, about the pairs final, the track in Eskilstuna, Joel's tough practice sessions and his father's expectations and demands of his own riders.

Cyril talked about Wimbledon's season so far, about their next opponents Wolverhampton and reminded Tommy that he had to sign his new contract the next day. Tommy was happy with their agreement – he made 25 Swedish kronors (approx. £2.50) per start and the same amount per point. He didn't receive a signing-on bonus from the club, as many other riders did at the time, but he didn't care. "That's good, then I won't have the same pressure on me," Tommy had told his family before leaving for London.

Money didn't matter to him then and if Cyril had offered him only a pound per point, Tommy would have taken it – that's how eager he was to race with the best and show everybody that he was ready to compete on the highest level, week after week. To prove that he was a winner.

And nobody put as much pressure on him as he did himself. He was there to make a statement on the track, that was his mission and that's what he demanded of himself.

Backstage at the pub, four women waited to get out on stage. Cyril hadn't informed his companions about the imminent 'entertainment.' This place was more than a pub where men gathered to sink a few pints of lager.

During a conversation about football – among other things, they had discussed that year's centenary FA Cup Final at Wembley, where Leeds United had beaten Arsenal 1-0 – all of a sudden, without warning, it was showtime. And since Cyril was the only one of the three who knew what was about to happen next, he studied his two companions when the four women emerged on stage.

Former World Finalist Cyril Maidment pictured riding for Wimbledon in 1971, his last season as a rider before he became the Dons' manager the following year.

Four topless go-go dancers!

Darrell smiled and so did Cyril.

But Tommy wanted to get the hell out of there!

In Eskilstuna, he was very cautious about what he did. At the same time as he considered a drunken walk across the main square in Eskilstuna in the middle of the night a no-no, he took the view that a strip-joint was the wrong place for a professional speedway rider to be seen.

"Let's go home, I need to sleep," Tommy said to the others.

★★★★★

Double World Champion Ronnie Moore understood that his Wimbledon team needed a boost and it wasn´t enough that the legendary Kiwi was racing almost as well as he did in his glory years.

Cyril Maidment introduced Tommy to the veteran Moore, saying: "Tommy is one of the best riders in Sweden, very professional on and off the track, and we're going to get a lot of help from him."

Tommy, of course, remembered when he and Ronnie had been standing together on the infield during the presentation before the World Final in Gothenburg in 1971. It was a magical moment for Tommy, one that he would never forget, and he could still name all the other riders in the event. Ronnie remembered the meeting and that he had ended up in 10th place with five points but he hadn't paid that much attention to his 15 opponents on the big night. Great riders seldom spent time thinking about lesser opponents.

"Welcome and good luck," Ronnie said but, at the same time, he questioned whether this new signing, very young and somewhat frail looking, was really tough enough to make it on his own far from home. It's easier to qualify for a World Final at home compared to racing full-time in the British League. Was a 19-year-old from Sweden really the right solution for Wimbledon? Ronnie Moore was not so sure about that.

The opponents from Wolves noticed the newcomer in the pits and Ole Olsen told his team-mates that young Jansson was for real.

Tommy was calm before his first start. Here he was, in a team together with guys like Moore and 1970 World Finalist and England star Trevor Hedge.

It was June 15, 1972 and the start of a great love affair between the fans in their red-and-yellow hats and scarves at Plough Lane and a kid from Sweden named Tommy Jansson.

'This is where I belong,' he thought, looking out over the track and onto the packed terraces. He was impressed by the atmosphere in the neatly enclosed stadium, which was so different from the natural track in the shadow of the pine trees in Eskilstuna. Just to be at a stadium with a fine restaurant overlooking the main straight, a place with a fountain surrounded by a neatly cut centre green, to Tommy it was all so wonderfully different. He even preferred the music in England compared to what was played at tracks back home.

Cyril, who had retired as a Dons rider only the previous year, was his usual nervous self before the first meeting. It took a while for him to get used to his new position, managing on behalf of the Greyhound Racing Association (GRA) bosses, but the new speedway manager could start celebrating after Tommy's first race.

The newcomer with number five on his back was in second place coming out of the last turn on the final lap when he made a smart move to pass Dave Gifford right before the finish line. The fans went wild with delight.

"I told you, the kid is great," Cyril said to skipper Ronnie Moore.

Moore smiled and thought to himself that maybe he wasn't going to feel as lonely

as he had feared that season. Privately, Cyril felt a great weight lift from his shoulders, his life had suddenly become so much easier. Anders Michanek, and the others who had recommended Wimbledon's manager to sign Tommy, had been right. The young Swede might not look that tough, and he said no to beer and strippers, but he could race fast – and that was more important than anything else.

Olsen looked at his stunned team-mates, including the angry Gifford, and said. "I told you Jansson is for real."

The rest of the night was the Olsen show. The World Champion won all his heats, ended the night with a maximum 18 points and the only time he was really put under pressure – by Tommy – he broke the track record.

Wimbledon's Kiwi legend Ronnie Moore was delifghted when young Tommy arrived at Plough Lane in 1972 to share the burden of leading the south London team.

Gifford lost for a second time against

With his Wimbledon 'star' front fork cover, Tommy sets off on turn one in pursuit of the leading Poole pair during his first season at Plough Lane.
Right: How the front cover of the Dons' match programme looked in 1972. Ronnie Moore is the featured rider but Tommy would replace him as the 'cover man' in each of his subsequent seasons with the club.

Tommy and after also getting excluded from one race for a tape violation, the fiery Kiwi almost got into a fight with Cyril Maidment.

Olsen's one-man show wasn't enough for Wolves. Wimbledon won their first match with Tommy in the line-up, 45-33, and besides Olsen's brilliance the spectators also talked about the new great Dons duo of Moore and Jansson, who had both scored 10 points each.

The old maestro shook hands with Tommy, congratulated him, thanked the newcomer for his effort and said: "Great to have you here. You'll definitely take some pressure off me."

Tommy loved the praise and attention, and he also pocketed some money out of it as well. His first payment from his British League debut was 560 Swedish kronor (approx £56).

'Now I can buy more stuff for my bikes,' he thought.

But not all the other Wimbledon riders were happy and when Tommy's bike broke down during a match a couple of weeks later, one of his team-mates refused to lend Tommy his bike. It didn't take long for him to realise the cold, harsh reality of trying to make it in this league, where success for one rider inevitably meant failure for somebody else.

For Tommy, racing speedway was a way out of Eskilstuna and out into the real world. For many of his fellow riders in the British League, escaping a lifetime in a factory was truly a blessing. The everyday life in England was much tougher for workers compared to Sweden, where strong unions had negotiated more favourable deals for working hours, holiday time and other benefits.

This background made tough characters of most of the British riders and this was something Tommy and his future friend and fellow rider, USA star Scott Autrey, would talk about. Scott said: "Many of the Brits had nothing to lose on the track. To many of them it was either race speedway or go back down the mines, or work in the factory, and live life like their fathers and grandfathers had done before them. Of course, those kids did all they possibly could to enjoy a better life. It was all or nothing, do or die, out on the track. Of course that meant it became dangerous sometimes, really dangerous."

Tommy was a quick learner. He knew instinctively which riders he was supposed to look out for. Back home in Eskilstuna, he commented that some British-based riders were a safety risk to themselves and everybody else.

Tommy also quickly discovered that the attention he had attracted from girls back home, which was quite a lot, was nothing compared to the female adulation that came his way in England. While the riders were braver and more physical on the track, the same could also be said about the women who went to watch them.

More and more girls approached him after meetings and soon a group of them formed the Tommy Jansson Fan Club – most of the members were girls who couldn't stop talking and dreaming about the Swedish heart-throb. He was bombarded with all kinds of interesting offers – dates, marriage and some of them told him they'd do whatever he wanted them to, whenever he wanted it.

To Tommy, it was all very bizarre, maybe a little shocking, but also a lot of fun.

The youngest girls, of course, were very innocent. Surrounded by giggling teenagers, he readily signed autographs and gave them his most beautiful smile, which made them all happy. The older female fans wanted more – but he politely said no to all offers! "I'm here to race speedway," Tommy said.

That he was shy and always very polite just made him even more attractive to his adoring fans.

A young girl who fell for Tommy from the first moment she laid her eyes on him was Shannon Ruane. She was just thrilled with his debut, when she stood in the crowd during the match against Wolves, together with her mother's friends. Shannon had loved speedway since she attended her first meeting – and after every home meeting she was one of the young fans who always waited for the riders outside the pit gates at Plough Lane.

Tommy's long, dark hair, his eyes and that smile . . . the night when she made him sign her autograph cards 'To Shannon', she was the happiest 10-year-old girl in the

All-time Dons heroes Ronnie Moore and Barry Briggs took a keen interest in young Jansson.

world. She immediately became a member of Tommy's English fan club and made her mother agree to let her attend every meeting at Plough Lane. Shannon's mother was a widow, the family lived in a rough part of the capital city and were not exactly rich. But because Shannon's mother had friends who followed Wimbledon Speedway, they didn't mind bringing the young girl along every Thursday night. Shannon's mother was glad that she could help fulfil her daughter's dreams in that sense.

Shannon's friends adored Donny Osmond, David Cassidy and the Bay City Rollers and had the walls of their bedrooms plastered with posters of those pop stars. Shannon put up photos of Tommy instead and she bragged to her friends that she could actually meet her big idol almost once a week.

She thought that everything Tommy did was great, on and off the track, and all the clothes he wore seemed cool to her. While some of Tommy's new friends in London would laugh at his attempts to try to find outfits in trendy stores in London, in the end he wore a mix of the latest jeans from fashionable stores on the Kings Road in Chelsea . . . and then shirts from the most unfashionable shop possible in his native Eskilstuna.

Shannon and other girls stared at Tommy's different-looking shirts: "Look at him! Is that shirt super-cool, or what?" they'd say. If Tommy's friends from Eskilstuna had heard those kind of compliments, they would have laughed their heads off.

When Tommy faced Ivan Mauger for the first time in the British League, he learned another important lesson about life in England.

A smart way to success was to be ruthless and daring at the gate.

Anders Michanek's had studied Mauger's way of controlling the gate, by going in to the tapes, distracting the others, messing around and making everybody, including the referee, nervous . . . and knowing all the time that the moment he moved back, the tapes would fly up. Anders and Ivan mastered this technique and were able to control races from the beginning.

Ivan never backed away from all the people that criticised him for this behaviour – some called it gamesmanship, others preferred to call it plain cheating.

Six times speedway World Champion, Ivan once said: "If you have a meeting with 16 riders and none of them touches the tapes one single time, then you know that you've got a meeting with 16 riders who don't really want to win. The rider who says that he doesn't try anything at the gate is either a liar or an idiot."

Tommy listened to those words carefully, because he was neither a liar – except for some conversations he'd had with reporters – nor an idiot. Tommy learned from the best and he was ready to do whatever it took, even use some dirty tricks if necessary. Later on, his antics at the gate would infuriate some of his opponents so much that they wanted to start a fight with Tommy.

An opponent who liked racing against Tommy was four times World Champion Barry Briggs. One of Barry's biggest nights in his career was his triumph at Wembley 1958, and in his first heat that night he was alongside Joel Jansson. Briggs paid attention to Tommy Jansson for the first time when the Swede made his debut in the 1971 World Final. The fact that Tommy was the first son of a former World

A couple of weeks after making his Wimbledon debut in the summer of 1972, Tommy scored 18 poiints for this Swedish team against an England side drawn from second division sides at Canterbury. Also in the touring team that was narrowly beaten 55-53 that night were: Bengt Larsson, Soren Karlsson, Christer Sjosten, Karl-Erik Claesson, Lars-Inge Hultberg and Kall Haage and (on bike) Lars Jansson.
Below: Tommy on his way to that impressive maximum at Canterbury.

Finalist to emulate his father had impressed Briggo.

Briggs and Jansson had one more thing in common – both of their respective mothers hated watching their sons race. Just like Tommy, Barry had understood the value of training and keeping fully fit in the off-season – the Kiwi great had even trained and worked together with footballers from Chelsea, Millwall and Southampton. Tommy thought that sounded more impressive than skiing in Eskilstuna.

When Ronnie Moore first told Barry about Tommy, it was the will to train hard and the ambition to do things perfectly in all aspects – training and taking care of his bikes and equipment – that impressed the two New Zealand veterans the most.

But both of them held the strong opinion that the youngster still had much to learn. He had the talent, but now he had to start to work at it very hard and the best place to do that was England, where the sport continued to grow and every week meetings all around Britain drew a combined quarter-of-a-million spectators. Only football attracted greater public support in the UK.

"Something amazing about Tommy is how quickly he learns to deal with new tracks. He rides like a veteran on tracks he's never even raced on before," Ronnie told Briggo.

"That proves how smart he is. He's got some talent and it's going to be fun following his progress," Barry added.

Tommy himself was grateful for all the previous practice time back home in Eskilstuna, where his father had forced his riders to try different lines, by positioning cones on different parts of the track in order to make the scenarios different and to teach the riders how to adapt to new lines. That way, Tommy had learned to read tracks and adjust to new challenges fast.

Tommy's only problem at the time was all the travelling he had to undertake.

He had a tough schedule with team matches all the time in England and Sweden. In between, he took part in individual events all over Europe and also represented Young Sweden on second division British tracks for a third successive season. Right after his debut at Plough Lane, he had a spell of nine meetings in 10 days and during one weekend he went from racing in England one day to racing in Sweden the next, and on the Monday he boarded a flight to Holland to defend his Golden Helmet. And yes, he won that meeting as well.

"I've lost count of how many meetings I've been in this year. I get tired sometimes but I'm living my dream, this is what I live for. It can't be better," Tommy would say to everybody who asked how he coped with his hectic, new schedule.

"The racing has gone better than I'd expected. When you get into it, it's no problem. Sure, some meetings are extremely tough and competitive, but that's how it should be. It's just fun," he said when he posed for photos for the local newspapers in Eskilstuna during one of his rare return trips home during the summer of '72.

The papers gave a lot of coverage to the wonderkid who was so celebrated in England and he showed them articles written about him that had appeared in English newspapers and magazines. The Swedish reporters quoted headlines like 'Fine debut for Jansson' and 'Super Swede Tommy makes great start'.

When reporters and photographers left the Jansson family's apartment, Joel and Inga-Lill wanted to know more about Tommy's life in England, but he promised to tell them more later. First, he had to go to sleep.

Another time, one of the local papers even published a photo of Tommy sleeping in his bed at his parents' home. England took its toll on him but he loved it.

All the travelling had just started for him.

He knew it was a price he had to pay and those late-night flights were tough. But at least he didn't have to go back and forth between Sweden and England by sea or in private aeroplanes, like many of his older colleagues had done before him.

Even though Tommy was always travelling from one place to another, he kept winning – in Sweden and in England, where he made everybody happy.

Most of all he delighted Cyril Maidment and the fans – like 10-year-old Shannon.

"How can you like speedway so much?" her friends asked her.

"It's exciting, it's dangerous and Tommy Jansson rides like nobody else. And then he's good looking – the best-looking man in the world."

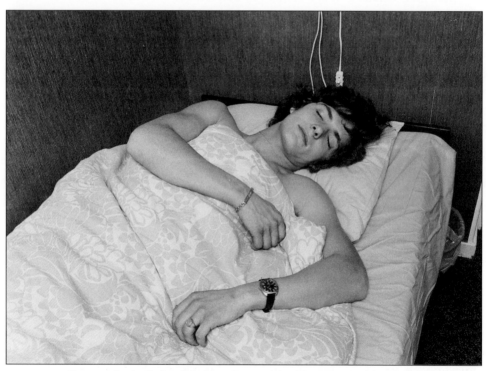

Tommy posing for the Swedish press, who reported on his gruelling travel schedule.

7
The Russians are coming

"Tommy Jansson is going to become Sweden's next World Champion."

Arne Bergstrom

The scrapbooks at the Jansson family home continued to grow. The red one was already full and a new, blue binder held together the latest stories about Tommy. In addition to all the reports that he kept from the local papers in Eskilstuna, Tommy had a lot of stuff sent to him from other places in Sweden and he himself made sure he brought home everything he saved from papers and magazines in England.

During the 1972 season, when he was racing regularly in Sweden as well as in England, he made a big impression wherever he went and one paper in his homeland wrote: 'Tommy Jansson races with his head and he's never out of line or reckless. He wins by being smooth, finding the right moments to strike and pass the others.'

A reporter at Gotland paid tribute to Joel Jansson for being one of the most elegant riders ever to perform at the track in Visby, but the reporter concluded that Joel's son, with his movie star looks, was going to become better than his old man.

Smederna finished the season in third place, their first year in the top division since the 50s, which made everyone associated with The Blacksmiths happy.

Tommy reached the Swedish Championship Final, where Anders Michanek was faster than anybody else on the night. Tommy lost in a run-off for bronze against Bernt Persson – his main rival from their home-town of Eskilstuna. Tommy viewed that race as his most disappointing defeat to date. Persson, the rider who Joel had introduced to speedway, the one Tommy always wanted to beat because of all the talk about who was the best rider from Eskilstuna.

Tommy had led the run-off all they way to the final straight, when Bernt passed him inches from the finish line. Tommy became so furious and distraught by this defeat that he cried. He threw his helmet down in the pits and cursed loudly. "How could I let him pass me like that?" he said.

Bengt Jansson tried to comfort his team-mate from Smederna by saying that Tommy's time would come.

But it was going to take a while for Tommy to get over this bitter defeat. It didn't matter that Persson had probably never been in better form – the same year he was beaten in a run-off against Ivan Mauger for the 1972 World Championship.

★★★★★★

At Wimbledon, everybody was happy with Tommy's first season in the British League but the campaign proved a nightmare for the Dons, who ended up 13th in the BL – their worst finish to date. Tommy's average was 7.45 from 17 matches, which made him the third heat leader behind the veteran Ronnie Moore and Trevor Hedge. But they lacked support on a consistent basis from the rest – Graeme Stapleton, Peter Murray, Jim Tebby and Neil Cameron. John Dews quit mid-season.

Tommy's promise was such that when it was announced that Moore was finally retiring for good, there was no panic among Wimbledon supporters.

What did concern the Dons' fans in south London, though, was news of Tommy's upcoming military service. Newspapers in England even suggested that Tommy should marry an English girl, in order to avoid his compulsory stint in the Swedish Army. His No.1 fan in England, Shannon Ruane, thought that was a great idea – until she reminded herself that she was still only 10-years-old.

If he'd wanted to find an English girl to marry, that wouldn't have been a problem. The upside of being a world class speedway rider was the chance to see the world far away from home. Tommy had travelled all over Europe and he had recently accepted an offer to visit Australia for a spell of racing in the European close season.

The world could also come knocking on Tommy's own front door. In October 1972 the Soviet Union national team toured Sweden, with one of the three Tests scheduled to take place in Eskilstuna. The Russians arrived in a beaten-up, old bus and inspected the facilities at Motorstadion with deep curiosity. Among the group were some well dressed, serious-looking gentlemen – just lurking in the background but always present.

"KGB," guessed one Swedish rider.

And he was right. The men were plain-clothed security officials from Moscow, sent on a mission to control the group and make sure no riders escaped to the west. For the Soviets and their leader Leonid Breschnev, sport was a way of showing the rest of the world what Soviet superiority was all about. Success in sports was perfect propaganda and at the same time as the speedway team was visiting Sweden, the Olympics in Munich had just ended with the Soviets again winning more medals than any other country.

The red Soviet flag, with its yellow hammer-and-sickle symbol, never went unnoticed. The Swedes looked twice when the Russian riders visiting Eskilstuna put on their racejackets. With the exception of their body colours, the team was dressed all in black – from their clothes to their bikes. Young Smederna rider Percy Lundkvist worked in the pits that night and he heard a lot of stories about Russians trading goods, especially items with a bit of colour to them. Percy collected some racing saddles and other colourful items that might interest them and, in return, he received a Soviet racejacket as a souvenir. Other Swedes secured Czech-made Jawa engine parts, to which the Russians had ready access.

The KGB officers turned a blind eye to the sneaky dealings in the pits, or were busy trading goods themselves.

Five of the touring team – Viktor Trofimov, Gregori Chlynovski, Viktor Kalmykov, Valeri Gordeev and Anatoli Kuzmin – had been in the World Final at Wembley that same year, while Anatoli Mironov and Vladimir Zapleshny completed the team.

Lining up for the Swedes were: Tommy Jansson, Bernt Persson, Jan Simensen, Anders Michanek, Hasse Holmqvist, Gote Nordin and Bengt Jansson.

Despite icy, cold winds and the alternative option of live ice hockey on TV, an historic match between the Soviet Union and Canada, 3,000 fans showed up at the track in Eskilstuna to witness the speedway Test.

Like his fellow Swedes, Tommy was amazed by the Russians' tactics – or rather the total lack of them – out on the track. The touring riders were usually fast from the gate but before every turn they suddenly shut off the throttle, which made it dangerous for anyone right behind them.

The bravest Russian in Eskilstuna was Valeri Gordeev, brother of Vladimir, who was so aggressive that he crashed badly. For a change, the other riders in the pits didn't even flinch. By then it was just a resigned feeling of 'here we go again' – Gordeev's spill was the fourth time that night that one of the Russians had gone to ground. But this time the rider had really hurt himself, a collar bone was broken and all the Russians became very concerned, especially their security people. What were they supposed to do? They couldn't let Gordeev leave the track in an ambulance and end up all by himself at a hospital in the 'evil West', with all its temptations? No way. One of the KGB people accompanied Gordeev to the hospital.

None of the Swedes were going to see Valeri any more that night, because the Russians only wanted to show the world tough and strong athletes – not an injured speedway rider with a bandaged shoulder – so during the official post-match banquet he was forced stay in his hotel . . . in the company of a KGB man, of course.

"Isn't he going to get something to eat?" Joel whispered to the other Swedes around the table.

"Oh, yes, some of the Russians went up to his room with a plate of food," somebody answered.

Sweden beat Russia in Eskilstuna, 55-53, and best rider of the night was Bengt Jansson with a maximum. Tommy had machine problems and scored only 10 points and some fans, with the characteristic accent that made them sound like they were always complaining, said: "Tommy's got a lot to learn."

Arne Bergstrom didn't listen to the doubters, saying: "Tommy Jansson is going to become the next World Champion from Sweden. In two years time he is going to be on the podium after a World Final. Maybe on top. The kid has progressed as a rider in a remarkable way. I have always believed in him and even if he wasn't on top tonight, I know how highly I rate him."

Bergstrom continued: "To become a speedway rider at the very top level you need to focus on speedway and nothing else. Hanging out with friends and family life, it all has to take second place. I hope dearly that Tommy is going to put speedway before everything else in the coming years."

Bernt Persson was a superstar already – and now that he wanted to return to his old team Smederna, Joel Jansson wasn't prepared to pay the money Bernie wanted.

"This season I won each and every race I was in with my Swedish team Indianerna in the second division – I had a 3.00 race average – and I was in a run-off for gold at the World Final. I deserve a good salary," Bernt said.

"Nobody should believe that us speedway riders make big money – we're not even close to earning what company directors are paid. All the talk about money is so wrong. If you end up second in a World Final, it's all about how much money I make. I work extremely hard for my income," continued the Cradley Heath superstar.

Joel didn't care.

There was another rider he'd rather bring to Smederna – Bengt Jansson. When Benga accepted and Eskilstuna was named Swedish City of the Year for 1973 by Expressen newspaper, Joel said: "Okay, then 1973 will be the perfect year for Smederna to become Swedish Champions."

One thing was for sure, 1973 was going to be a year to remember in Eskilstuna.

And in Wimbledon.

But the foundations for Tommy's success were going to be laid far away from home. His family and friends were going to go through one more tough winter while he was off to race speedway on the other side of the globe.

Next stop, Australia.

Ever the stylist, Tommy and Wimbledon race partner Graeme Stapleton combine for a 5-1 as they squeeze out King's Lynn's England star Malcolm Simmons.

8
In the footsteps of Ivan Mauger

"There must be a pride in winning. There must be more to it than making money. You must be able to look your team-mates and supporters in the eyes."

Ole Olsen

One of the first things that surprised Ole Olsen when it came to Tommy Jansson was something that made Tommy stand out from most of the other Swedish riders.

"He was never partying like crazy," Ole observed.

The Swedish riders had a bad reputation – and they deserved it – because some of them were as wild off the track as they were on it.

During a trip by the Swedish national team in the 70s, some of the riders grabbed fire extinguishers and started spraying each other in the departure lounge at Sydney Airport. The mayhem didn't end until the cops came and stopped the unruly Swedes. Swedish embassy officials were called in to mediate before police let the touring riders out of Australia.

Bernt Persson could be the wildest of them all.

As tough as he was on the track, he was as formidable in holding up the bar afterwards. Olle Nygren praised his friend's stamina but it was a back-handed compliment: "Bernt Persson is stronger than anybody else. He doesn't care who he's up against on the track, he isn't afraid of anybody. Tough, strong and very, very good.

"But he doesn't always carry his liquor too well. At the same time, he never raced better than the day after a wild night out. He can party until five in the morning . . . and then beat everybody out of sight the next day," Olle added.

At this point we are back to what's called 'The Law of Jante', attributed to Danish writer, Aksel Sandemose, who declared: 'You shall not believe that you are somebody', and: 'You shall not believe that you are any better than us'.

Swedes very much lived by those rules and even some 30 years after these wild parties in the 70s, people in Bernt Persson's home-town still talk more about his drinking habits than about his success as a speedway star.

Bernie Persson – one of the finest sportsmen to come out of Eskilstuna.

"Bernt has been a wild child over the years."

"Bernt never missed out on any party."

And so on.

In reality, Bernt Persson wasn't unique in any way. Thousands of men his own age, right here in Eskilstuna, behaved exactly like him, especially during the 70s. If it was party time, those Swedes partied like there was no tomorrow.

Bernt Persson was partying like a Swede.

Nobody was thinking about the morning after. A 'real man' could always drink and a 'real man' never said no.

That was the mentality most men in Eskilstuna had back then.

That's why it's a little tragic to hear those statements about Bernt today, all the talk about his drinking, when fans in Eskilstuna should be talking about something else, about something that was truly unique.

For many years Bernt Persson was one of the best speedway riders in the world.

While others drank like fish and then went to work at the assembly line at Volvo in Eskilstuna, Bernt was competing in a run-off in the World Final against mighty Ivan Mauger, in front of 75,000 fans at Wembley Stadium.

Bernt is one of the best Swedish speedway riders of all time and one of the best sportsmen who ever came out of Eskilstuna.

But Swedish speedway riders liked to have fun. A lot of crazy stunts happened, especially when they toured around Australia. During one particular trip Olle Nygren was in charge of the invading Swedish Vikings when, one day, while travelling between cities, they stopped on a bridge, 25 feet above the water.

Olle suddenly said: "It's warm, I need to go for a swim."

He screamed like Tarzan, ripped off his shirt, stood up on the railings along the top of the bridge and dived into the water. He almost got stuck on the bottom. When he came back up to the surface, he was covered in mud. He had effectively 'drilled himself' into the bottom of the river. A different, less forgiving river bed and he would surely have broken his neck and died instantly.

But, instead, he washed himself clean of all the mud, while all the others cheered him on.

Later during the trip, the Swedes were invited to stay at the home of one of the Australian promoters. His wife had gone on a trip, so late one evening Nygren opened her closet and tried on some of her clothes. The bearded Swede, the notoriously tough-guy of speedway, ran out to the others dressed in a lady's nightgown. He looked like a transvestite – but the others loved it, of course.

When Tommy Jansson travelled to Australia in the early winter of 1972 he had heard all these stories, and more. Before this trip Tommy had never been outside of Europe. He had also never been on a flight longer than the two hours separating Stockholm from London, which was nothing compared to the 23-hour flight to Sydney. On one leg of the trip he had the window seat and next to him were two other passengers, both of them pretty overweight and used to travelling. They'd found their seats, got themselves comfortably positioned and didn't show any willingness to move an inch until landing.

When Tommy felt he needed to go the bathroom, he looked at his fellow passengers and their trays full of food and drinks and decided that these two fat guys had been around the block a bit. They had it all taken care of and didn't want to be disturbed by some kid making his first long-haul flight. Tommy decided to delay the bathroom visit until the plane was back on the ground.

Ole Olsen liked it that Tommy was a little shy, that he was always friendly, curious – and, of course, serious with a strong desire to win. And Olsen also liked it that he didn't party like a typical Swede.

Tommy found it unbelievable that he was really going Down Under. He hadn't even had to pay for the air ticket himself. That was all taken care of by Melbourne Speedway Club, who considered it a good investment and knew they were going to get their money back promoting meetings involving the kid from Sweden.

They were right. He proved that he was very good value much faster than anybody could have expected.

"Looks good, eh?"

The promoter with the big smile and the uplifting "G'day, mate" greeting showed Tommy the advertisement in the local newspaper with the announcement aimed at drawing the public to a shopping mall in the city the day after at 12 o'clock: 'Meet the young man who has charmed all of Europe and lit up the fans in Melbourne,' it read.

"We'll let you go there tomorrow and sign autographs and give out free tickets to fans," the promoter said.

"Do you think any fans will show up?" Tommy asked.

"There's going to be a long line of fans wanting to meet you. We have 200 free tickets to dish out and they will disappear fast. This is the home of speedway and you are a world class rider," the promoter enthused.

He was right.

The next day it was chaos at the mall, where posters plastered everywhere told fans about the 'Swedish Sensation, World Finalist and Swedish Champion' – a bold statement that embarrassed Tommy a little, but the promoter just smiled and said: "You won the Junior Championships, right?" The promoters throughout Australia were smart in their marketing techniques and this scenario was repeated everywhere Tommy went.

Bert Harkins, who was reunited with Tommy at Wimbledon, seen here leading Belle Vue's Soren Sjosten.

He loved the attention, cut out all the articles in the papers and saved them for the scrapbook at home. He was interviewed by newspapers, radio stations and television crews.

Everybody wanted their piece of 'The Swedish Sensation.'

He was presented variously as 'Swedish Champion', 'Future World Champion', 'The Next Ove Fundin' and 'The Flying Swede´. His spoken English had improved dramatically since his first trip to England and the Swedish/English dictionary cum phrase book that he'd borrowed from Bosse before his move to Wimbledon was no longer required.

The board of Melbourne Speedway Club held a meeting and congratulated each other on their smart move to bring the fast-rising Wimbledon star to Australia. Tommy had not only raced brilliantly, he had the looks of a pop star, presented a great image wherever he went and all media reporters and teenage girls loved him at first sight.

Tommy attracted fans in great numbers and after only two weeks of racing he had an offer to return during the British winter of 1973-74 and the year after that. In high spirits, he called home and told them about the offer to sign a two-year deal to race in Australia.

"If I can race all-year round for years to come, my chances of winning against the best will definitely improve," Tommy said.

"How is life over there otherwise?" Joel shouted, feeling that he had to sound strong on the line from Down Under.

"Everything is perfect here . . . it's sunny and warm. The other day it was 80 degrees and when we're not racing or working on the bikes, we're at the beach. How about you?"

"Here it's 14 degrees."

Tommy laughed.

A week later he visited Sydney and his former Wembley team-mate and future Wimbledon colleague, Bert Harkins, who had been out in the sun so much that he had turned red and was nicknamed 'Barbecued Bertie' by his friends in Australia. The Scotsman took Tommy to the famous speedway track at the Sydney Showground. Tommy wanted to take a photo of the vast Royale arena but even though he climbed the stairs up to the top of the stands, he couldn't fit the whole stadium in his view-finder

"What a place!" Tommy said.

Bert knew that Tommy had a great future in this sport but the popular Swede's feet returned to the ground when he pointed out: "The only problem is that I'll have to do military service at home for 10 months. All Swedish men have to do that."

"Well, that's an offer you can't refuse!" Bert joked.

"Nice suntan you have, by the way," Tommy laughed.

"Oh, yes, the other day I was out doing some motorcycling on the road, wearing a fully-enclosed full-face Bell crash helmet and red shorts. My body and legs were so red, though, that when a passer-by noticed me standing on a the corner, he stopped and popped some letters into the open visor of my helmet . . . he'd mistaken me for a pillar box!" added the typically wisecracking Scot.

Bert made Tommy laugh a lot. He liked Bert Harkins with his trademark spectacles and goofy smile. His attitude was something to admire, Tommy thought. Even when the Scot was sat in the heat with a bandaged body after a crash, he didn't complain to anyone.

Tommy had noted that many riders had a knack for finding excuses for their own failures. In Australia, where they then staged only individual races and the riders travelled from all over the continent, the least successful ones tended to blame their poor showings on the fact that their bikes hadn't arrived in time – which is something that happened now and then – or they were unable to score many points on the long, unfamiliar tracks because they were victims of the handicapping system that also operated at many meetings..

When things didn't go right, Tommy never blamed anything other than himself. He could be angry over dropped points, even though that didn't happen often. This was a learning period for Tommy – that's how he treated his first adventure Down Under.

He accepted life with motorcycles that went missing in transit or having to ride borrowed bikes of such a poor quality that would have made Joel Jansson furious and forced the owner to go back home and not come back until his machine was in order.

Joel, by the way, would have been extremely proud watching his son win races in Australia dressed in his racejacket of Smederna. Tommy loved wearing the Smederna logo outside his homeland.

Among the riders who had a tough time catching up with the young Swede were the 1971 World Champion, Ole Olsen, and the reigning world title-holder, Ivan Mauger. Ole and Ivan were both fierce competitors and good friends. Ole looked up to Ivan, who had pulled all the strings when Newcastle Diamonds had the guts to recruit the then unknown Dane in the spring of 1967. Ole Olsen had learned a lot from his mentor and maybe the most important lesson of all was that no-one could teach anybody else how to become World Champion.

In order to reach the top you needed talent and a will to win that was impossible to learn. It needed to be ingrained in you from the beginning, because without talent and determination there was no way you were going to be successful no matter how many pieces of good advice you received.

Now Ole Olsen had the feeling that Tommy was doing exactly as he'd done with Ivan years ago. Tommy studied Olsen's every move and he loved to hang around Ole and Ivan, just listening to them talk. On buses, during flights and at barbecues after meetings in Australia, he always tried to get close to these two superstars of the sport. Tommy couldn't think of a better way to gain the education he wanted.

One evening Olsen talked to Tommy about the pride in being successful with your team. "There must be a pride in winning. There must be more to it than just taking the money. You must be able to look your team-mates and supporters in the eyes.

"The fans at home in Eskilstuna always demand that I win every race I enter," Tommy said.

"They should. That's what they have paid to see," Ole told him.

"Sure, and I always want to win with my teams – Smederna as well as Wimbledon. In Eskilstuna we have a team good enough to win the Swedish Championship this year and it would be fantastic to win with my home-town team – to win it all in front of my home fans."

Olsen said: "Unfortunately, the money has destroyed the sport in some ways. When I started racing, and earlier when Ivan Mauger and Barry Briggs came in to the sport, we were all amateurs, we raced because it was fun. Now many riders are

Ole Olsen hated postponements.

too comfortable, too lazy. But you can never lose your hunger. If you do that, you are finished as a rider."

Tommy decided that he was never going to stop trying, or sit back and relax and become indifferent.

And then he thought about the weather, which was a classic excuse for some. 'The weather was too bad, the track was poor,' was what he heard all the time – from losers. Winners never complained about bad track conditions.

Ole Olsen hated it when meetings were postponed because of bad weather. He always thought it was unnecessary, no matter what the conditions. A little rain wasn't enough to stop a meeting but too much water made it impossible to ride properly on most tracks. Olsen was one of the last riders who accepted that a meeting had to be stopped.

"We are already wet and can't get any wetter," he would say.

When Ole Olsen was in the zone, as he he described it himself, then nothing was going to get in his way – not even a monsoon. In his eyes, the fans had come there to see him race, so what else was he supposed to do but fulfil their expectations?

Even the Brits who were used to rainy weather were astonished once during a British League match, when Ole just refused to park his bike for the night and ended the meeting in a run-off for the title with Hans Holmqvist – the two of them looked like they were riding around on a boating lake.

Afterwards Ole said: "If I'm here to race, I am here to do my best, and nothing is going to stop me. Bad weather doesn't exist for me in those moments. That's only a bad excuse from riders who failed. But this is also what separates the men from the boys – and the real men who become World Champions."

Tommy was a devout listener to statements like this. When Olsen told him, during a barbecue in Australia, that he kept a diary in which he carefully noted details after all his meetings – describing exactly how he'd set up his bike and facts about all different tracks in terms of preparation, surface and everything else, Tommy immediately started keeping his own invaluable reference book.

He realised that you could never prepare too much.

★★★★★★

In Australia, Tommy got to stay at home with Johnnie Jones's family. He was one of the top men in the Australian speedway federation whose family had a house on the outskirts of Melbourne.

Tommy liked his occasional trips into the centre of Melbourne, a colourful city populated by immigrants from Italy in the 50s, and while downtown he found cafés where he could unwind from all the races and life on the beach in the middle of winter. To Tommy, Melbourne and Australia were a lot like England, except for the guaranteed great weather. Melbourne was definitely more like London than Eskilstuna.

Away from the most populated areas and it immediately became a totally different story, of course. Like when Tommy ended up at the track at Jerilderie Park in Newcastle, two hours north of Sydney – the only track in the world that had real live koala bears as spectators! The koalas were up in trees around the track, looking down at the humans making plenty of noise below them.

A couple of weeks after new year, Tommy travelled to the old gold mining town of Bendigo, 100 miles from Melbourne. The heat was almost unbearable, very dry and dusty. When the racing started and the wind started blowing around the track, the sand clouds became like a red fog that blinded the riders and made it hard for the fans to see the action. In the middle of one race, including Tommy and his friend Bert Harkins, a violent wind erupted and it was like a mild sandstorm for a short moment, the riders having totally disappeared from view.

It was the worst drought in the area for many years and during the car journey there from Melbourne, the temperature outside had been over 95 degrees, although going home it dropped to a more cooling 77 degrees.

It sure beat Sweden in the winter!

"I prefer this over the Swedish winter, though," Tommy said.

The next day was race-day race in Melbourne and this time the heat soared to more than 100 degrees fahrenheit, an all-time record for the city. Ole Olsen and Bert Harkins had been sharing a hotel room and at breakfast they felt like grilled fish.

Bert recalled: "The air conditioning broke down and the temperature in our room was 100 degrees. We had to get up in the middle of the night to repair the damned thing and bring the room temperature down to 80 degrees. That was just lovely!"

A promoter in town wanted to lift their spirits and told the rider a story: "A man came to hell and complained to The Devil that it was too hot.

"The Devil said: 'If you think this is hot, you should be in Melbourne'."

Tommy couldn't stop thinking, though, that he'd rather spend time in 100 degrees heat in Melbourne racing speedway, than in freezing conditions and the dark winter back home in Sweden, getting up early in the morning for another shift working as a mechanic.

He couldn't even get upset over the fact that the bikes had problems functioning normally in the intense heat, and that he had blown one motor and suffered another engine failure. To ride borrowed bikes was another step in his education and forced him to meet new challenges and different conditions.

Tommy was sure that these experiences were going to be invaluable as soon as next season started. Even when he heard the news that Ronnie Moore wouldn't be returning to his beloved Wimbledon for the 1973 season, Tommy didn't worry at all. On the contrary, he welcomed the fact that more was going to be asked and expected of him. He was ready to take on the extra responsibility and assume the No.1 mantle in the team.

Moore was tired of racing in England while his family lived in New Zealand, and he had secured a deal with Kawasaki to ride in exhibitions and promote their bikes. A perfect job for an accomplished rider who could feel proud of what he had achieved in his illustrious career.

Tommy Jansson was just beginning his career and he had the hunger that Ole Olsen had talked about. It was a burning hunger not even his new favourite dish of roast beef could satisfy.

Johnnie Jones, who had let Tommy stay at his home, had also seen the driving ambitious within his temporary lodger. He'd taken Tommy along on fishing expeditions and they had also attended some of those brutal Aussie Rules matches together. Tommy had enjoyed everything during his stay but he liked nothing better than to sit down with Johnny and talk about speedway late into the night.

Tommy could sit and talk forever about his favourite subject.

★★★★★

Even the most serious guys could have fun and you could have fun without getting drunk. One weekend the promoter, Cyril Hitchcock, brought along Ole Olsen, Tommy Jansson and some other riders in his van with loudspeakers, that he used to publicise forthcoming meetings while driving through cities. 'Don't miss tonight's speedway event, with world class competition.'

Ole took the microphone when they were passing a shabby and dirty character who was stood hitchhiking by the road. "You can't look like that if you expect to get a ride!" Ole joked over the loudspeakers.

Later they came to a steep downward hill and Ole grabbed the microphone again and yelled: "Mayday! Mayday! . . our brakes don't work!"

A few days later the meeting ended late at night and on the way to the regular barbecue party, Ivan Mauger grabbed the microphone and screamed to all the cars around them: "Attention! Watch out . . . our driver is about to fall asleep!"

★★★★★

Olsen won one event in Melbourne with 12 points, one ahead of Mauger and Tommy. In the final heat Olsen came first, followed by Mauger and Jansson – but the fans celebrated the young Swede as much as the others. The Aussies liked Tommy's attitude about never giving up no matter how far behind he was and throughout all four laps he gave it as much as he possibly could.

His personality helped as well. One paper in Australia wrote: 'Next time you see Tommy in the pits, don't be

On tour Down Under . . . Ivan Mauger with Tommy, John Louis and Egon Müller.

Soaking up the sun and surf in Australia, where Tommy enjoyed water skiing.

afraid to walk over and say hello, as he will return your greeting with a smile. That's just the kind of man he is."

Tommy also earned a lot of respect from the others after a crash when he burned his leg on the exhaust pipe. He refused to miss his next race, so while a doctor took care of his leg and bandaged it, he continued working on his bike, before ignoring the pain and going back out again.

He wasn't only good looking, he was tough too.

Back in England, Wimbledon Speedway manager Cyril Maidment had done all he could to sign Ivan Mauger from Belle Vue. But the four times World Champion asked for more money than the Dons could afford, so Cyril had to give up on the idea of bringing back the man whose amazing British racing career had begun as a raw rookie at Plough Lane way back in 1957.

After all, he had Tommy, who ended his first time in Oz by qualifying for the Australian Championship at Sydney Showground – the place that had so impressed him during a visit together with Bert Harkins. In the advertisement for the Aussie final, the promoters used a cartoon of some speedway riders, one of them sporting a racejacket with three crowns, the Swedish national emblem – and it was all done in honour of Tommy. It was, naturally, a gesture that made Tommy very proud and capped his wonderful first trip to Australia.

But it had not been all fun. During his time Down Under, the sport had been dealt a tragic blow with the sad news that veteran Jack Biggs had suffered an engine failure during a race in Bendigo, on the same night Tommy was racing in Melbourne. Biggs, who had been racing for 25 years, crashed and the riders following behind were unable to avoid him. The former World Finalist and Aussie international was killed.

Every time somebody brought up the subject of this and other tragic accidents, Tommy and his fellow riders repeated what they always said in such circumstances: 'Sure, speedway can be a very dangerous sport. But you run a bigger risk of being killed out on the streets driving your own car.'

Speedway riders knew that talent and hard work wasn't enough. You needed some luck also – or, more crucially, you needed to avoid any bad luck.

At Sydney Showground, where the sheer speed of the vast 600-yard track almost scared him, Tommy dropped five points and ended the night in sixth place.

During the long flight home to Sweden, Tommy reflected on his four months in Australia, the 40 meetings he'd been in . . . and how he was still a little slow out of the gate. But instead of being home in the bitter cold, he had been able to race full time and made some good money as well – even more than he'd expected.

He glimpsed inside his passport and realised that he'd travelled a lot for a 20-year-old – to Norway, Denmark, Britain, West Germany, East Germany, Poland, Holland and now he was on his way home from Australia.

'This is just the beginning,' he thought.

9
Mr Nice Guy

"I went where I wanted to go on the track. Anders Michanek used to push people around but by racing like that, you can really hurt somebody else or crash yourself. I didn't want to take those kind of risks.
"I didn't want to make enemies."

Bengt Jansson

Back in Wimbledon, the first pre-season practice of 1973 at Plough Lane saw Tommy crash straight through the collapsible wire mesh fencing that separated the speedway track from the surrounding greyhound circuit. Track staff, who had spent hours putting up the fencing, cursed the reckless Swede who made them have to do all their hard work again.

Bert Harkins, who had just signed a contract with Wimbledon after a season with Sheffield following Wembley's closure, smiled when Tommy came back to the pits – unhurt, except for a little burning sensation on his backside.

"Tommy, don't you remember what I told you in Australia? You can't continue racing as fast as you did over there now you're back in England."

Tommy had totally misjudged the difference between racing on the big, long tracks Down Under compared to the smaller venues in Britain and the rest of Europe. He decided to regard his mishap as a sharp reminder that he still had much to learn. Tommy recognised again that as soon as you became a little cocky and thought you had it all under control, something could literally jump up and bite you on the backside. He knew it was important for him to remain humble and never lose focus.

After that first practice session the riders all discussed what they had been up to over the course of the winter. Australian Neil Cameron told the others about the shock he had when he went to pick up his car, after returning to England from his native Australia.

"I had it parked in a garage in Wolverhampton, a nice V 4 Corsair, but my garage was vandalised and my car totally smashed up. Some football hooligans from Liverpool, whose team had just lost to Wolves, terrorised the whole neighbourhood and vandalised everything in their way – including my car," Neil said.

The story about his car even appeared in the papers. Newspapers in England published more and more about speedway and although at one time the Sunday

Mirror was the only paper regularly covering the sport, more had latched onto the early 70s boom period. The Daily Mirror sponsored the International Tournament in 1973 that culminated in a dramatic, televised England v Sweden final at Wembley, while the Daily Express annually sponsored an individual competition, the Spring Classic, staged at Wimbledon.

In March, Speedway Star even reported that Bosse Jansson 'might show up to race in England pretty soon.'

Bengt Jansson started writing his own column in The Star and in his first piece he attacked all the people who had questioned the commitment of the Swedish riders when they sometimes missed meetings in Britain in order to race in their homeland. 'We have signed contracts with teams in both countries, and we really want to be there for everybody as much as we can,' Benga wrote.

Tommy read most of the stories he could find on speedway and was in an excited mood as the new season in Britain was about to dawn – as always, a few weeks before the campaign got underway in Sweden.

Wimbledon's '73 team consisted of: Tommy, Bert Harkins, Neil Cameron, Graeme Stapleton, Tony Clarke, Reg Luckhurst and captain Trevor Hedge. Luckhurst also had something interesting to tell his team-mates – how he'd recently managed to capsize his motorboat off the Kent coast! It meant Reg had to agree to a clause in his contract, that he was not allowed to go out to sea by himself. The veteran Reg was a true character, who had been in the recording studio to make two singles and even produced an album with his country and western band, The Huntsmen.

It all started well for the Dons, who started with a home win over Ipswich Witches, a team with Olle Nygren and John Louis in their line-up. Wimbledon supporters had waited almost two years for a victory on the road but the Dons won two of their first three matches away from Plough Lane.

Captain Hedge crashed a couple of times but still managed to show the way. "Hedgie is important for us," Tommy told fellow countryman Bengt Jansson, when the two boarded a plane back home to Sweden.

"By the way, how was Australia?" Bengt asked.

"Even though I travelled a lot, it was perfect to be based at one location, like I was in Melbourne," Tommy told him.

"I've been there with the national team a few times but I mostly found it too hectic. A lot of travelling, bad meetings and things didn't work out at all for me. It felt like a waste of time," Bengt said.

"It's best to go there by yourself and freelance – you should try it,"

Reg Luckhurst also had some trouble at sea!

Tommy was very happy with third place in the prestige Internationale, even though he finished behind Ole Olsen and Anders Michanek.

Tommy said.

He told Bengt more tales about his adventures Down Under and Tommy was glad that he didn't have to talk about his own bad start to the season in England. The team had been doing great, but Tommy had been no better than average.

He had counted on being in top shape from the start, but he'd had difficulty readjusting to the smaller tracks in Britain. His usual ability to read tracks and spot weaknesses in his opponents wasn't really there yet.

Bengt didn't want to remind him about their last get-together either. His team, Hackney Hawks, had won 42-36 and even if Tommy had been the best Wimbledon-rider with 12 points, it was a total he achieved from six rides, so he'd been disappointed to drop six points.

In the prestige Internationale individual meeting at Plough Lane, Tommy had been the only rider to beat Ole Olsen in front of 20,000 fans. But it had been Olsen's night and in a breathtaking run-off victory against Anders Michanek, the Dane had lowered the track record.

In a run-off for third place, Tommy had beaten World Champion Ivan Mauger. That performance left the Swede feeling even happier than anybody else among the big crowd at Wimbledon that night, including Ole Olsen.

"Tommy will become World Champion one day, I'm sure about that," predicted Wimbledon boss Cyril Maidment.

★★★★★★

Back home in Eskilstuna, Tommy was reminded yet again of the other side of the coin of being a celebrity. The local newspapers had their usual big stories – if he wasn't pictured posing with his parents and showing off souvenirs from Australia, he was quoted on his latest successes and the glamourous life of being a professional speedway rider in Britain. Tommy loved to see those stories in print and he was very proud of all the coverage he was attracting.

But walking the streets of his home town . . . that was something else. He didn't mind when total strangers came over and congratulated him or just wanted to chat for a while and get an autograph. He was used to that.

What he didn't like, however, and what he realised was the downside of being famous, was the attention from all the people who pretended to know him, people who acted like they were his best friends and who wanted to rub shoulders with him, just because he was a celebrity.

Tommy took a step back from the hangers-on. He wanted to keep them at bay and though he was polite, he never allowed them to get too close nor invited them into any conversations or in any way encouraged them. Tommy even warned his brother: "You have to learn the difference between who your real friends are, and those who just want to be your friend because you are a famous speedway rider."

He knew there were some back-stabbing people from his own home town who talked behind his back, accusing him of turning cocky and alleging that he was not a team rider and only interested in winning for himself.

Joel had heard the talk as well but he didn't take it seriously. Joel had raced against Ove Fundin, who was always in his own little world, not caring about other people, and extremely selfish on track. You had to be like that to be very successful.

Olle Nygren was the total opposite – always happy-go-lucky and loved to talk to anybody at any time. Tommy had been surprised by Nygren's laid-back approach and even asked his father: "Isn't it better to be open and friendly like Olle, rather than moody and introverted like Ove?"

There is another major difference between Ove and Olle. Fundin won the World Championship five times but Nygren never won it once.

Joel had always wanted to have fun riding speedway, while at the same time doing whatever he could to win as a rider. He had the same attitude when he became a manager. As a rider he had been forced to accept his shortcomings – he was never good enough to go all the way and conquer the world, but he went as far as he could. And that's exactly what he demanded of the riders in his own team.

Responding to his ambitious leadership, Smederna were shooting towards the Swedish League Championship.

Back home after spending the winter in Australia, Tommy shows Inga-Lill and Joel some souvenirs.

When Joel arrived at the speedway track in Eskilstuna, he checked that everything was running smoothly.

"Are the programmes ready?"

"Oh, yes, we've got line-ups showing all the riders' name and numbers."

"Concession stands?"

"All taken care of. Fans can buy hot dogs, snacks and coffee."

"Great."

There were already hundreds of people making their way into the stadium. It was an early evening in May, midweek, and in a short while there were long queues forming outside the concession stands and around the hot dog vendors.

The first bikes roared.

Tommy Jansson had landed in Stockholm the same day. He was tired, all the travelling was taking its toll on him. He was also in a bad mood for a different reason.

"I'm so unhappy over my bad gating," admitted Tommy.

"You know what I have told you . . . it's bad starts that make you so popular with the fans. When you have to pass others all the time, that's the kind of speedway the fans love to see," Joel responded.

Tommy shook his head, while Joel just tried to calm him down.

"I was the same when I was racing. I had problems making consistently good starts – but then I went past the others on the outside!" Joel said with a smile.

"But against the best riders in the world, I can't afford to be slower than them from the gate," Tommy pointed out.

Tommy always wanted to make a good impression in Eskilstuna, where he knew that many of the fans in the stands had come there just to see him.

In 1973, he was not aiming to race as well as he had done the previous year – he was determined to perform even better. The fans demanded that from him and he couldn't let them down. There were around 1,000 spectators in attendance, a decent number for a meeting in Sweden and they were curious to see just what Tommy could do.

Tommy was up against Sven-Olof Lindh, Bosse Jansson and Ake Doved. That's right - all four riders rode for Smederna.

1,000 spectators, long queues to get a hot dog and printed line-ups in the programmes. But for a real meeting?

No, this was only a practice session!

There wasn't another team in Sweden at the time, in any sport whatsoever, that attracted a crowd like this for an ordinary practice/training session. It was totally unheard of.

And it was all because their world class superstar was back in town.

Tommy Jansson's return trips to Eskilstuna were always a big thing.

His bike was in tip-top condition but, once again, he was behind from the gate. The fastest away was Sven-Olof Lindh, who had a great knack of finding openings and exploiting them.

Joel loved to watch his team practice. It was at these times, more than in matches, that he could really identify who the best riders were and who had the best attitude.

He never hesitated to replace a better rider with somebody who still had to lot to learn, as long as that rider was very willing to learn and strive to become better. There was nothing he disliked more than those who wasted their talent or just didn't care about themselves or their bikes.

Joel would pick an ambitious youngster over a lazy veteran every time.

Now and then he would tell riders to go home and fix their bikes before returning to his team. He never backed down from a confrontation and many riders got an earful from him and were told to get their act together.

He demanded that all riders maintained their equipment to the same high order, whether it was for a league match or just a practice session. He often invited riders from other teams to practice with his Smederna riders, to make the sessions more competitive.

He loved to position cones around the track in order to create new racing lines and to make the Motorstadion circuit in Eskilstuna ride like other tracks. Prior to every away match, he tried to imitate the track they were going to next and he always talked to his riders about the most important aspects and characteristics of the different tracks they visited.

Joel didn't doubt that Tommy was in good shape and, of course, he knew what Tommy could do. Instead, he paid attention to another rider during this particular practice, the winner of the first race – Sven-Olof Lindh.

Sven-Olof was flying and back in the pits afterwards, Joel couldn't help himself when he uncharacteristically yelled to Sven-Olof: "That's how you're supposed to ride in real competition. During practice you are the best speedway rider in the world, so ride like that against other teams as well," Joel said.

Sven-Olof removed his helmet in the pits and smiled but Tommy was not amused.

He hated losing at any time.

It was the same during actual racing. Tommy and Sven-Olof often rode as a pair and while Tommy was the one who won most of the races, for Sven-Olof it was mostly a case of just trying to keep up and collect any possible points behind his much more illustrious team-mate. If he happened to win, everybody was all smiles. Well, perhaps not everybody – not if Tommy felt that Sven-Olof had impeded him in any way. Tommy had complained to him about this a few times: "You have to be more alert out there," he'd tell him.

Sven-Olof listened and tried to learn but, really, he was just thrilled to be where he was. It was him, and nobody else, who was riding in partnership with Tommy Jansson – one of the best young riders in the world.

Sven-Olof Lindh was typical of riders to be found in most teams – a bread and butter performer. In his home town of Haparanda, in northern Sweden, he had started work at a travelling fair, riding the Wall of Death. But when he had the chance of another job and a better future in Eskilstuna, he packed up his Ford Mercury and drove south.

He worked at Volvo, got a small place to stay in town and pretty soon decided that he was going to stay in Eskilstuna for the rest of his life. He loved cruising around town in his Mercury, loved the work he had and the money he made. Looking back on his time as a Wall of Death rider, he enjoyed telling stories about cheering fans, about how he used to sit on the handlebars of an Indian motorcycle, while his colleague steered — and there were some spectacular falls too.

But nothing made him as proud as being a rider for Smederna.

It all began after he'd attended a few meetings and gained the inspiration to try the sport himself. He found a bike under the classified ads section of a magazine and attended an open practice with Smederna. The next day he went alone to a gravel pit outside of town, to try his new machine. Later he tried it for real with Smederna again and did well immediately. One veteran even commented to him: 'You must have been racing in the past!'

Sven-Olof and Tommy came into Smederna at the same time and the former Wall of Death performer was now an important part of one of the best speedway teams in Sweden.

Sven-Olof could live with some verbal abuse from Tommy if he, as the secondary rider in the pair, got in the way of the No.1. He could live with some stick from Joel now and then – like the time, during a meeting far away from Eskilstuna, when Lindh had started dismally with two last places.

"You haven't travelled all the way from Eskilstuna to end up in last place in every race, have you?" Joel asked. After that, Sven-Olof won three straight heats. To be a rider in the shadow of stars suited Sven-Olof perfectly, because he got what he felt was the biggest reward possible. He got to experience something only a select few in the world got to be a part of – and there was nothing he loved more than for his close companion Tommy Jansson to walk over to him in the pits before a race and say: 'Okay, Sven-Olof, now you have to go for it.'

And he was thrilled afterwards, following another 5-1 victory, when Tommy had taken charge by closing the necessary gaps to allow Sven-Olof to move alongside him and into his favourite position on the outside. A smiling Tommy walked over to him and said: "Lindh . . . we did great!"

Sven-Olof Lindh lived for those moments.

So did the fans.

In the fifth round of Swedish League matches, Smederna broke the team record for a home match with 4,000 fans in the stands to watch them face Getingarna. Star visitor Anders Michanek was man-of-the-match but since Smederna had the powerful trio of Tommy Jansson, Bengt Jansson and Gote Nordin, the Blacksmiths won.

"To lose against Anders is nothing to be ashamed of. It's no exaggeration to say that he's the best speedway rider in the world right now," Tommy said.

Joel Jansson was happy as well.

"Now we're getting closer to the number of fans we had here in the 50s. We're approaching an average of between 4,000-5,000 and if it continues like this, there's going to be little room left around this track."

Joel was much happier after victory over Getingarna than he'd been after his team had crushed Njudungarna, 50-28. That was too one-sided for the manager, who wanted to see closer matches that excited the fans. He also demanded the highest standards of organisation and presentation – the sound of the two-minute buzzer was unusual in Eskilstuna, where he ran a slick operation.

He once said: "Fans come here to see speedway, they come here to be entertained – not to see staff working on track preparation."

One night, when the track had to be watered and the driver of the water truck had disappeared for a moment, Joel took his place and went out and took care of the track himself. He always led by example.

★★★★★★

Bengt Jansson quickly became one of the most popular riders at Smederna – especially among his own team-mates. Like during one race with Sven-Olof Lindh, when Benga showed an opening for his team-mate by pointing with his finger . . . and then closed the gap behind to ensure another Smederna 5-1.

Bengt lived in a suburb of Stockholm and commuted between Hackney and Eskilstuna. The offer to ride for Smederna was one he couldn't refuse. Sweden had no Rider Control restrictions that so irritated people in Britain. Riders could make their own choices all the time and sign for any team they wished.

Bengt became attracted to Smederna thanks to the Jansson family. His impression of Tommy was that the youngster had racing in his blood, even before he'd ridden a bike himself.

When Bengt and Tommy travelled together to Poland for a meeting, they removed the rear seat from Benga's Mercedes 200 Diesel and put their bikes in the back. They drove all the way from Stockholm to Leszno, a round trip close on 2,000 miles. Apart from Bengt's failed attempt to make Tommy understand his second passion in life, country and western music, the only thing they talked about during all the hours together in the car was speedway.

Tommy wanted to know all the details about Bengt's machines – set-ups, how he worked with his compression, gears, clutch settings – everything.

He wanted to know what Bengt thought about the future, how the sport would develop and how the machines were going to get better and faster.

Bengt knew that Tommy didn't have the best equipment at that stage. Bengt had been a world class rider for a number of years and had some of the best machinery money could buy. During a London derby clash between Wimbledon and Hackney, he had trouble with his bike and nothing worked for him at all. He complained to Tommy, who didn't care that Bengt was racing for the opposition and the young Dons rider offered him the use of his own bike.

Reluctantly, Bengt relented, agreed to borrow Tommy's two-valve Jawa, and then got a shock – the Hawks' No.1 ended up last in his first heat.

But that made him even more impressed by Tommy, because his young compatriot's bike was much inferior to his own normally reliable Jawa machine. In that moment Bengt realised again what a unique talent Tommy was.

"Not only did he ride very well, but he did so on a piece of s**t," Bengt said.

In Poland it was the usual routine. The Polish girls surrounded Tommy but he didn't seem interested.

"I don't think he cared about girls. It was just speedway on his mind – nothing

Above: Benga Jansson proved a great signing for Smederna.
Below: Anders Michanek, Bengt Jansson and Terry Betts after the Daily Express Spring
Classic at Wimbledon in 1973.

else," Bengt added.

Bengt and Tommy Jansson often travelled together between Sweden and England. At the airport they always started their conversations the same way: "How'd you do last night?"

"Dropped two points. How about you?"

"Dropped three."

The Swedish stars never talked about how many points they collected, it was all about how many they'd dropped. For both of them scoring a maximum was always their main goal. To them, a second place – even against giants like Ivan or Anders or anybody else for that matter, was not two points gained. It was one dropped point.

Bengt Jansson rode in six individual World Finals, never finished lower than sixth and won one silver and one bronze medal. He forced a run-off for the world title against fellow Swede Ove Fundin at Wembley in 1967.

In that particular final, Bengt had missed every start, but raced excellently after that, passing great riders like Barry Briggs, Michanek and Fundin in extraordinary fashion.

But in the final analysis, Ove was more ruthless, he just wanted it more than Bengt and did so to collect his fifth crown. Ove was ready to do whatever it took to win, whereas Bengt's only weakness was that he could sometimes be too much of a Mr Nice Guy on the track.

He admitted: "I went where I wanted to go on the track. Anders Michanek used to push people around but by racing like that, you can really hurt somebody else or crash yourself. I didn't want to take those kind of risks.

"I didn't want to make enemies. I'd rather wait for the right moment and then go for it. I liked to pressurise others into mistakes and then pass them."

Michanek obviously had a different attitude.

"Nice guys never win World Finals – and Bengt was too nice," said Mich.

Bengt Jansson was in more than 20 Swedish Championship finals, without ever winning a single one, though he did finish second twice. Coming out of a turn there was nobody better in the world and Joel told Tommy to study Bengt, the way he came out of a bend and raced into the straight with great speed and with his bike's wheels perfectly in line.

In team events, Bengt was priceless. The perfect team-mate, he had problems dealing with the most egotistical riders, like Anders Michanek and Ivan Mauger, both on and off the track. Surprisingly though, Bengt still remains a very good friend of Ole Olsen's – they share a love of country and western music.

What Joel Jansson liked about Bengt were his skills as a rider, the way he passed others and they way he handled himself in the turns. He also valued his upbeat personality, saying: "He is the nicest person you can meet – always positive, a manager's dream."

Besides that, Joel had detected something few people understood.

Just exactly how tough Bengt Jansson really was. He had a high pain threshold and once, when he came back from England for a meeting with Smederna, he could hardly walk.

But Benga ignored his pain and raced with his customary class. Later the same night he had to see a doctor and it was revealed that Bengt had a severe fracture in one of his legs, which had to be put in plaster. The doctor was shocked to hear that Jansson had been racing speedway with a broken leg.

"It must have hurt badly?" said the medico.

Bengt didn't say anything.

He just smiled.

★★★★★★

Smederna's quest for gold even caused strained relations between father and son a couple of times during the year. In one match Joel ordered the water truck out onto

The ever-studious Joel talking tactics at Smederna with Tommy and Benga Jansson.

the track because the flying dust made it uncomfortable for the fans. The result of all the watering was a totally different racing surface and completely new conditions for the riders.

It seemed to unsettle the home riders and Tommy was so erratic in such heavy conditions that he returned to the pits and threw his helmet down in frustration.

"How can you water the track like that? This is my livelihood. This is what I do, so don't ruin it for me. If the track is like this, I don't want to go out there at all."

"I admit, it was wrong of me to water it like that," Joel conceded.

In another meeting Tommy was the one not paying attention to detail. In one heat partnered with Bengt Jansson, he lost control and allowed Hans Holmqvist to squeeze between him and Benga to snatch the win. Smederna, in turn, dropped points they should definitely have had.

"That's not the way to ride if you're a professional. You're supposed to know where Bengt is in on the track," Joel complained to his son.

This time the roles were reversed and it was Tommy who would feel stupid and remorseful.

"I know, I made a mistake," he agreed.

10
Respect for Michanek

"Just hang on to me. Then at least you'll end up second."

Anders Michanek

Anders Michanek was never popular among his peers. When Olle Nygren had a huge birthday bash, many years after his career had ended, he wanted to invite all his old friends from the world of speedway.

He called Anders Michanek and said: "I've always thought you are a mean bastard, the meanest bastard I've ever met. But I still want you to come to my birthday party."

Anders agreed to come . . . and he showed up.

That little story says a lot about the world class rider Tommy Jansson had to partner for the World Pairs Final in Boras, Sweden, in June 1973.

The first advice Michanek gave his new partner was: "Just hang on to me. Then at least you'll end up second."

Nygren had a name for Anders Michanek. Olle called him 'The Cobra', for Anders' ability to strike in all situations and for his total lack of fear.

Nobody had ever been able to scare him. Anders Michanek didn't only push around nobodies out on the track, he ran straight into superstars like Ove Fundin and Barry Briggs as well. Nobody could relax for a second with Anders around.

Nygren agreed: "Anders Michanek was a real tough guy."

That toughness, and the way he treated everybody the same way, earned him respect as well as invitations to parties.

Tommy was full of respect for the big city man from Stockholm and curious about how Anders worked with his bike and how he set it up for races. In Boras, Tommy walked over to Anders' bike in the pits and touched his throttle. But Anders got mad and pushed Tommy's hand away.

"Don't f****** touch that," snapped Mich, who explained to Tommy that nobody was allowed to touch his machines.

When Anders heard the story about how Tommy had passed his own brother Bosse inches before the finish line in a match against Bysarna – a move many others thought unnecessary and despicable – Anders just smiled. He loved it.

Anders also had a brother in the sport and Lennart Michanek was a rider like Bosse Jansson, one class below his more famous brother, and Anders was as

Anders Michanek had respect for Tommy.

uninterested as Tommy had been in lending his brother a helping hand.

"Pass my brother right before the finish line? Tommy did the right thing, of course. I'd have done the same thing without even thinking about it," Anders agreed.

Anders liked Tommy, which surprised a lot of other riders since Anders was well known for loving nobody except himself. Later on Anders would let Tommy use one of his bikes in the middle of a meeting – talk about giving everybody else in the pits a shock. It was totally unheard of.

The reason behind Anders' generosity was the respect he had for his younger colleague.

He explained: "Tommy never liked to go out for a couple beers. He was extremely serious. He would even have stayed in the pits and polished his spokes while the rest of us went out for dinner and a night out. He was very careful. And just the fact that he had the guts to always walk his own way, do his thing, that's what I thought made him tough."

Many other Swedish riders had strong opinions about the home pairing for this final in Boras and the widely held view among them was that Tommy wasn't the best rider to partner Anders.

However, Arne Bergstrom, the man behind the selection, didn't care. He thought it was a clever move to combine a hardened veteran with a hungry youngster.

Anders wasn't complaining either. On the contrary, he couldn't agree more with Bergstrom's view. He thought it was a smart decision and in the pits before the final he was very confident of a Swedish victory on home soil.

Tommy went to Boras with mixed feelings – his last visit to this venue had ended in tears. In the Swedish Final the year before he had lost the run-off for third place against Bernt Persson. The bumpy track around the football pitch was often difficult to handle.

"I'm surprised that we don't see more accidents here," Anders complained. "It's not a nice track at all. It's annoying and trying to ride here is never good for your nerves."

What gave Tommy increased confident, though, was his recent results. After beating Getingarna – Anders' team – at home, Smederna continued their impressive league form by taking two points on the road against Bysarna, inflicting the team from Gotland's first home defeat in three years. After that match, the Bysarna manager, Tore Attlerud, walked over to Joel, shook his hand and said: "Congratulations on winning the championship."

Although he knew that there were a number of other battles still to be won, deep down Joel knew his team was in title-winning form and he was very optimistic.

At the Nordic Final in Norrkoping, where Ole Olsen won with maximum points, Joel had witnessed impressive performances by three of his riders who qualified for the next round, the Nordic-British Final, another step closer to the World Final in Poland. With Bengt Jansson (beaten only by Olsen), Tommy and Gote Nordin in such strong form, nothing could stop Smederna from winning the league title.

In World Pairs Championships, the outcome was often settled by the secondary man of the partnership. Ivan Mauger, Ole Olsen and Anders Michanek almost always delivered and collected their expected amount of points – but what could their compatriots do? Tommy's recent success made the Swedes pre-meeting favourites to win on home soil.

Mauger raced side by side for New Zealand with Tommy's team-mate from Wimbledon, Graeme Stapleton. Mauger was furious at the SAD airline who, for the second year in a row, had misplaced his luggage and in order to race in Boras he had to borrow equipment – including boots and a helmet – from Olsen.

No matter, New Zealand still had a great chance of winning the whole thing – even though Michanek feared only one single opponent in the entire field: Ole Olsen. Luckily for his rivals, Olsen was a very lonely man on this occasion. Although the Wolverhampton No.1 scored an outstanding 18-point maximum, his Danish partner, Kurt Bogh, was out of his depth at this level and managed just three points.

Mauger felt sorry for Olsen. Like many others, Ivan had a hard time getting on with Anders Michanek, but Anders and Tommy clicked at once. Tommy followed orders and made sure he hung on to Anders' coat-tails in order to at least grab second place. They both had a good knack for spotting each other on the track and did what was best for the team in all situations. When Tommy won his first race and later on even managed to beat Mauger, it was no longer a contest.

Sweden won gold with 24 points – Anders scored 15 and Tommy nine – and finished three clear of Denmark. Olsen beat Poland's new 'wonder boy', Zenon Plech, in a run-off to decide who won the silver medal. New Zealand, with Mauger scoring only eight and Stapleton just two, finished last of the seven pairings.

Tommy – who competed in his newly-designed racejacket bearing the Smederna logo, Wimbledon's famous yellow star on red background and the Swedish flag – proudly stepped up onto the rostrum alongside Anders and the proud feeling Tommy had on hearing the Swedish national anthem was something he'd never felt before.

Celebrating with his parents on the centre green, he said: "Anders carried the heavy load, of course, but I'm more than happy with my performance. This is my best moment as a speedway rider so far."

Anders was equally happy, saying: "I was sure we were going to win tonight. We're in great shape, both Tommy and me."

The veteran Michanek knew he was the big star but he was aware of Tommy's

speedway star

W/E JUNE 23, 1973   12p

INTERNATIONAL LEAGUE PREVIEW

growing importance. "I really want to thank Tommy for this victory. We made a team in a way no other pair did tonight. And the way Tommy beat Ivan . . . that was great to see." Tommy loved to hear all the praise.

Besides the home pair's victory, most of the talk afterwards was about the reckless Polish riders. Zenon Plech was so tough in a race against Reidar Eide that the Norwegian had to be taken to hospital.

Mauger said: "Zenon Plech is one of the wildest riders in the world but he can become really, really good. Every time he stays on the bike for four laps, he gets good results."

Back in London, Tommy picked up a copy of Speedway Star. He was pictured on the front cover, in colour, together with team-mates Reg Luckhurst and Bert Harkins, while on the back of the same issue was a shot of Bernt Persson in Cradley Heath colours.

'Me and Bernt from Eskilstuna,' Tommy thought, 'we're doing a great job promoting Sweden's City of the Year.

11
Money talks

"Once a Smed, always a Smed."

Joel Jansson

One more day at work, one more flight between London and Stockholm. At Arlanda airport Joel waited for his son. This time Tommy dreaded what was about to happen. Normally, he looked forward to returning home, but this time he was walking into a minefield – he was going back to talk to his father about money.

Tommy had heard what riders from other teams were being paid and he knew of many, way below his own ability, who were making more money than he did at Smederna At the same time he knew that Joel looked after the club's finances and Tommy understood that one of the reasons why Smederna was in such a stable economic state was thanks to his dad and treasurer Olle Lundh running a tight ship and not allowing any unnecessary expense.

Tommy also knew his father had principles he lived by. There was nothing Bernt Persson wanted more than to race for his home-town team. He didn't ask Joel for a ridiculous amount of money, just standard pay for the market and what other clubs were prepared to pay him – and what Indianerna later ended up paying him.

Joel just plainly refused to even come close to lavishing that kind of money on any of his riders. It wasn't so much about having to balance the books, more down to his principles. Joel would never forgive Bernt for leaving Smederna, a club on its way up. Joel was the man who introduced Bernt to speedway. Bernt learned how to ride from Joel Jansson.

But Joel felt Bernt repaid him by leaving Smederna and that was a betrayal impossible for him to forgive or forget.

Tommy started the difficult conversation with his father, in the car on the way from the airport, by talking about other riders' salaries. Joel didn't take the bait.

He would have preferred to hear about Wimbledon's latest match.

"I really think I deserve to be paid better," Tommy started.

"You have signed a contract with Smederna," Joel reminded his son.

"But, next year . . ."

"We pay you only what we can afford to pay you," Joel explained.

"But riders in other teams, with smaller crowds than we have in Eskilstuna, they make more money than me. Much more," Tommy protested.

His father's resolve didn't weaken.

"Those teams don't take care of their finances the way they should. A team can't afford to increase its costs too much. We have plenty of expenses – salaries, equipment, material, rent of the track. This is a major operation we're running here and we can't let costs escalate out of control."

"But I should be paid the same as other riders of my calibre," countered Tommy.

"Your time will come. You are still young."

"But I can't wait forever, so I'll have to change teams and race for someone else in Sweden."

"Impossible!" Joel said.

"Why?"

"You just can't do that."

"Why not?"

"Once a Smed, always a Smed."

Tommy gave up. Deep down he also knew that he would never betray Smederna, never leave his dad's team. Not just because of his father, but because Smederna was the team from his home town. That's how strong his feelings for his team were.

That fans sometimes asked unreasonable things of him but, in the end, nothing was sweeter than winning at home, in front of his own fans in the town where he was born and raised.

No money in the world could buy that feeling of satisfaction.

Tommy put financial considerations aside and said to himself: 'My father is right. Once a Smed, always a Smed.'

★★★★★★

Eskilstuna is Worth a Melody, was a song recorded to honour The 1973 City of the Year in Sweden. It was not really rock 'n' roll. Far from it.

The Expressen newspaper's campaign for Eskilstuna in '73 sparked action among community leaders, who organised different kinds of activities, including a folk music festival. But the more cynical citizens of the town complained to the papers, claiming it was no more than a publicity stunt designed to sell more copies.

The biggest crowd of the year gathered when the politicians from the leading Social Democrat party had a start-up meeting before that year's election in the working class town between the lakes in the heart of the country. Sweden's Minister of Finance, Gunnar Strang, made the headlines with an uplifting speech in front of 10,000 people. Later, the Social Democrats stayed in power with the smallest margin possible – 0.11 percent more votes than the Conservatives. This was also the year of a famous bank robbery and hostage situation at Norrmalmstorg in Stockholm. It was also the year the Swedish King, Gustav VI Adolf, died and was replaced by Carl XVI Gustaf.

And 1973 was also the time for Tommy Jansson to begin his military service.

By the way, the Wimbledon and Smederna star was not the only celebrity they talked about in town that summer. A rock star was rumoured to be looking for a summer cabin in Kvicksund, a nice homestead by lake Malaren, just outside Eskilstuna. He was Rolling Stone Bill Wyman, who had a girlfriend from nearby Vasteras and had been spotted in the area, although he never did buy a property there. The sceptics of Eskilstuna just laughed about the whole thing and wondered: 'What the hell is a man like Wyman going to do here? He can do so much better than this town.'

The self-esteem among the downbeat folk of Eskilstuna was still at its normal low ebb. Despite the so-called celebrations in the City of the Year, the people there still felt small and nobody was supposed to believe they were anything special.

City of the Year? Nah!

In other words, everything was just like it always had been.

With one exception.

One night it all changed for a short while. One warm August evening Smederna won the Swedish Championship for the first time ever and, without feeling stupid, fans ran around screaming: 'We are the best!' Which was truly shocking behaviour in Eskilstuna.

Smederna beat Njudungarna 51-27 and even though the season hadn't quite finished yet, no team could catch them at the top of the league.

At long last, Eskilstuna had the best speedway team in Sweden.

Tommy was tired from all his travelling and his first months of military service. Fortunately, he had managed to arrange for a lot of official leave from the army to enable him to continue riding – thanks to one of the hot-shots of the Swedish speedway federation (SVEMO). Anders Thunborg, a politician who would later have a career as Minister of Defence, working as an ambassador in Washington and Moscow, was one of the most powerful men in the country. Thunborg called Tommy's officers at the barracks in Enkoping and asked them to release the young rider whenever he needed time off to pursue his racing commitments.

Tommy was grateful for that co-operation and didn't miss as much racing as he'd feared – he was even able to go to England occasionally.

What bothered him was that he felt he could have raced better, so he was also grateful for his father's talent in being able to assemble such a strong, well-balanced team.

Tommy remembered Ole Olsen's words in Australia, about always thinking about the team and never being happy with a personal maximum if the team lost. It was the same thing Joel had said to him many times. In team races the team had to come first, ego second.

But that phrase could also be turned around. Even if you'd had a bad meeting individually, but your team had won, then you could celebrate like everybody else.

After the victory against Njudungarna, who were skippered by Bo Wirebrand, it was easy to celebrate.

Even though Tommy had to wake up early every morning for exercises, dressed in army uniform and in front of screaming officers, and the fact that he'd missed a lot of meetings in England, that he always felt tired and that his bike had not worked

Wimbledon's improving 1973 team. Back row, left to right: Cyril Maidment, Graeme Stapleton, Pete Wigley, Tony Clarke, Neil Cameron, Bert Harkins. Kneeling: Reg Luckhurst and Tommy. On bike: Trevor Hedge.
Left: With Ronnie Moore back in retirement, Tommy's action picture adorned the front cover of the Wimbledon programme throughout the 1973 season.

WIMBLEDON SPEEDWAY
SPRING GOLD CUP
Dons v Kings Lynn
29 MARCH 1973

Official Programme 7p

properly on this memorable night . . . none of that mattered when the fans cheered and celebrated the new champions.

Tommy felt so delighted for team-mate Gote Nordin, one of the riders he looked up to the most, when Gote capped his last season as a top rider by breaking the track record in his last race in Eskilstuna. Anders Michanek's recently established record was shattered by as much as a whole second. Tommy couldn't have been happier even if he'd beaten the record himself.

At home on Tornerosgatan, Inga-Lill Jansson prepared a late-night supper and many riders and friends showed up for a party. Joel checked the programme and remarked: "Talk about a team victory. There is no doubt that we're the best team in the country."

Against Njudungarna, the Blacksmiths had five riders who scored eight points: Gote, Tommy, Bengt Jansson, Stefan Salomonsson and Ake Dovhed. It was so typical of their all round strength throughout that magical season.

"This season beats everything I've ever experienced in the sport." Joel added.

★★★★★★

In the British League, no team could do anything to stop Reading who won the first championship in '73. The 'Racers' were spearheaded by Anders Michanek, who was the best rider in the BL that year.

Another day, another journey ... Tommy prepares to re-load his BMW in pursuit of greatness.

It was a great achievement, especially as Anders was stubborn enough to keep racing with only one bike, while most of his opponents had at least two available.

"I don't want to have a trailer, because I hang my only bike on the back of my car," he explained.

"And besides, it doesn't matter how many bikes you have. As long as you have everything in order, you're just fine with one bike."

The few times when he had engine trouble, Mitch didn't even want to borrow anybody else's machine – especially if the match had already been won. In those situations he just felt he'd completed his work. His various managers over the years had disputes with Anders over this issue but Michanek was always his own man – very stubborn, always determined to do his own thing.

In Sweden as well as in England, many followers of the sport felt he wasn't team-orientated enough and was a rider who cared only about himself.

He answered that by saying he came there to do his job. That was it – over and out. He didn't care about anybody else, not even his team-mates' feelings.

And who could really blame him? He was the main reason for Reading's championship success.

Anders Michanek was a great rider. And he knew it.

Tommy couldn't stop admiring Anders for his ability to always reach his best when it mattered the most, his toughness on the track and for his sheer will to win.

Wimbledon had another disappointing season in the BL, the Dons moving up just one place to 12th. Tommy was the best rider in the team, even though he missed 18 out of 34 league matches. From the 20 official meetings he rode in, he averaged 9.19 points and took over from Ronnie Moore as the team's new No.1.

Tommy valued the advice and experience of Trevor Hedge.

The riders behind him were just not good enough and changes were needed. The Dons were reasonably okay at home, where they won 12 of their 17 BL matches, but their main problem was their inability to win more than two away fixtures.

Tommy's comrades in the army were envious that he was granted so much authorised leave to go and race speedway, while his team-mates in Wimbledon were fascinated how he could cope with his extra responsibilities and maintain such impressive form. Army routines one day, winning speedway races the next.

Team-mate Bert Harkins couldn't understand how Tommy could take the hectic schedule so lightly and without ever complaining. It was this attitude that made Bert like Tommy so much.

"How do you manage to cope without passing out?" Bert wondered.

"Being in the army is good for my speedway career, because I'm forced to do a lot of physical training and the strength it gives me is an advantage for me on the track," Tommy explained.

And he really meant it. He always said to himself that he had to stay positive and always do the best in his situation.

"Ask the Swedish Army if they can consider taking on a Scotsman!" joked the ever-ebullient 'Haggis' Harkins, who wore distinctive white racing boots.

Cyril Maidment continued to champion his Swedish ace and took every chance possible to give the fans what they wanted. When Wimbledon had to a race away at Swindon, Cyril could easily have saved some money and used a guest replacement instead, but he still flew Tommy back from Sweden to lead the Dons.

Swindon thanked the Wimbledon manager in their programme and the Robins' supporters also applauded the skill and efforts of the visiting superstar who repaid the Wimbledon management's faith and expense by putting on a quality performance. He collected a maximum after beating Swindon legend Martin Ashby in all three races in which they met, which was no mean feat around The Abbey Stadium in those days.

In England there were some real lunatics.

One of them was named Jack Millen, who was also a danger to himself.

They called him 'Crazy Jack' and during his long career this wild man from New Zealand had broken more than 30 bones in his body.

With an injury record like his, he was a cult-figure among fans at Sunderland and Crewe. He once raced with a foot in plaster and the steel-shoe screwed to the plaster cast on his foot.

Ironically, Millen was killed when his car careered off a main road and caught fire.

Some fans liked these 'hairy' riders the most – the crazier the better.

Injuries are common in speedway but the statistics for the 1973 season in Britain made scary reading. The number of riders who needed to claim on their personal insurance was 154, which equated to around half of all active riders.

No club suffered more bad luck than Cradley Heath, or 'United' as they started calling the club that year before the club reverted to its traditional title. Bernt Persson's team used a total of 42 riders in 1973 – enough to fill six teams. This was Tommy Jansson's new world.

He started to get used to life in England and he could handle the tough routine of being a professional speedway rider. He enjoyed life there and he was no longer surprised any more when Bengt Jansson was re-named 'Banger' or that Bernt Persson became 'Bernie' to his adoring British fans. Tommy liked the colourful racejackets and cool-looking team logos like Belle Vue's classic ace of clubs, or Ipswich's flying witch, the skull-and-crossbones worn by the Pirates from Poole, or the white elephant of Halifax Dukes.

Ivan Mauger was still riding for Exeter Falcons, thanks to a unique agreement with the management of the west country club who supplied him with a private plane so that he could commute from his home near Manchester to the big, fast County Ground track in Devon. That year alone, Ivan took part in 125 meetings across 16 different countries.

It was a great investment by the Exeter promoters whose team attracted record numbers of fans to the banked raceway venue and large crowds wherever Mauger, Scott Autrey and the rest appeared.

Ivan still kept track of Tommy and

Tommy challenges on the inside of Leicester's Ray Wilson.

he and his good friend and rival Ole Olsen were both expecting to face Tommy in the World Final at Katowice later that year.

One rider who was not quite so convinced of Jansson's credentials, though, was Barry Briggs. It seemed to some of Tommy's fans that the veteran Kiwi wanted to find fault with his successor to the throne.

Briggo said: "Tommy doesn't have enough ego, he's too much like Bengt Jansson. Tommy doesn't take chances the way he should do and is not aggressive enough. Besides, he depends a little too much on others, trusting his team-mates too much and he should care more about himself."

"Also, Tommy is a bit spoiled, used to being successful and mollycoddled. If he starts a meeting badly, he can get upset and continue riding poorly the whole night," Barry observed.

Shannon Ruane, who had celebrated her 11th birthday, and the other supporters in Tommy's fan club, didn't care what 'old man Briggs' said.

"There is only one fault with Tommy – he has to do his military service in Sweden and can't take part in all of Wimbledon's matches," Shannon said.

Dons' manager Cyril Maidment agreed with her and didn't take Briggs criticism too seriously.

"We shouldn't forget that Tommy is still only 20-years-old," said Maido.

The 1973 World Final in Poland was going to be an historic event.

Tommy was as surprised as everybody else when the final heat was done and home rider Jerzy Szczakiel was on top of the rostrum in front of more than 100,000 mainly jubilant spectators at the Slaski Stadium in Katowice. The impossible had just happened – a Polish rider had won the World Final for the first time ever. And it was the 'wrong guy', because other Poles – notably the popular Zenon Plech – had been more favoured to win the title over him.

Jerzy Szczakiel, the man with the name so difficult to pronounce. The one who scored zero at the final held at the Ullevi Stadium in 1971.

Now he was ranked the best speedway rider in the world.

Tommy was not the only one thinking: 'If he can do it, so can I . . . '

As rain fell on the uncovered, concrete bowl of a stadium, Polish girls in national costume danced on the centre green. In the pits the other riders couldn't believe what had just happened. What a strange final it had turned out to be.

The surface was slippery, tricky to handle, and Anders Michanek, the big favourite to win after his successive victories in the British-Nordic and European final rounds, missed his first gate completely and finished last. His chances of becoming World Champion that year disappeared immediately.

The German referee, Georg Transpurger, didn't have the best night of his life and missed the moment when Peter Collins got his helmet caught in the tapes. The ref made some other strange calls as well.

When Szczakiel later on received blatant help from his fellow Polish riders, his rivals cursed how the others held back to help their fellow countryman. But it was nothing unusual, not in a World Final where numerous riders from other countries had done similar favours many times before. Maybe not this obviously, though.

But, above all, Szczakiel rode brilliantly and his machine worked perfectly. The championship was decided in a run-off between Szczakiel and Ivan Mauger, who was bidding to equal Ove Fundin's record of five individual speedway world titles . . . until it all ended with Mauger and his bike in the dirt.

On the second lap Ivan made a rare error, crashing into Szczakiel's back wheel before falling a few feet from the pit gate.

Poland celebrated one of its country's biggest sporting victories. For one night the whole country could forget living under repression from the powerful Soviet Union.

A Polish rider had made it – from zero to hero.

Tommy was amazed and listened carefully to what Mauger said after the meeting: "It was stupid of me to do what I did. If I'd just waited until the next straight, I would have beaten him. I was just going too fast and for a hundredth of a second I thought I could pass him on the inside.

"I'd not have felt this terrible if I'd scored only seven or eight points. But to be this close . . . it makes me feel sick," said the Kiwi maestro.

Speedway could be cruel.

And the memory of the contrast between the winner and the man in second place was something Tommy brought home with him. It was still on his mind while doing his exercises back in the army barracks a couple of days later.

Tommy also felt bad that he had missed securing a spot in the Final and that he had only been in Poland as a reserve. He'd finished fourth in the British-Nordic Final at Coventry with 10 points after brilliantly passing Mauger. Bengt Jansson had been very impressed by Tommy that evening, when he felt the Wimbledon star showed more composure compared to many of his more experienced rivals.

The speedway world was in a state of shock when little known Jerzy Szczakiel won the 1973 World Final after a run-off against Ivan Mauger, with the more fancied Pole Zenon Plech having to settle for third place.

Above: Wheel-to-wheel, Smederna team-mates Tommy and Bengt Jansson racing as individuals in the tough British-Nordic Final at Coventry. Below: In the same qualifer, meeting winner Anders Michanek blasts clear of Aussie Bob Valentine, England's John Louis and fellow Swede Jan Simensen.
Inset: Mich after going on to win the European title in Germany.

The last step before the World Final was the European Final in Abensberg, Germany, where Anders Michanek – who finished three points ahead of Ole Olsen in the Coventry qualifier – again dominated the show. First off, he shocked all of his rivals when he decided to not ship a bike to Germany beforehand. Instead, he rode his one and only bike in Reading's match at Oxford before starting his journey to Germany.

He travelled by ferry from Dover to Zeebrugge and then continued on by car through Belgium and Germany, arriving the day before what was effectively the semi-final of the World Championship. The others had all shipped their bikes there by airplane and then travelled by air themselves to arrive in time without any hassle. They spent the few days before the meeting getting their bikes and themselves in perfect order. Michanek arrived after many long hours spent in his car but he was certainly flying on the track, winning the European Championship with a another emphatic maximum.

Tommy couldn't live up to his own expectations and he under-performed. Unable to relax on his bike, he managed only six points, with Ray Wilson, who also scored six, just pipping him to the 11th, and last, qualifying place for the World Final. On a rough Abensberg track littered with pot holes, it was Willie's two second places in his opening couple of rides that ultimately edged him through at Tommy's expense, although the Leicester and England skipper had finished ahead of the Swede when they met in heat six. Tommy needed to win heat 19 to qualify for his second World Final but could only finish second to Russian Vladimir Paznikov, whose win clinched him the bronze medal.

In 1973, Tommy twice appeared at Wembley representing his country. Shortly after sitting out the individual World Final as reserve, he made his World Team Cup Final debut and scored six points as the Swedes finished half-a-dozen behind Great Britain, who tracked an all-English team for the first time.

For the final of the Daily Mirror International Tournament staged earlier that summer, it finished very much closer between Sweden and fast-emerging England.

Some 50,000 fans at Wembley and millions watching at home in England on ITV were enthralled by one of the classic confrontations of the 70s – the infamous run-off between Peter Collins and Anders Michanek after the countries had drawn 39-39 at the end of 13 heats.

The Swede was disqualified for allegedly causing Collins to fall as the two raced hard into the pits bend, leaving England to be awarded a highly controversial victory. Tommy Jansson was the youngest rider in the starting line-up and not that successful either, scoring five points from his four heats, although Swedish team manager Christer Bergstrom replaced the veteram Olle Nygren with the young Jansson in one heat.

Tommy proved that he was on his way up even if the lasting memory of the final for him was that Sweden lost and that he got fooled, big time, and passed by Malcolm Simmons in one heat. "S**t, I should have beaten Simmons," he grimaced afterwards.

Before the year was over Tommy appeared in two more major meetings. Over 5,000 fans headed for Eskilstuna to see Sweden beat USSR in a Test match. Michanek dominated yet again with a maximum 18 points, while Tommy was second best with 17. Swedish team manager Eric Karlsson said: "That Anders Michanek was going to collect a maximum was not surprising but 17 points for Tommy was way better than anybody could have expected. I'm brave enough to say that Tommy is a future World Champion. Not since Ove Fundin has Sweden had a future World No.1 of this calibre."

What Eric liked most about Tommy during the match against Russia was the youngster's will to win. Tommy became angry every time Sweden dropped a point.

"The guy really has a temper. When he's a little upset and fired up, he can race away from anybody."

Missing qualification for the World Final had upset Tommy and made him even hungrier for success. He never wanted to be 'just a reserve' on the biggest occasion again. He felt at least the equal of Szczakiel and – though he never said this aloud – to see a rider he considered below his class, win the world title, was too painful to bear. He realised again how tight and how tough it was at the absolute top. And how luck – good and bad – could ultimately determine everything.

Tommy also knew, though, that he was getting closer to the best riders in the world and that he could compete on their level. He definitely had the ability. That year he had spent months in the army – and still managed to win the World Pairs Championship, become a member of the team that was pipped to the Daily Mirror Tournament final and, of course, he was the leader of the Swedish Championship-winning team.

In the Swedish League, he had the third highest average, after Michanek and Tommy Johansson.

In the British League, he was the third best Swede, behind Mich and Christer Lofqvist. Tommy was the 15th highest placed rider in the BL charts.

Unfortunately, though, he couldn't end the '73 season on a high.

He finished third in the Swedish Final, behind new champion Tommy Johansson and former Poole rider Bo Wirebrand.

But late that night Tommy almost didn't have time to think about his own achievement, because two other riders had stolen the show in a way they wish they hadn't.

Anders Michanek and Bernt Persson became enemies for a long time. It was during the Swedish Championship final in Gothenburg that Michanek was so far behind that he lost control of himself and crashed into Persson. The Cradley Heathens hero broke his arm in the incident, while a remorseful Mich hung up his leathers for the night and cried like a baby.

"This is the most bitter moment of my career, I just can't understand how I could be so stupid," said Mich. "Worst of all, Bernt is my best friend. I don't know how I'm going to be able to look his wife Monica in the eyes after this."

Bernt was sitting next to Anders in the dressing room under the grandstand of Ullevi Stadium, with a cigarette in his mouth and with dark eyes, while a doctor took care of his broken arm.

"I can't blame anybody else but myself. If I hadn't raced like a rookie this wouldn't have happened."

Winners and losers. Triumph and heartbreak. Summer became winter. Australia was further away than ever for Tommy.

In the midst of it all, doing his military service, Tommy came to think about something his father had said. The sport had two big winners that year, two guys

Above: The Swedish team before facing USSR in the Daily Mirror International Tournament at Hackney in 1973.
Standing, left to right: Olle Nygren, Bengt Jansson, Christer Bergstrom (manager), Anders Michanek, Christer Lofqvist. Front: Tommy, Bernt Persson, Soren Sjosten.
Below: On his Wembley debut, Tommy chases after England's Malcolm Simmons in the Wembley final.

Above: This Swedish team had to settle for the silver medal after England again beat them at Wembley, this time in the 1973 World Team Cup Final. It was Tommy's first appearance in the WTC final. Full line-up: Bernt Persson, Bengt Jansson, Anders Michanek, Tommy, Arne Bergstrom (team manager) and Soren Sjosten.

who hadn't received the recognition they deserved during the year. With all due respect to the dominant Anders Michanek and Swedish Champion Tommy Johansson, 1973 was the year in which two riders made history in the shadows.

Nobody paid attention to their achievement. Their unique statistics weren't mentioned in the papers, nor by anybody else.

Gote Nordin, who had decided that this was his 21st and last season, and Bengt Jansson had both won a Swedish League championship medal for the eighth time in their careers.

It was unheard of at the time. Not even legends like Olle Nygren or Ove Fundin had come close to emulating Nordin and Jansson's amazing feat.

Speedway was, first and foremost, an individual sport. While all riders took part in team events, at the same time everybody wanted to win for their own sake. Tommy remembered all the talk about Bernt Persson and other superstars linked to Smederna. Now he really understood why Joel brought Gote and Bengt to Smederna before everybody else.

With a very impressive eight league championships each, they both had Tommy Jansson's full respect.

12
Tommy Jansson
versus
Bernt Persson

"The first time I saw him race he was very young. But I said immediately: this kid is going to be a star."

Gote Nordin talking about Bernt Persson

Bosse and Tommy Jansson worked on their bikes in the garage at home in Eskilstuna. The whole town was talking about the forthcoming showdown between Tommy and Bernt Persson, as Bernie was about to return home with his Indianerna team to race against Smederna.

Everybody asked the same question: who is the best speedway rider in Eskilstuna? Tommy or Bernt?

"Aren't you nervous?" Bosse asked.

"No, why should I be nervous? He's got two wheels and one engine, just like me," Tommy replied.

"We're talking about Bernt Persson, here."

"I'm not so impressed."

"You're not very impressed by any of the top riders, right?"

"No, not enough for them to make me nervous in any way," Tommy answered.

Bosse thought about how Tommy never complained about any tracks. Other riders would blame their failures on what they considered very bad track conditions but Tommy never did. He never complained about the weather either.

It started to get late in the evening and Bosse was hungry.

"Are you ready?" he asked.

"I'm just going to measure the pressure in the valves."

"Is that really necessary?"

Tommy knew that if he wanted to become the best speedway rider in the world, he had to pay careful attention to details and leave nothing to chance. At the highest level all riders are equal, all bikes are of the same standard, so it's the minute details that separate the very best from the rest.

Bernt Persson and Tommy – a couple of speedway legends from Eskilstuna.

Bosse was proud of his little brother. Of course, he still had dreams of beating Tommy, but since his spectacular crash two years before, he'd fallen a few more times, injured himself and therefore missed out on the opportunity to claim a place in Smederna's championship team of 1973.

He was forced to watch the club's greatest season from the stands. Now it was 1974 and Bosse had finally made the team. Best of all, he now had a unique opportunity to learn from the best – his own younger brother.

Throughout all Bosse's setbacks, Joel repeatedly explained to his eldest son the importance of racing with his brain more than his heart. There was nothing wrong with Bosse's will to win – and he was tactically smart too. His problem was that he wanted it too much sometimes. Some riders questioned his decision to ride at all, while others respected him for his courage.

Some people, though, had problems with Bosse's personality off the track. Very few were aware what a victory it was that Bosse was racing speedway at all given the fact that he'd managed to leave his previous wild lifestyle behind him. That accomplishment gave him a belief in himself that could easily be misunderstood.

In that respect he reminded people of his mother. He never excused himself, always said what was on his mind and he never backed down.

Tommy was more like his father – more laid-back, the silent type.

The Jansson speedway family had adjusted to its new life. Tommy and Bosse enjoyed spending so much time together and Tommy, who had felt for Bosse after all his previous crashes, was now more than proud of his big brother's progress.

Joel might not have been that optimistic when it came to Smederna's chances of successfully defending their league title in 1974, but he demanded the same effort from everybody involved with the team, on all levels, and he wasn't going to be satisfied with anything less than another championship win.

Even mother Inga-Lill had taken a position in the club, running the supporters' stand underneath the referee's box that overlooked the starting gate. She still closed her eyes during racing, especially when Bosse was riding since he had been so unfortunate of late. She was a little less nervous when Tommy was in action and trusted his ability more. She was not as scared as she had previously been when Tommy raced but she still kept her eyes closed during every race involving her two boys.

Sometimes she had her back to the track on purpose, chatting with friends just to try and take her mind off the action. She enjoyed the company of her friends around the club. Smederna had become a way of life for her as well.

But the whole family had a special feeling when the Indianerna team came to town. It was no ordinary day.

Not when Bernt Persson arrived.

Bernt Persson liked Tommy Jansson. Yes, he really did.

Many fans didn't believe that to be the case and, admittedly, it wouldn't have surprised anyone if Persson had disliked his biggest rival. For Tommy had turned into exactly what Bernt had always dreamed of being – a hero in his home town.

Tommy got most of the local newspaper headlines, he was the big fan favourite and he was especially loved by the female fans.

He was the big hero of Eskilstuna.

Bernt Persson was the man from town who had decided to leave for greener pastures elsewhere and now he was back as the enemy, a member of the team trying to take points away from Smederna.

Tommy was well aware of all the pre-match talk and he always viewed his meetings with Bernt as prestigious clashes that he had to win.

It was Inga-Lill who was in charge of putting his scrapbooks together, but during the 1971 season Tommy couldn't help himself after a successful race against Bernt. Besides a newspaper clipping about the match, he gleefully wrote in ballpoint pen: 'Oh, boy. I beat Bernt. Great!'.

Team-mate Sven-Olof Lindh had noted Tommy's obsession with beating Bernt. Against others, Tommy could relax during races if he was leading by a large distance or even if he was behind the leader. Instead of chasing the front-runner like a maniac, he concentrated on holding his position and not letting anybody pass him. But, when up against Bernt, he never sat back.

"On the track they were never friends and both of them knew how the fans in Eskilstuna loved to watch them do battle. Tommy and Bernt loved those meetings as well – they were never more focused than when they were alongside each other at the gate," observed Sven-Olof.

Bernt remained the coolest of the two, though. When he beat Tommy in the run-off for third place in the Swedish Championship Final at Boras in 1972, Bernt returned to the pits without making any spectacular gestures.

On the other hand, Tommy went over the top in his reaction, threw down his helmet and became so angry that he cried.

Bernt simply took off his helmet, lit a cigarette, smiled and said: "Nice to show who's the best."

Bernt Persson was born on June 24, 1946 in Eskilstuna. In his younger years he worked with Joel at a mechanical shop in town. This was before the Smederna team had been revived by Jansson senior.

"I would like to try a speedway bike one day," Bernt said.

Joel tried to arrange for practice rides at the defunct Tunavallen stadium, the same track they subsequently returned to, but at the time they were refused entry. The athletes working out nearby didn't want to be disturbed by the noise from the motorcycles.

Everything changed when Arne Bergstrom handed Joel the mission to turn Eskilstuna into a speedway town again. Joel initially rejected his offer but Arne talked him into it during a meeting at a hotel in the city of Katrineholm, where the powerful Mr Bergstrom also promised to help out in any way possible. It was an offer Joel couldn't refuse and that's when he started working as a manager for the club.

That same year, in the summer of 1963, a 17-year-old kid made his debut for Smederna. His name was Bernt Persson.

Two years later he joined the newly-formed British League, signing his first professional contract with Edinburgh Monarchs. Another two years on, he made his World Final debut at Wembley in 1967, causing uproar when he was controversially excluded for bringing down Ivan Mauger.

He managed to do all this while at the same time racing in the third division in Sweden. With the help of Joel's coaching and advice, the talented young rider progressed faster than anybody could have expected and Bernt was forever grateful for what Joel did for him. To Joel, Bernt was his major role model.

That's why Bernt felt so bad after his unhappy split from Smederna and his falling out with Joel. At that time Smederna were still in the second division and Indianerna in the top flight.

Joel offered Bernt five Swedish kronor (50p) per point, Indianerna gave him an unmatchable 20 kronor (£2) per point. Bernt felt he had reached a point of no return and left town saying: "This is an offer I can't refuse."

Then he said some things he would subsequently regret. Many years later even Joel admitted – but only to close friends – that in the end the main reason for the falling out between him and Bernt was down to pride. The reason Bernt never received any offers to re-sign for Smederna during Joel's time as a manager was Mr Jansson's strongly held opinion that if somebody closed the door on him, then that person had to re-open it again if the situation was to change. Otherwise the door would remain forever closed.

And that's what happened in the relationship between Joel and his former protégé. Bernt was not going to return to his home town team – well, not as long as Joel Jansson was in charge there.

★★★★★★

Despite Swedish television broadcasting the European Cup Final between Bayern Munich and Atletico Madrid – a form of entertainment very uncommon on Swedish TV in those days – more than 4,000 fans showed up in Eskilstuna. Those people decided to avoid watching West German football giants Bayern, with their galaxy of world stars like Sepp Maier, Gerd Müller, Uli Hoeness, Paul Breitner and the elegant Franz Beckenbauer.

But in Eskilstuna nothing could outshine their own clash of the giants: Bernt Persson versus Tommy Jansson. Even the major newspapers from Stockholm sent reporters to Eskilstuna, with Bernt and Tommy posing together for photos before the start. Neither of them refused media requests for photos and interviews, because they knew that their rivalry was good for the sport. They were also proud of themselves – for being the main attractions. Two regular, working class lads from Eskilstuna.

They both looked relaxed and ready to go. Bernt, with the coolest sideburns and the most impressive pedigree, against the clean-cut, fresh-faced youngster.

Both of them had suffered the consequences of a strange season, especially Bernt. This was 1974, the year when Swedish riders were unfortunately banned from competing in England. The British promoters had had enough of high costs for bringing in commuting Swedes and the relationship between the BSPA and SVEMO was at an all-time low, especially with fixture clashes happening all the time.

Bernt had bought himself a truck for road construction and started his own business, to find another source of income.

All the top Swedish riders were saddened and troubled by the BSPA's ban. By not racing in the British League, against the best riders in the world, week after week, the Swedes knew they were going to lose ground on their main rivals. However, Tommy felt he could afford to be more patience than many others, as he was still a few months away from completing his national duty in the army. He was in close touch with Cyril Maidment, who worked hard to try and lift the ban. His efforts made Tommy feel better and besides returning to Wimbledon, his main goals that season were to qualify for the World Final at Ullevi Stadium in Gothenburg, and challenge for the Swedish Championship, the final of which would be held at his home track.

So a new heavyweight battle with Bernt Persson was just what the doctor ordered.

"How are you?" Tommy asked.

"Just fine," Bernt answered.

"It's boring not being able to race in England. I'm okay, though, since I'm still in the army. But all of you, who have a family to support . . . " added Tommy, thinking about Anders Michanek who made a decent living competing in as many grasstrack and longtrack meetings in Germany, along with speedway's other big guns.

Tommy avoided the subject of Michanek in the conversation with Bernt, given their bad crash in the Swedish Final the year before, when Michanek made a dirty move and deliberately rode into Bernt, breaking his arm. Bernt was still a little weaker in that arm.

Smederna had started the season with one victory and one defeat, while Indianerna had won one of their two matches. The main men were up against each other in the first heat of the night – Tommy riding with Sven-Olof Lindh, while Bernt partnered Bengt Eriksson.

Tommy lined up at the gate and he knew that nothing was going to stop Bernt from giving it all he had. He knew Bernt could fly but he also knew that Bernt was a fair rider, never dirty, and they had a lot of respect for each other. In one race, when Tommy's chain broke and his bike stopped, Bernt was right behind him and made a quick turn to avoid a crash. Afterwards, Tommy walked up to him in the pits, held out his hand and said: "I'm glad it was you who was right behind me. Great move."

This time Tommy flew from the gate and the fans roared their approval. Bernt didn't have a chance.

Of course, nobody in Eskilstuna cared a damn about Beckenbauer and the other German footballing greats on TV at that same moment. This was the year when Bayern Munich won the European Cup and Germany beat Holland in the World Cup Final. But, in Eskilstuna, nobody was bigger than Tommy Jansson.

Smederna won the match, with Tommy scoring a maximum. He said: "Sure it's fun to beat Bernt. Too bad I wasn't a little faster in the first heat, when I was so close to the track record. I want that record."

Bernt was humble in defeat, saying: "It's just hopeless trying to catch Tommy and Bengt Jansson at the moment, especially here in Eskilstuna."

Joel talked mostly about his eldest son. Five points and a regular spot in the team. No crashes. And, what's more, no injuries.

"Bosse is on his way to overcoming his fear, which was natural after all his previous crashes. You can never be afraid out there, you have to be physically and mentally strong and have the courage to go as fast as you can. Otherwise, you're asking for trouble and the risk of getting hurt is greater. Considering all this, it's really impressive to see Bosse come back in this way," Joel said.

Bosse was as humble as Bernt. He was just proud to be there, even if he was still a bit shocked at the speed and the amazing battle between the two giants, Bernt and his little brother.

"I'm never going to be as good as my brother but Tommy has taught me a lot. He always tells me if I do anything wrong and gives me good advice when I need it."

Life in the army – and speedway. That was it for Tommy and it was fine by him. Sometimes he accompanied friends to the movies, to see blockbusters like The Exorcist and The Sting. But when he came home after a night out, he didn't go straight to bed – he went down to the garage to work on his bikes. He tried not to do too much, because that would be counter-productive. His team-mate, Stefan Salomonsson, could sometimes seek perfection way beyond what was possible and the result was that his machines performed even less efficiently. An old saying among speedway riders in Sweden, a phrase that Tommy loved too, was: 'Better to ride the s**t to pieces, than work the s**t to pieces.'

But Tommy hated negligence and disorder, so he took great care of his bikes and did everything he could to maintain the highest standards he'd set himself.

Bosse took notice, although his problem was his temper. When his bike broke down during a practice, he just left it on the centre green and walked across the football pitch back towards the pits area, leaving it for his mechanic to collect.

Joel had other ideas: "Go back and get your own bike," he told his son. "If you don't, you have no business being here at all."

Bosse walked back in shame and picked up his bike.

Nobody was going to act like a prima donna in Joel's team.

★★★★★★

Tommy didn't make it to the World Final in 1974, agonisingly losing out by just one point in the Swedish domestic qualifiers that would determine which gfive riders qualified for the Gothenburg finale.

The rider who snatched the final spot from him was none other than team-mate Bengt Jansson, who tied for overall fourth place with Tommy Johansson. Benga Jansson and Johansson, who had spells in the BL with Ipswich and Hull, both scored an aggregate 33 points from the three Swedish qualifying rounds held at Stockholm, Norrkoping and Gothenburg . . . with Tommy a heartbreaking point behind them on 32. They went direct to the World Final at Ullevi, along with overall winner Anders Michanek (42) and the runners-up, Soren Sjosten (41) and Christer Lofqvist (35).

A sympathetic Benga said: "This was brutal for Tommy but my experience made the difference. I had to be at my very best to be successful tonight. I really wanted to reach the Final and I'm just sad that it was at the expense of my own team-mate. I feel for Tommy and understand his disappointment."

Tommy was both sad and angry – at himself. Without the red-hot weekly competition that the BL provided, he'd lost his touch a little bit in the summer and during his last months in the army. He wasn't happy with his bike either.

Michanek was so superior in the Swedish rounds of the World Championship that year that rumours started to spread about him using illegal fuel. 'Something's got to be wrong,' the jealous few whispered behind his back.

Anders wanted to tell them to go to hell, but he just smiled and said: "Give me whatever machine you want . . . I'll beat anybody, anywhere."

Joel Jansson was not easily impressed but Mich made an impact on him. Partly because of Anders' personality – every second time they met Mich said 'hello' and

The depleted Swedish team that was smashed 5-0 by England on British tracks in 1974. Lining up before the first Test match at King's Lynn are (left to right): Soren Karlsson, Tommy Nilsson, Bengt Jansson, Christer Bergstrom, Tommy, Thomas Pettersson, Olle Nygren and Kennet Selmosson. On bike: The outstanding Soren Sjosten.

Anders Michanek and Soren Sjosten on their way to the 1974 World Pairs Championship at Belle Vue.

talked briefly. On other occasions he totally ignored Joel, as if he'd never seen the Smederna boss before.

Joel knew that Anders had enemies among his own team-mates and that he very seldom allowed anybody else to use his bike, or dispensed advice to lesser team-mates.

Anders Michanek was his own man.

Tommy Jansson was an exception.

Anders helped him with both machines and advice.

But what Joel liked most about Mich was his uncompromising will to win.

Anders said it himself: "Ego and will to win . . . it's the same thing."

While other riders thought hard about who they were up against, Anders couldn't care less.

He said: "What are you talking about – Jan Andersson and Per Jonsson? I never paid attention to the riders coming up behind me, I didn't need to worry about them. I checked the programme before every match and came to quick conclusions: Okay, today we are racing Indianerna and they have only one guy who can really race. That's Bernt Persson. I don't need to waste my time thinking about any other rivals.

"When we came to Eskilstuna, it was Bengt and Tommy – the rest of the team were a bunch of nobodies. I don't remember any one of them," he added dismissively.

Anders' strategy was simple: 'First out of the gate, first over the finish line.'

But Tommy and Bengt were the type and quality of riders who made him pay attention to what was behind him.

"I hated having Bengt breathing down my neck. And Tommy was tough, he never gave up," Anders admitted.

The reason Anders helped Tommy was that he saw a little bit of himself in young Jansson, his World Pairs-winning partner of 1973. Just like Ole Olsen had found a personal favourite in the young Swede. After all, a champion could always recognise a future champion.

Tommy had learned to toughen up after some close encounters with Anders on the track. Anders had used his elbows and shoulders against him and merciless Mich had even used his front wheel to pinch Tommy a little on his left leg. It could be scary stuff at that speed but Tommy never backed down or showed fear.

When he didn't get the chance to represent Sweden in the World Pairs Final, Tommy was deeply disappointed. The year before he and Anders had struck gold in Boras, Sweden. Now the final was going to he held at Belle Vue, Manchester – a familiar track for Aces legend Soren Sjosten, who took Tommy's place alongside 'Mighty Mich'.

Members of Tommy's UK-based fan club had to postpone their trip to Manchester, deprived of a rare chance to see their idol that season. Although Tommy complained unsuccessfully to SVEMO, he felt the top brass had gone behind his back.

He said: "I've had a string of bad luck this season. I've not lost my ability but my bikes haven't worked properly. Things like this can happen to any rider, at any time, and it's no reason to kick me out of the team."

Anders was surprised as well, but there was nothing he could do.

Tommy continued: "It's just time for me to look forward to the future. I'm going to show those old fellows at the federation what I can do. My goals for the season are to win the league again with Smederna and to win the Swedish Final for myself. I'm not going to dwell on this setback."

To be fair to Sjosten, he had carried the Swedish team single-handedly throughout the summer Test series in England, where he was the only tourist to score double figures in all five matches, of which all were lost by a considerable margin. Compared to Sjosten's outstanding 71 points haul, Tommy contributed only 25 points in the series, with Michanek and Persson absent from all matches.

England, continuing to tighten their grip on world supremacy in the mid-70s, went on to win the World Team Cup Final at Katowice, Poland, where Tommy's seven points made him third top scorer for the silver medalists, behind Sjosten (10) and Michanek (nine).

Anders liked Tommy even more for his attitude. He was not only a great rider, he had the guts to say what he thought to the old boys in charge of the sport in Sweden. Michanek wasn't the biggest fan of that bunch of men in grey suits either. He never backed down from stating his opinion, like when he said that managers shouldn't tell riders how to ride.

"The best riders don't need any coaching. To become great, you need to learn the ropes on your own," he insisted.

On the other hand, Anders actually had a brief stint as a team manager after his career was over, when he took over at Rospiggarna in the Swedish first division. He tried to get the riders to learn how to tune their bikes, how to set them up properly for different tracks and gave them advice on how to select the best wheel sprockets, etc, etc. Little things that can make a big difference.

"But the riders couldn't care less," he sighed. "They found it more interesting to wear flashy leathers and run around flexing their biceps for young girls in the crowd. I totally lost it after that and left the sport," said a disillusioned Anders.

It takes a lot to impress Michanek: "There are so many riders in this sport but very few of them can actually ride well. Maybe two or three guys per team, but the rest should really be doing something else," he added.

★★★★★★

The whole speedway world stood still and took notice when Anders Michanek won the 1974 World Final.

He broke the track record at Ullevi Stadium in four of his five heats in front of a record crowd of 39,000 fans – an attendance that still stands as the highest ever in Swedish speedway.

Tommy Jansson was there only as a reserve. He participated in three heats and ended the evening with three points. Bengt Jansson was placed fifth with nine points.

For Anders, the ultimate victory was not the start of a ferocious quest to do it again. In fact, on the contrary. For him, one World Championship was enough.

He said: "Now I've proven that I can be the best speedway rider in the world and nobody can take this away from me. And that's enough for me – now I don't need to prove anything else."

Smederna had the chance to retain the Swedish League championship but failed to do so after losing at home for the first time in four years. That same night all the other results went against Joel's team, who had to settle for fourth place in the

Four of the Swedish contenders before the 1974 World Final in Gothenburg: Tommy, Benga Jansson, champion Anders Michanek and Tommy Johansson.

Wimbledon had to persuade Barry Briggs (on bike) to come out of retirement to replace Tommy when the commuting Swedes were banned from the BL in 1974. Joining Briggo in the Dons line-up were: Cyril Maidment, Rob Jones, Bert Harkins, Neil Cameron, Reg Luckhurst, Graeme Stapleton and Trevor Hedge. Roger Johns was injured when this picture was taken.

standings. Michanek's Getingarna were champions again.

Michanek, who also won the World Pairs Final with Soren Sjosten instead of Tommy, had only one thing left to win that season – the individual Swedish Championship.

But it didn't happen for him.

That night belonged to Tommy.

The day after winning the Swedish Championship, Tommy flicked through the morning papers to read about his greatest triumph and look at the photos from that wonderful Friday night at his home track.

He read the final score:

1. Tommy Jansson, 15 points (maximum)
2. Anders Michanek, 14.
3. Tommy Johansson, 13.
4. Christer Sjosten, 11.
5. Bernt Persson, 11.

Other riders further down the scorechart included: Hans Holmqvist, Bengt Jansson, Stefan Salomonsson, Christer Lofqvist and Bengt's brother, Lars Jansson.

After breakfast, Tommy jumped into his car and took his father and mechanic Kenneth Swedin along to Mariestad, almost three hours from Eskilstuna, for a match between Sweden and Soviet Union. The Swedes won 66-41, Tommy dropping his only point when he covered behind a team-mate.

On home territory again, Tommy was back in business, doing the same things as

Tommy and another Wimbledon hero, Ronnie Moore, at the airport and set for another Aussie tour.

before and spending even more time in the garage. His team-mates at Smederna couldn't believe their eyes.

Stefan Salomonsson said: "He doesn't even talk about it, you can't tell that he's the new Swedish Champion,"

For most riders, the season was over, but not for Tommy. He was back off to Australia for a second time.

13
Love letters, marriage proposals and pictures of naked ladies

"We in Tommy's fan club wanted to do something special for Tommy, so we arranged a disco in his honour. Oh yeah, he came there. But I think he was a little embarrassed, because everybody wanted to dance with him."

Supporter Shannon Ruane

Kenneth Swedin was a mechanic who worked with cars for a living and liked speedway. In many ways he was the typical supporter, at least on the outside.

But when Tommy met Kenneth he identified more qualities in him. On one hand Kenneth was comfortable within himself and he never tried to befriend the star riders like many other hangers-on did. Kenneth was seriously interested in the sport – not in the way that many fans collect memorabilia and memorise results and all other details. He loved working with engines and he was fascinated with different ways to make machines perform to their maximum capacity. He was stubborn as well as smart and was constantly exploring ways to improve his work.

That's why Tommy and Kenneth became great friends and why Tommy decided to hire Kenneth as his mechanic.

Before the 1975 season one of the local papers in Eskilstuna had a story about Kenneth with the headline: 'Tommy's unknown mechanic'. Tommy loved to see that story in print, because he felt it was about time that Kenneth got the recognition he deserved.

The two friends from Eskilstuna had spent the winter together in Australia. Jealous friends in Sweden had 'congratulated' Kenneth on his holiday in the sun but he had just laughed at them. Vacation? Forget it.

There were some lazy days on the beach, though, and Kenneth would never forget one day in the 100-degrees heat when they stood in the shade, wearing only swimming trunks while working on Tommy's bike and enjoying the good life.

But they worked a lot too, driving across the continent in a small truck to get to meetings all over Australia. They stayed either at cheap motels or with friends Tommy knew from his previous trip Down Under.

Tommy with Hasse Holmqvist, who received criticism from the British speedway press.

The fan hysteria was the same as the last time he visited the schedule just as gruelling. The average crowd at meetings was around 6,000, although some attracted as many as 10,000.

Back in Sweden, he not only brought home unusual souvenirs like a kangaroo-skin, which he showed for the benefit of local photographers in Eskilstuna, he also brought back a feeling, based on his great results in Oz, that 1975 was going to be a year to remember for him.

He was going all the way to the Wembley World Final – he was absolutely sure of it and nothing was going to stop him. Sure, he looked forward to defending his Swedish Championship too and he also wanted to do well again with Smederna.

There was another big boost when it was confirmed that Swedish riders were welcome back in the British League after the ban on commuting foreigners was lifted by the BSPA. "Now the fun can start for real," said an excited Tommy when he heard the good news.

At Wimbledon, Tommy was reunited with a legend – Barry Briggs was back for his second consecutive season at Plough Lane. It didn't take long for Barry, who the year before had spotted faults in Tommy, to start changing his opinion of the Swede. That Tommy was now firmly established as the fans' No.1 favourite didn't bother the four times World Champion and New Zealand great.

In a meeting with Cyril Maidment, Briggo said: "The best thing about Tommy is his sheer determination to reach the top. He considers himself a world class athlete – you have to be these days, otherwise you don't stand a chance of being successful. The fact that he doesn't drink or smoke is a good sign. Tommy is serious about his sport."

The only lingering weakness Barry could detect in Tommy was that he was still liable to fall apart if he started a meeting with a couple of poor rides. On the other hand, Barry was pleased to note that Tommy no longer had too much respect for any of his on-track opponents.

"That could've been the case in the past. Sometimes he was beaten before the tapes went up but, nowadays, Tommy knows he can beat anybody in the world. If he keeps racing like this, he will become the World Champion one day," added Barry, who had been tempted back after a year off to plug the gap left by Tommy during the BL ban on Swedes in 1974.

But neither Wimbledon, nor any other team in the BL for that matter, could do anything to stop the rampant Ipswich Witches that season. The Dons, who had moved up the table to eighth in '74, would end the '75 campaign in ninth place.

The Swedes were mostly welcomed back with open arms by their clubs and supporters, but not all of them. The riders who under-performed got to hear about it in the papers. Among the high profile riders in the Swedish League who received most bad press in England were: Bo Josefsson, Bengt Larsson, Bengt Brannefors and Hans Holmqvist. Poor 'Manolito' got one unusual beating in a paper who compared him to the evergreen Bernt Persson.

'Holmqvist is the total opposite of Bernie Persson,' wrote one journalist and that was not fun for Holmqvist to read.

One reason English journalists – and fans – had a hard time accepting that the Swedish stars missed important meetings in England to race in their homeland was the poor crowd levels in Sweden. In his book, Speedway and Short Track Racing, published in 1974, journalist and author Dave Lanning wrote: 'Without a doubt, Sweden could be the dominant force in world speedway today but for the lack of

Ronnie Moore, Barry Briggs and Cyril Maidment in the pits at Plough Lane.

one vital commodity: fans!

'For despite an international record which bears comparison with any other nation in the world over the past 20 years, public response in this crisp, clinical Scandinavian country remains outrageously apathetic. Box office returns in excess of one thousand pounds at a track, where even a reigning World Champion is appearing, is good reason to crack open a bottle of schnapps. Sweden's top track stars – and they have reeled off the production line like Hong Kong dolls – are more popular and better known in Britain than in their own backyards.

'Virtually any other country in the world would be shouting hallelujahs if their riders were as consistently successful as the Swedes. If an Iron Curtain or Latin country had done nearly as well, speedway would be their number one spectator-pulling sport.

'But without the financial encouragement that in speedway only healthy crowds can bring, the sport in Sweden lurches along on the breadline.

'So it's a bitter Swede situation.'

That was the reason many people around Plough Lane had difficulty getting excited when Tommy talked about the fans back in Eskilstuna. Most people around speedway in England had the same feeling: the people of Sweden should be ashamed for not having the decency to celebrate their speedway heroes properly.

Not that they had anything to cheer when Sweden met England, home and away, in 1975 Test series – and lost both of them 5-0. Tommy top-scored for the tourists at Poole, Leicester and Belle Vue and was second highest scorer behind Christer Lofqvist and Bernt Persson at Hackney and King's Lynn respectively.

It wasn't only the girls who appreciated Tommy's talent at Wimbledon.

Tommy (inside) and Anders Michanek try to beat Dave Jessup (outside) to the first bend at Poole, with Peter Collins trailing, during the 1975 Test series.

On home territory the following month, the results were much closer but Sweden still slumped to consecutive defeats at Kumla, Eskilstuna, Stockholm, Vetlanda and Mariestad. Once again, Tommy topped the Swedish scorechart in three of the five matches and only in the third Test defeat in Stockholm did he fail to hit double figures for his country.

Not surprisingly, it was England who went on to win the World Team Cup Final at Norden, Germany, where the dispirited Swedes were even pushed into third place by the USSR. Tommy scored four points in a miserable total of 17.

The 1974 ban on Swedes in Britain had clearly taken its toll on the track, if international results for '75 were anything to go by.

★★★★★★

In a match against Halifax Dukes, Tommy collected 17 of Wimbledon's meagre 31 points. No wonder Tommy's UK fan club arranged a disco in his honour. He had to keep his phone number and address a secret in order to keep his growing army of female fans at arm's length. Even if he lived for the sport and loved the attention and adulation, sometimes feeling more like a rock star, he still valued his privacy.

Of course he dated sometimes – but he was very discreet about it and he had no long-lasting relationships. What he liked most was when he met women who didn't know who he was, which did happen occasionally

He got a lot of fan mail, many of them love letters. Some women proposed marriage, while others sent photos of themselves naked.

But Tommy stayed away from all these women. The girls that he spent time with, and they were few, were not speedway fans at all. He treated them with respect but was also very frank about his lifestyle.

He'd say: "I'm here in town for a few days but I'll be leaving soon. And as a professional speedway rider, there is no room in my life for a steady girlfriend."

Some women held back. Others liked his honesty and were just happy for the little time they were able to spend with him. Nobody got hurt – but maybe some were sad realising that he was gone after such a short while. Nobody could get angry with him, since he was always straight with everyone.

Tommy had listened to the veterans in the sport, who often talked about the importance of living on your own while on your way up in the sport.

Ole Olsen once said that "speedway is my best mistress." Ivan Mauger said that "speedway must be the love of your life, if you want good results," and Barry Briggs' words of wisdom on the same subject were: "If you want to become the best in the world, then you'd better stay single."

Having said all that, all three former World Champions have enjoyed long and loving relationships with devoted wives!

Tommy himself was quoted in a Swedish tabloid and he loved the headline: 'Yes to Speedway – no to Chicks.'

The story had a great beginning: 'He is well aware of the importance of not looking too deep into any cleavage, like many other top athletes have done before him with disastrous results. He is not going to make the same mistake. That's a promise he has made to himself and his closest friends.'

He was quoted as saying: 'If I'm going to reach the top, my mind has to be on one thing and one thing only – my bike.'

Hanging on during the disappointing 1975 World Team Cup Final at Norden.

Some riders just talked about how things were supposed to be and how they should conduct themselves – and then did the total opposite. Tommy never cared about what others got up to, he just let them get on with their own lives.

But he couldn't help feeling anything other than contempt for the Swedish rider who had a girlfriend in Sweden and another in England, the two of them not knowing anything about each other, of course.

In Tommy's eyes, that kind of duplicity showed no class at all.

Riders drinking heavily was another thing he disliked, although he never tried to dissuade those who liked a beer or six.

"Everybody has the right to live their life as they please but I can't understand them. Nobody races better with a hangover, that's just rubbish," he'd say.

Tommy stayed away from drugs, too.

For some riders, drugs – or alcohol – was a way of cooling nerves and summoning the confidence and courage to race at the very top level. Tommy had the guts to do what was needed to be done without any form of artificial help.

He didn't believe in God, or in finding 'inner peace' with the help of a bottle or a pipe, nor in finding the meaning of life through love. He viewed himself as a realist and felt that his fate was in his own hands.

But he was curious, so when he and his good friend, Speedway Star photographer Mike Patrick, spent an afternoon browsing in shops in and around London's Kensington High Street, Tommy stopped at a fortune teller and said: "I want to go in here."

"Why? Do you believe in that stuff?" Mike asked.

"No, I'm sceptical, but it's fun to try it."

They went in to meet the clairvoyant and she immediately reacted to Tommy and said: "You're a racing driver of some sort."

That certainly grabbed Tommy's attention and he listened carefully to what the woman had to say.

In the end he couldn't help himself from asking her: "Will I ever become a World Champion?"

She answered: "You will go as far as it is possible for you to go."

★★★★★★

For Tommy's Swedish team, the 1975 season was no better than average. He and Bengt Jansson remained the top two but this time the supporting cast wasn't strong enough for them to mount a serious championship challenge.

Smederna finished in second place but Bysarna – with their top trio of Christer and Soren Sjosten, together with Christer Lofqvist – were unstoppable.

It didn't matter that Tommy's 14.21 average was the best in the Swedish League. While he was happy with his own figures, he was disappointed that the team couldn't repeat its glorious feat of 1973. Tommy still had a problem dealing with defeat and, to him, a season ending without victory was a season lost.

What really gave Tommy joy in Sweden that year was Bosse's success in having the fourth best average of the Smederna riders. Tommy knew that some people within the organisation had difficulty dealing with Bosse, thinking that the older

Smederna with their three heat leaders – Tommy, Bengt Jansson and Stefan Salomonsson – on bikes.

Jansson brother was too cocky and full of himself. In reality, Bosse's pride in his accomplishments sometimes showed in wrong ways – he was so happy that he didn't realise when he stepped on other people's toes . . . or literally ran over them with his bike!

For him, it didn't matter. He wasn't racing speedway to gain new friends. He was in the sport for the same reason as his father and brother – to win. The fact that he didn't possess as much talent as the other men in the family, didn't stop Bosse from trying.

During the Swedish Junior Championship Final in 1974 he'd been so sure of winning that when he failed completely, even some people in his home town laughed behind his back. The year after, it was his turn to shine – at the Gubbangen track in Stockholm.

Tommy and Joel helped him before the final, giving him all the backing they could. They worked on his bike and gave him advice that he listened to. Bosse dropped just one point and won the final.

He'd finally got his chance to show everybody that he was for real, not just another Jansson riding in the shadow of his father and brother.

But what Bosse valued most that night was not the feeling he had standing on top of the rostrum or the attention he got from the spectators in this, the biggest moment of his career. What made him most proud was that he finally felt that Tommy had a new-found respect for him.

He even said as much to his friends: "Now Tommy understands that I'm serious about speedway."

At the same time Tommy had told him that in order to achieve success, he had to learn for himself as he went along. In a match against Ornarna, the Jansson brothers rode together against Borje Klingberg (who later rode briefly for Eastbourne in the BL) and Karl-Erik Claesson, two top riders in the Swedish League at the time.

"Okay Bosse, you can pick your gate," Tommy said to him.

Bosse went for the inside position, so Tommy ended up in gate three, of course. Normally the weaker of the pair got the least favourable gate, except in this case it was the other way around. The least experienced rider had the best chance to win.

Bosse was, in fact, fastest from the gate, but Tommy passed him in the first turn and then just took of. 'Bye, bye, big brother, you are on your own,' was the message.

Bosse was second, but realised that Tommy had no intention of helping out in any way, as his team-mates usually did in those situations.

Tommy's only thought was, 'this time Bosse has to make it on his own.'

Bosse cursed as he had the chasing home riders all over him for four laps. There were some hairy moments and he had to do everything in his power to hold on to second place.

Afterwards Bosse confronted his brother in the pits: "Why didn't you wait for me? Why didn't you team-ride?"

"You have to learn this sport on your own," reasoned Tommy. "If I slow down and help you, then you won't learn a thing."

In contrast to that meeting in Visby, when Tommy passed his brother just before the finish line because he wanted to win all his heats, Bosse stayed calm this time.

He knew Tommy was right.

★★★★★★

"Towel," Gavin said.

"Twel," Tommy said.

"Come on, Tommy, it's t-o-w-e-l," Gavin said.

"Give me a break. Try to say seventy-seven in Swedish," Tommy said.

Tommy had problems saying the English word towel and messed it up all the time.

On the way to a Wimbledon meeting, he was sitting in his car being tutored by his good friend Gavin Elms. Gavin worked as a teacher, he was a native of Australia and he loved speedway. He and Tommy shared an apartment together with two other people, in Putney, south-west London, right near the River Thames and fairly close to Wimbledon. Tommy had moved in there during the 1973 season and, following his year out of England due to the ban on Swedes, he returned there for the whole of 1975, by which time he and Gavin had become really good friends.

Gavin travelled to a lot of British meetings with Tommy, helping to re-fill the bike with methanol and oil in the pits and generally running errands for him.

But he was most valuable as a language teacher. Tommy often encouraged Gavin to teach him new words and he wanted his friend to point out every time that he made a grammatical error. He wanted him to correct him and teach him the right words to use.

Except once.

The two of them were out driving in London and got lost, Tommy was behind the wheel of his Swedish-registered BMW and Gavin was in the passenger seat with a map on his lap.

"So where am I going at this intersection?" Tommy asked.

"Left."

"But it's a one-way street . . ."

"Oh, don't worry."

Tommy turned the corner and a police car stopped them immediately.

Gavin kept a straight face and quickly told Tommy: "Whatever you do, don't speak any English."

An angry police officer walked over to the car, Tommy rolled down his window, gave the officer his Swedish driving licence, smiled and muttered: "Sorry, can't speak English."

Gavin looked as lost as Tommy and said: "No English. No English."

The police officer didn't want the hassle and just waved them on their way.

Tommy pulling into the pits at Wimbledon.

Many people came in to see Inga-Lill at the store were she worked to get the latest news about her famous son.

"Do you get the chance to see him at all, when he spends so much time in England?" they'd ask.

"Oh, yes, every time he comes home to Eskilstuna he stays in his old room. But most of the time he's in the garage, of course. Sometimes I wonder if that's his home but we have installed a phone down there now. It was about time too – our phone has been ringing off the hook with people from England wanting to talk to him. And I can't speak English," Inga-Lill said.

"How is Tommy's English?"

"Good. In the beginning it was fun to watch him speak English on the phone. He made all these gestures while he was talking to somebody who couldn't see him. But he speaks English fluently now," Inga-Lill said proudly.

Customers in the store where she worked left Tommy's mother with their new clothes and a glimpse of the glamourous world of a sporting celebrity.

Back home at Tornerosgatan there was always a full house after every meeting. Inga-Lill made sure everybody got something to eat. One day she said: "Tommy, now my food money has gone."

"Oh, yeah. so what am I supposed to do about that?" Tommy smiled.

A couple of days later he gave her £50 – a quarter of the amount he had received when he won the World Pairs Final in Poland with Anders Michanek.

Forty thousand fans in Wroclaw, Poland, wanted to see home duo Edward Jancarz and Piotr Bruzda win the World Pairs Final.

The Swedish speedway riders who got the chance to enter behind the Iron Curtain always felt sorry for the people living in Poland, where the citizens suffered at the hands of the rigid Soviet regime.

The demoralised Poles sought refuge in sports and their speedway riders – always racing fast and aggressively – understood that the way to national glory was a route via Britain. In order to compete with the best, Polish speedway's governing body had to allow their best riders to come to England and in the 60s the export started. Of course, their movements were all controlled by the authorities, although one rider managed to defect to the west. Tadeuz Teodorowicz started a career in Britain with Swindon but died after crashing at West Ham in 1965.

Anders Michanek hated travelling to Poland. He didn't like the food, the standard of hotels or the bureaucracy and visa trouble that annoyed him most.

During their trip together to Poland, Anders and Tommy talked about the World Final in 1973, when Mich arrived at Katowice as the big favourite, only to finish last in his first heat, get disqualified in another and end the night with a hugely disappointing 10th place, with a lousy (for Anders) six points.

Mich admitted: "I was so sure about winning that first heat. I had gate one but I was too sure of myself and not focused enough. The gate was just terrible and I could never catch the other three."

In many ways Tommy was typical of the kind of rider that Anders disliked. He never warmed to those riders who he thought were too serious and just worked on their bikes. Practice, race, work some more on the bike, race some more . . . no, according to Anders, that was not the way to live.

Ole Olsen and Anders Michanek.

He wanted to have fun, not test the track before a major meeting like the World Final. He thought that was useless and considering the fact that he was fastest of all in practice before that infamous 1973 final, maybe he had a point.

Anders wanted to just sit back and relax, have a couple of cold ones, laugh and tell stories. He looked at speedway as a way of making a living, a sport. Certainly not life and death.

Of course, he always wanted to win and most of the time he did. But he felt many of the boys were hungrier than him. He thought to himself: 'I'm still smarter than most of the new guys and

Smooth and stylish, Tommy looking totally at ease on the Wimbledon track in 1975.

nobody beats me from the gate.'

The reason why Anders still liked Tommy – even though he was not, to quote Anders "the kind of guy you brought with you when you went out to dance" – was that Anders knew he and Tommy had a great chance of success together.

They won the Pairs Final in 1973 and now they'd won it again – by the smallest margin. Only one point separated the triumphant Swedes from the host nation, although the Polish fans sportingly saluted the winners anyway.

Tommy was happy about his seven points on the night, even though he was far behind Anders, who scored 17, and the undefeated Ole Olsen.

One reason for Tommy's upbeat mood was that he felt he was not in the same league as the others because he still didn't have a four-valve engine like many of the top riders. The English-made Weslake was introduced in 1975 and revolutionised the sport in which two-valve JAP and Jawa motors had been used exclusively for decades.

Tommy still rode an old two-valve Jawa machine in the '75 World Pairs Final but he recognised the new trend and told Anders: "I need a new bike if I'm going to have a chance against the best."

"Yes, you're right, but thinking about that makes our victory tonight even sweeter. This is the best of my three pairs final wins, because nobody expected us to win – not even ourselves," smiled Anders.

He had a lot of good things to say about his young partner after their triumph in Wroclaw's Olympic Stadium. Anders was amazed by Tommy's ability to ride totally according to plan. While Anders always looked for a win in every heat, Tommy's

Role model Tommy advertising the US aerosol deodorant in the Plough Lane pits.

aim was to try to beat at least one of their opponents and make sure that nobody got a chance to challenge Anders at the front. Tommy made life miserable for their opponents and only maximum man Olsen got too close to Anders. Their gameplan worked perfectly.

That they earned only 2,000 Swedish kronor (£200) each for their victory, compared to the 120,000 (£12,000) kronor Bjorn Borg got for winning the French Open that same weekend, was something Anders and Tommy had learned to live with. Speedway was not a big-time sport.

So when they travelled by ferry between Sweden and Poland, Anders felt they hadn't done anything wrong when they tried to avoid paying their bill after dinner. But the restaurant staff made an announcement over the ferry loudspeakers that no passenger would be allowed to leave the boat until the Swedes' dinner was paid for.

"Of course we're going to take chances like this, when we only receive small change for winning a World Final," Anders muttered.

Back in Eskilstuna after his second World Pairs victory, risk and reward was something that Tommy had in mind when talking to the local media. "Some people think that I live like a rock star but it couldn't be further from the truth. They don't know how much time I spend working on my bike – I take it apart piece by piece, everything needs to be looked after and cleaned.

"A rider without a perfect machine doesn't stand a chance at the top level. It's down here in the workshop that I win my races," Tommy said, posing for the photographer.

He didn't say anything about a large hangover after returning from Poland. For once, Anders had managed to persuade Tommy to join him for a night on the town.

Tommy couldn't say no this time . . . they had another World Pairs Championship to celebrate.

14
When Tommy 'mugged' Jan

"Sure, some riders became mad at others. I remember one rider who had a gun in his toolbox. I asked him: What are you planning to do with that? He said: Nobody is going to beat me up in the pits again."

Anders Michanek

In the space of 12 days Tommy Jansson rode a sequence of eight meetings in three different countries. He was a member of the Swedish team that, for the second year in succession, lost five straight Test matches in the series against England.

In a Swedish League match against Vargarna, Thomas Pettersson was so reckless in a battle with Tommy that the Smederna star's wrist watch snapped off and was later found in the shale.

Tommy had recently lost badly against his big rival Bernt Persson, forcing him to read local papers proclaiming Persson as the 'best speedway rider from Eskilstuna' in large headlines.

Like an increasing number of top riders at that time, Bernt had one of the new four-valve engines, but Tommy still had his conventional, old two-valve Jawa.

So after all the travelling, and struggling against his biggest rivals on that old machine, he was upset big time. Somebody was going to have to pay.

That somebody turned out to be Jan Simensen, when he visited Eskilstuna with his Dackarna team from Malilla.

Normally Tommy was a gentleman who'd seldom been involved in any arguments at the track. Sure, some riders had got mad and yelled abuse at him, especially in the early stages of his career when some veterans had shouted at him to show better control of his bike and himself.

One rider who already had a grudge against Tommy was Simensen.

Once they got tangled up and crashed, which led Jan to give Tommy an earful. Another time, Simensen walked over to Tommy in the pits in Norrkoping, after Tommy had broken the track record.

"What have you done with your engine?"

"Nothing that's against the rules," Tommy answered.

"You must have done something," Simensen persisted.

"No."

"You are full of s**t," added Simensen.

Tommy could recognise the type – most veterans hated being defeated by an up and coming rider like him and Simensen was certainly in that category.

Dackarna's 31-year old star had been riding professionally in England for many years, having also represented Sweden in numerous Test series and individual events all over Europe and the rest of the world.

He had been in one World Final (1972) and was infamous for his temper – both on and off the track.

He could be dirty and didn't hesitate to fence others when he felt it was necessary. He could be as rough away from the speedway as well – when he and Bernt Persson were briefly team-mates at Cradley Heath in 1970, it meant big business for pub landlords in the Black Country region of the West Midlands.

In a good mood, Jan Simensen was the best drinking pal a man could have.

He was also a man worthy of praise for his remarkable strength in maintaining a speedway career at all, considering that he'd suffered a severe case of rheumatism. Fact is, he was often in so much pain that he couldn't do any physical training and doctors had told him that the best thing he could do was quit racing altogether.

Against all the odds, it was fantastic that teams from England still called him repeatedly to ask him to come back to Britain, and that he was still a star in the Swedish League.

Jan Simensen deserved a lot of respect.

But, in a bad mood, he was hell to deal with.

During a tour of Australia with the Swedish national team, things turned ugly when best friends Jan Simensen and Bernt Persson, who shared the same apartment, got into a fight. Flour, syrup and all kinds of food made a total mess all over the floor before the two brawling Swedes were finally pulled apart by their team-mates. It was total chaos.

Speedway riders could get very angry with each other at times – all those close encounters on the track could easily spark trouble in the pits.

"It could be wild sometimes. I once saw somebody take off his steel shoe and knock somebody else over the head with it," recalled Persson.

Michanek will never forget a meeting in Sheffield when he discovered a pistol in Aussie star Garry Middleton's tool box!

"What the hell are you doing? . . . what are you planning to do with that?" a stunned Anders asked the former Hackney star.

"Nobody is going to beat me up in the pits again," explained the fiery, outspoken Middleton.

Another Swedish rider who could lose his temper and issue threats to others was that explosive, little Swede Soren Sjosten.

But now it was Jan Simensen who visited Eskilstuna with the intention of teaching young Jansson a lesson. Tommy knew that Simensen desperately wanted to beat him and a personal triumph was as important to the older rider as winning the match

Tommy looking unflustered on his bike, while Jan Simensen (foreground) just gets angry.

itself. Simensen wanted to show Jansson what he could still do – and to do it at Tommy's own home track would be all the more sweeter.

But Tommy had other plans.

And he was mad, so he didn´t even come close to considering the consequences. Just like his father, Tommy seldom became angry but whenever it happened, sparks would fly.

Joel had been just as impulsive during his active racing career. During a Test match with the Swedish national team in Kumla, an inexperienced Joel Jansson had been partnered together with World Champion Ove Fundin. Joel was fastest from the gate but never looked round, assuming that Fundin could take care of himself.

The fiery Fundin completely lost it. Back in the pits, he chased Joel with a sledgehammer in his hand and all hell broke loose. When the two of them met up the next time, at Motorstadion in Eskilstuna, Ove felt it was payback time and rode right into Joel.

This time Joel reacted furiously. He jumped up on his feet with only one thing on his mind – he was going to give Ove Fundin the beating of his life. World Champion or not, he decided it was time Mr Fundin got his comeuppence

But Ove had hurt himself in the crash and Joel calmed down.

'Ove got what he deserved anyway,' Joel thought, looking down at Fundin who was clearly in pain.

★★★★★★

In the match between Smederna and Dackarna it was 33-33 before the 12th heat. Tommy was pushed out onto the track by his mechanic Kenneth, where he had inexperienced team-mate Kent Pettersson for company. Jan Simensen came out with his partner, Stephan Johansson.

Tommy and Jan were side by side.

Tommy knew that Jan was watching him as closely as he was looking for the green

One of the many marriage proposals Tommy received from his huge female following at Wimbledon.

light to go on and the tapes to rise. And that was exactly the moment when Tommy decided to make a fool of Simensen, in a way Tommy had never done before.

He quickly let go of the clutch so that he jumped a bit, but not enough to take him into the tapes. Simensen, spotting Tommy's slight forward movement, went full blast, straight through the tape and got disqualified. He was mugged, made to look a fool by the kid.

Naturally, he erupted in fury.

Tommy was sitting still on his bike and shrugged his shoulders as if to say: 'I didn't do anything,' which of course made Simensen even angrier.

"What the hell are you doing? What kind of s**t is that?" Simensen yelled while walking back and forth on the track, trying to get the referee to change his mind.

Tommy just sat there looking innocent.

Simensen had enough and came over to Tommy and threatened to get physical with him until others had to jump in between them to avoid a fight breaking out. When the race finally started, Tommy wanted to make a final point by pushing Kent Pettersson forward to victory and settling for second place himself

Tommy was mean, he was cocky – and he enjoyed it.

★★★★★★

Shannon Ruane had become a familiar face to Tommy. She was one of the supporters who always waited for him outside the main entrance at Wimbledon Stadium after every home meeting.

MEMBERSHIP No. 72

Tommy Jansson
"Fan Club"

Secretary: Lynda Slack
61 Westcombe Avenue
West Croydon
Surrey, CR0 3DE

Signed

He called her "Curly Head", because of her bubbly hair, and when he happened to comment on the fact that she'd had her hair cut one time, she became terrified that he'd liked her previous haircut better and vowed to grow it longer again.

Tommy liked hanging out with the kids, because they didn't ask impossible things of him. They were natural and didn't try to befriend him by acting falsely.

Tommy himself came from a tough town but he knew his background was nothing compared to the reality for many of these working class kids in England. Eskilstuna was a safe haven compared to the inner-London suburbs.

So every time he could give these kids something to cheer about, he was pleased to see their happy faces.

Shannon gave him a love-letter with the lines:

'Tommy you are wonderful
Tommy you are great
Oh Tommy, Tommy, Tommy, Tommy
May I have a date?'

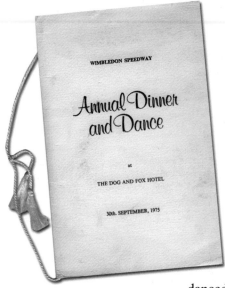

WIMBLEDON SPEEDWAY

Annual Dinner and Dance

at

THE DOG AND FOX HOTEL

30th. SEPTEMBER, 1975

The letter ended with a marriage proposal and the text was surrounded by painted flowers and a couple of suns. It was signed: 'Love Shannon, Age 13.'

Tommy was happy and a little flattered. Even superstars could sometimes wake up in their own world and realise just how unnatural their life really was. Like when Tommy's first fan club secretary Lynda Slack, from West Croydon, arranged a disco at the Merton Hall on Kingston Road, Wimbledon. Girl members paid their 50p entrance fee, then surrounded him and asked for a dance.

He felt a little embarrassed – but he still danced with them to the sound of some of that year's hit songs – Donny and Marie Osmond's Make The World Go Away and, of course, those from Abba who followed their 1974 blockbuster Waterloo with two more hits the following year, SOS and Mama Mia. Mud, who also had hits that year with The Secrets That You Keep and Oh Boy, were not favourites of the teenyboppers but the band lived local to the Wimbledon track and were occasional visitors to the speedway. They were even once pictured on the back cover of Speedway Star with Tommy, Peter Collins and Martin Ashby.

Guess who Shannon Ruanne is supporting!

All the girls in Tommy Jansson fan club seemed to like Abba – if for no other reason than for Tommy's sake, as a sign of their love of all things Swedish. Many of them had even called the Swedish Embassy in London to try and figure out where they could buy Swedish wooden shoes.

The year's smash hit in England was Bay City Rollers' cover of the Four Seasons' song Baby Bye Baby. Yes, they certainly partied that evening in Kingston Road.

Between the dances Tommy taught his English fans some Swedish words. They explained what they wanted to be able to say and he duly spelled it out for them.

"Kärlek (love)."

"Kyss (kiss)."

Fan club members received a birthday card signed by their hero.

Shannon wished that her friends in school should see her at that moment. Most of them loved the tartan-clad boys in Bay City Rollers, while Donny Osmond and David Cassidy had been the main two female heart-throbs when Tommy first arrived at Wimbledon.

But these pop stars were so far removed from their fans and from reality. The closest the teeny-boppers could get to their pop idols was putting up posters on their bedroom walls and buying their 45rpm vinyl singles or 33-inch LPs.

Shannon could actually get to meet, and talk to, her idol almost every Thursday night, from March to October.

To her, he wasn't only the most beautiful man in the world, he was polite and nice and always said: "Hello, Curly Head."

He also thanked her for her childish poems.

He was one of the best in the world at doing what he did. He showed everybody that if you were serious and focused, you could accomplish anything you wanted.

Talk about a perfect teenage role model.

15
The Wembley Roar

"The best thing about racing at Wembley was the crowd. You could really hear the fans there. They were so lively that you heard them over the roar of the bikes. It was just great to come out of a turn and see everybody in the stands get up on their feet."

Bengt Jansson

If there was anything speedway riders almost always had under their control it was their nerves. It didn't matter what happened around them, they usually didn't concern themselves about their opponents or what the fans got up to. They did their own thing no matter what.

Of course some riders had more respect among their peers than others. A few even provoked fear in their rivals and had races in the pocket before the gate went up.

There were some special places that could evoke feelings of fear and a great deal of respect, even among the absolute best.

One such venue was Wembley Stadium.

No speedway meeting in the world created such a buzz of excitement as a World Final at the most historic and atmospheric stadium in Britain and the most classic speedway venue in the world. In the shadows of the famous Twin Towers and in front of 80,000 fans, many experienced riders had crumbled into nervous wrecks.

The stadium – spiritual home of the FA Cup – became an even more electric place when the speedway riders made their entrance. Football matches were between two teams and two set of fans. Depending on the outcome, half the crowd could be silenced pretty quickly. If it was a boring or tense game, many fans were biting their nails instead of making a loud noise.

During a speedway final, all 16 riders had their fans cheering them loudly from the stands. Everybody wanted to be seen and heard, there was never a quiet moment – always a reason for some group of supporters to either celebrate or boo.

With one or two very rare exceptions, speedway fans also showed good behaviour and respect towards their sport, the dignity to celebrate a champion whoever he was and whichever team or country he rode for. In their eyes, a true champion always deserved recognition and acknowledgement.

Ove Fundin had heard the noise from 80,000 fans many times and been celebrated at Wembley like few others. On the other hand, he actually managed to create friction among the fans as well. In 1957 he lost the title after a tough run-off against Barry Briggs – it didn't matter that Ove tried all his tricks. He came out late to the start, he tried to rattle Briggs in every way possible and when he chased Briggs like a maniac, he tried too hard and almost knocked the Kiwi down. But instead of Briggo falling, it was the desperate Fundin who crashed to the ground.

Heat 2 of the '75 World Final and Tommy finds himself shut out on the outside of leader Ivan Mauger, Malcolm Simmons and Ray Wilson, although he did manage to pass Ray.

Barry Briggs won the championship.

The crowd went nuts.

Half of them cheered for Briggs, the other half booed the referee and demanded that Barry should be excluded, especially the very vocal supporters from Norwich, where Fundin was a God.

One fan even slapped Mrs June Briggs in the face and she stood there crying when husband Barry took his lap of honour.

Wembley was a place like no other.

Or as Arne Bergstrom put it: "Wembley is the Mecca of speedway."

Tommy Jansson loved racing at Wembley.

On the morning of September 6, 1975 he left his apartment in Putney to go to Wembley and once inside this old stadium graced by many sporting legends he had to take a deep breath and try to take it all in. He stood in the pits thinking about his journey from Eskilstuna to what he felt was the most impressive stadium in the world.

He had high hopes, even if he wasn't among the favourites. This was his second World Final as one of the main 16. He'd made his debut at Gothenburg in 1971 but had been only a reserve for the final at Katowice (1973) and the next one back in Gothenburg (1974).

In the starting line-up there were three world champions – defending No.1 Anders Michanek, Ole Olsen and Ivan Mauger, who had won six of the previous seven finals between them.

Tommy had ridden in a few previous meetings at Wembley and he loved it. To him, all the noise from the crowd was just awe-inspiring, it gave him extra energy. He loved to show what he could do in front of so many people. Sure, like everybody else, he'd been amazed by the place the first time he raced there, in 1973, when he he could hear the noise of the fans over the roar of the bikes.

Peter Collins eventually edged clear of Tommy when they met in heat 14 of the 1975 World Final.

This was even better, though, because his parents were in attendance, along with lots of fans from Eskilstuna – at least six buses had left town for the ferry to England. Knowing Joel and Inga-Lill were in the stands made Tommy very proud.

They had arrived in a private Cessna. Tommy went to meet them and laughed as he stood watching the little plane from Sweden tax between two giant jumbo jets at Gatwick airport.

Joel had been there before – not only to England, but at Wembley to ride in the World Final. "It looks the same," he said after taking his seat beneath the Twin Towers that had witnessed so many memorable moments in sporting history.

The track surface seemed to be in pretty bad shape – just like he remembered it. Since Wembley was only an occasional speedway venue, after the Lions finally quit BL racing at the end of 1971 (due to a lack of dates made available by the Football Assoiciation), the track often became bumpy, rutted and inconsistent.

When Joel rode there in the 1958 final he'd been up against Barry Briggs in his first heat. He came in last, Barry won the race – and all his other heats thereafter to become World Champion for the second consecutive year.

Around 61,000 supporters had celebrated Briggs' victory, except for a few Swedish fans and those from Norwich rooting for their man Fundin. Joel had considered it an honour just being one of the finalists. The other riders had been in the pits benefiting from a lot of back-up from mechanics and promoters but Joel was there on his own, having travelled to England with a group of supporters. He was the only one of the 16 riders on show not competing regularly in England. Not surprisingly, Joel finished last in all five of his heats but he hadn't been too down about it. He knew he'd done all he could – he just wasn't good enough to compete with the world's best.

Tommy was in a totally different situation in 1975. He was not out of place – he was one of the big boys.

Inga-Lill was taken aback by what she witnessed on the walk along Wembley Way towards the stadium. She had seen groups of fans wearing t-shirts with her son's face on them and others with red-and-yellow satin and woollen scarves with 'I like Tommy' printed on them.

Inside the stadium, she was a little disappointed about the decaying state of the old place. "I thought it was going to be nice here but I'm surprised by these hard, uncomfortable seats and the lack of room. I'm going to go numb sitting here the whole evening," she said.

"Look there," Joel said, pointing at more fans wearing t-shirts bearing a picture of Tommy's smiling face.

"I can't believe he's so popular here. I mean, this is London," added Inga-Lill.

They couldn't understand that their son was one of the fans' big favourites. A working class kid from Eskilstuna, far away from home, at the world famous Wembley Stadium, the Janssons were clearly filled with pride as well as amazement.

Ivan Mauger was sure that Tommy would win a World Final one day. Ivan had seen many promising riders doubting their own ability in high pressure situations like this. He thought that Tommy, with his 'pretty boy' look, could be underestimated. The old maestro knew that beneath that gorgeous smile and beautiful face was a racing heart of steel.

He had also said that Tommy could be rough out there. Not reckless or dirty, but very determined. If Tommy saw an opening, he went for it. Tommy was never afraid. That's why he had a bright future, according to Mauger.

Another characteristic that made Tommy such a likeable person was his openness and polite manners. Every time Ivan met the young Swede, Tommy was always very courteous and the Kiwi maestro remembered with a smile how eager to learn and how full of questions he'd been the first time their paths had crossed.

The boy had become a man – and Ivan thought that Tommy was not far away from reaching the top of the podium in a meeting of this stature.

Ivan had won two World Finals at Wembley, in 1969 and 1972, when he won a run-off against Bernt Persson.

Another rider who loved Wembley was young Peter Collins who held the track record and won a great victory for England in the run-off against Anders Michanek that decided the Daily Mirror International Tournament of 1973.

Bernt Persson was also happy to be back. At Wembley he had been acclaimed for his brave actions and also loudly booed, after being blamed for causing the horrific

crash in the '72 final that put Barry Briggs out of the meeting and into hospital where he had a finger amputated. Even though he had been heckled by the fans that night, he had kept on racing and was unaffected by his second race drama that also involved two Russians. Few riders in the world could handle getting booed by some 60,000 fans, so Persson was impressive all right.

Tommy was thinking about Bernt and Bengt Jansson, who hadn't made it to the final this time. Benga loved Wembley and Tommy had enjoyed hearing him and others talk about old races at the world famous venue. Benga had also been in a run-off for the championship, against Ove Fundin in 1967, the same year a kid named Anders Michanek made his World Final debut.

Bengt had told Tommy about the agony of getting so close to the title, which left a deep impression on the young man most observers expected to take over from Mich as the top Swede in 1976. But Tommy knew that if even a rider as talented as Bengt Jansson hadn't been able to win a final, then it said a lot about how difficult it was to achieve.

Joining Tommy and Bernt in the '75 final was their fellow countryman and the reigning champion, Anders Michanek, who couldn't wait for the night to end. For a change, he didn't expect victory and, after all the pressure and attention the previous year's championship success had brought him, he looked forward to no longer being the champion everybody wanted to beat.

But when Ole Olsen walked down the long, dark pits tunnel, out onto the track and into the light, where the the fans were getting so hyped up for the meeting to start, he thought the total opposite to Anders. Olsen was fired up like never before.

Wembley had not been kind to him in the past. He had crashed there a few times, and also suffered a very costly engine failure in the final heat of a crucial World Championship qualifier.

After going so close to defending his title in 1972, when a first race fall was followed by four straight wins, this time he intended to show the world some Danish dynamite. He had the look on his face that he had when he was at his best. It was as if his eyes had got bigger – he had an intense, almost crazed look about him.

And that look was not going to change all night.

While other riders complained about the scandalous condition of the track, which was first dry and dusty and later over-watered in certain parts, and still hard to handle, Olsen just saw opportunities – and grasped them.

Throughout the whole night there were precious few clean passing movements that were not down to the poor state of the track. One of them came when Tommy Jansson tricked Ray Wilson and went by him on the inside in the second heat of the night. But Tommy still managed only third place in his first race. Not a good start and he continued to have problems at the gate. He soon gave up all hopes of an ultimate victory this time and accepted that it was another case of look and learn.

It was a terrible track, one of the worst he'd ever ridden. But he tried hard not to lose confidence and thought that if he could cope with a sandstorm in Australia, he could handle the Wembley dust bowl too. In his second heat he came second behind Michanek and ahead of Henryk Gluklich and Vladimir Gordeev.

1975 World Champion Ole Olsen is congratulated by third pl;ace man John Louis, with Anders Michanek looking relieved not to have the carry the burden of being world No.1 any longer.

In the 11th heat Tommy finished second again, although it felt like a victory because Olsen was flying on the night and in unstoppable form. Bernt Persson trailed in third place in that heat, which was some consolation for Tommy, who wondered what Joel was thinking about the track that had turned from a dusty dirt road into a sticky mess.

The 14th heat started well, Tommy leading before he was bumped by Edward Jancarz. England's big hope Peter Collins won, although Tommy managed to fight back to claim two more points.

In his last ride Tommy was in the lead again and heading for a top five spot when he ended up in a hole in the ground. His handlebars broke in half and he slid off into the mud – uninjured, but dirty and without a point to his name.

Tommy finished in ninth place overall with seven points. Considering the circumstances, he was not unhappy with his efforts in his second individual World Final appearance. He never lost his ability to remain positive and just the fact that only seven speedway riders in the world could claim that they were better than him that year made him feel better.

'My time will come,' the 22-year-old reminded himself.

"How do you feel after your crash?" asked Inga-Lill.

"I'm glad I didn't go down more often – it was like a moto-cross track out there," Tommy said.

Ole Olsen was doing his lap of honour, celebrating his victory with maximum points and his second world title success. The World Champion was thrilled, of course, but he had already started to think about a different World Championship system – along the lines of a Grand Prix, with the riders' cumulative points being added together from a number of 'finals' held in different countries over the course of the whole season.

He felt the system of the traditional, one-off World Final was an injustice. In 1976, Olsen failed to qualify for the final, even though he was the reigning champion, after bowing out in the Inter-Continental Final at Wembley. In subsequent years he was among the most prominent in lobbying the FIM to adopt the Grand Prix formula used today and, since its belated introduction in 1995, Ole has been one of the main driving forces behind the BSI Grand Prix organisation in his role as Benfield Sports International's GP Race Director.

The 1975 World Final at Wembley marked the second of Olsen's three individual World Championship victories and his words afterwards inspired Tommy. The Dane talked about the importance of being a real champion.

He said: "The World Champion has to perform with class – every time. That's what the fans expect from the World No.1 – they expect you to beat their own favourites.

"And that's what you have to live up to. You have to race well and set an example all the time, otherwise you're a bad representative for the sport.

"If the best speedway rider in the world loses too often, it's a bad sign for the whole sport. For the champion there are never any excuses: Sweden, Poland, England or Australia – wherever you go, you have to be at the top."

The Wimbledon heart-throb posing on the centre green at Plough Lane.

16
Love at first sight

"You can be hit by a car walking down the street. You can get sick, so you shouldn't worry for my sake. I'll be fine."

Tommy Jansson

It was November 1975 and Bosse Jansson was gearing up for a party in his apartment in Eskilstuna. The music was important. Most guests liked Abba, of course – Annifrid, who came from Torshalla, outside Eskilstuna, had conquered the world with the group after winning the Eurovision Song Contest in Brighton with Waterloo the year before.

Another popular Swedish artist was Bjorn Skifs, whose band Blue Swede had made a version of Hooked on a Feeling that made it to No.1 on the Billboard-list in America. His song Michelangelo was a hit in Sweden.

Bosse liked Abba, Bjorn Skifs and Rod Stewart, with his new hit song Sailing.

Sailing was blasting out in Bosse's apartment when the guests arrived and the first drinks were poured. Everybody was there to 'warm up' before going to Smederna's party at the local Stadshotellet.

Tommy didn't care too much for music, even though he had a few Cat Stevens cassettes he played while driving his car in England.

Not even Bengt Jansson's hard work and influence towards the country and western beat had cut any ice with Tommy. If it sounded great and he tapped his foot to the floor, then it was simply okay. He never bought pop records.

Pouring drinks down his throat wasn't what Tommy favoured either. Bosse had even asked him: "Don't you find it boring to never be able to just let go and party once in a while?"

Tommy explained: "I'm a professional athlete, I can't stumble all over the town square in Eskilstuna like a drunk. I have to show more class than that."

Tommy arrived at Bosse's party on his own and took a seat in the living room. When Bosse poured himself a drink, Tommy looked at his brother and said somewhat sarcastically: "Don't I get one?"

"What? You want a drink?"

"Yes, please."

For a change, Tommy had decided to have a couple of drinks this time, to enjoy a fun evening and not worry about always being so careful. The season was over. In a few weeks he was going back to Australia. It was just a great feeling being at home in Eskilstuna, relaxing and knowing he didn't have to fly to England or some other place the next morning. It was time to have some drinks, listen to music, try to catch up on what was going on in the world outside of speedway.

He felt great and, just like he did on the speedway track, he felt in total control.

That's when Eva-Lotta Lindh entered Bosse's apartment.

All that talk about speedway being the only love in life, about the sport being the best mistress, and all that advice he'd been given by the older generation . . . in one instant it had all gone.

It was Lotta's fault. She had long, dark hair, sparkling eyes and the most beautiful smile Tommy had ever seen. Lotta's friend, Kristina, was dating the mechanic Borje Lundqvist and he had brought both girls along to Bosse's party, before heading on to Smederna's bash later on.

This was Tommy Jansson, the man the whole town talked about, who had won the Swedish Final in front of 12,000 fans at home and, in this same year, had competed in the World Final at Wembley.

Lotta didn't care about all that.

But she remembered when she'd seen him racing on his back wheel down Torncrosgatan and her boss going on and on about how gorgeous he was. Lotta recalled looking out of the window and thinking that he was not for her.

Now he was sitting on Bosse's sofa staring straight at her.

When their eyes locked, that marvellous thing, which few people ever get to experience, happened to them – both knew they were made for each other. Everything around them ceased to exist. They didn't talk to each other at first, but on their way out of the apartment Tommy approached her and asked: "Do you know my brother?"

"No, it was Borje who brought us here," she explained.

They introduced themselves. Tommy was born and raised in the northern part of town and went to school there. Lotta was from the other side of town and she had attended different schools, so their paths had never crossed.

On the way into town, while walking through a park, Tommy took Lotta's hand and they walked hand in hand together towards Stadshotellet.

Bosse almost fell backwards.

First the drink, now this – what was going on with his little brother?

Inga-Lill and Joel were at Stadshotellet, along with all the other people involved with Smederna, and when Mrs Jansson saw her youngest son together with Lotta, she couldn't believe her eyes either.

"Why is Tommy holding that girl's hand?" she asked.

Even Lotta herself couldn't believe what was happening. Is this really true, she thought, but she was all smiles.

Tommy just didn't want to let go, he felt it was the most natural thing in the world to walk around holding Lotta's hand. As natural as following her home that night. Sure, it was all innocent, but she still lived at home and imagine the surprise her parents would get, sitting down in the kitchen for breakfast when Eskilstuna's most famous man walked in, extended his hand and said: 'Hi, my name's Tommy Jansson.'

Lotta was going to drive Tommy home in her old Volkswagen but it refused to start.

'Oh, my God, this is so embarrassing, he's never going to want to see me again,' she thought.

But he just smiled, push-started the car and told her that he wanted to see her again – every day.

All of a sudden he wasn't that happy about the prospect of travelling to Australia for a couple of months and getting ready for the 1976 season.

It wasn't long before he had to explain his speedway plans to Lotta.

So in love . . . Tommy and Eva-Lotta.

"But I have to go there if I'm going to be as good as I want to be. My goal is to become the best speedway rider in the world and that's what I'm going to be one day," he said.

He liked the fact that she wasn't impressed by his achievements and celebrity status. It wasn't the international speedway star she had fallen in love with – it was Tommy Jansson, the person.

He hadn't even landed in Melbourne before he wrote his first letter to her – his first-ever love letter and one of many he would send during that winter of 1975-76.

The dangerous elements of the sport was something they seldom talked about, although she once admitted that she worried about the risks involved in speedway.

"But you can be hit by a car walking down the street. You can get sick, so you shouldn't worry for my sake. I'll be fine," Tommy said.

His words comforted her. Nothing was going to happen to him, she thought. Nothing could be dangerous in their beautiful world. She loved his long letters where he sometimes described the speedway tracks in detail – how long they were and how he prepared himself to race on them. And then he wrote, 'I love you' and 'I miss you' many times on each page.

Their time together was intense, full of nice conversations and experiences, a lot of laughs and wonderful feelings neither of them had ever been close to experiencing before. It was just like a romantic movie, where all the fun happened so fast.

Throughout this strange and lovely autumn, before Tommy left for Australia, neither of them could possibly have imagined that their time together was going to be so very short.

17
Returning Down Under

"After a crash, you always have to call home and tell your family that you are okay, so they don't have to hear about the accident from somebody else and get worried."

Ole Olsen

Tommy was sitting on the flight to Australia reading Speedway Star, which he always read from cover to cover every week. Partly because he wanted to know what was going on in the speedway world, but also to improve his English.

He kept a close watch on his biggest rivals. He knew the averages of most riders and that the 1975 season had seen him finish 12th in the overall standings with an impressive Gulf British League Calculated Match Average (CMA) of 10.06 (from a maximum 12.00) in his 28 league matches for Wimbledon.

The only riders ahead of him in the charts were:
1. Ivan Mauger, Exeter, 11.45.
2. Peter Collins, Belle Vue, 11.27.
3. Phil Crump, Newport, 11.17.
4. Anders Michanek, Reading, 11.03.
5. Ole Olsen, Wolverhampton, 10.78.
6. John Louis, Ipswich, 10.67.
7. Dave Jessup, Leicester, 10.45.
8. Malcolm Simmons, Poole, 10.39.
9. Dag Lovaas, Oxford, 10.22.
10. Reg Wilson, Sheffield, 10.18.
11. Martin Ashby, Swindon, 10.13.

Tommy studied the list of the best riders in the world, shook his head and said to himself: 'I should have ended up higher on this list.'

The personal highlight was his triumph in the World Pairs Final with Anders Michanek. In England, Tommy had won two individual meetings on his home track, the Marlboro Southern Riders' Championship Final and The Laurels, a traditional end-of-season event staged annually at Wimbledon. He was second in the two

Welcoming Larry Ross to south London.

memorial meetings, in honour of Geoff Curtis (Reading) and Peter Craven (Belle Vue), as well as in the London Riders' Championship at Hackney.

He knew that ninth place in the World Final was nothing to brag about.

In Sweden he wasn't able to defend his national championship. In the final he ended up third on another night that belonged to Michanek. Behind Anders, three riders had to contest a run-off to decide the runners-up places, won by Hans Holmqvist from Tommy and Bernt Persson, who just missed out on a rostrum position.

Tommy got the chance to shake hands with the Swedish King, Carl Gustaf, who took part in the award ceremony. Shaking hands with The King was fun but Tommy believed that third place was not worthy of congratulations. To him, second place was first loser. The position on top of the podium was the only place worth celebrating.

Smederna had been in the fight for the league championship before having to settle for second place behind Bysarna, although in England Tommy and Barry Briggs had been out on their own at the top of the Wimbledon scorechart, so the team had no chance of competing with the big boys. Most annoying were the three home defeats and a draw at Plough Lane which resulted in the Dons slipping one placve in ther table, to ninth. From 29 official matches, Tommy averaged 10.12 points a match out of a possible perfect 12.00. He was given most support by Briggo and Ed Stangeland, but Bert Harkins, Barry Crowson, Roger Johns and Reg Luckhurst were only solid without being spectacular scorers. The only newcomer to the side in '75 was New Zealander Larry Ross.

For almost every rider in the British and National League (second division), all thoughts during the winter of 1975-76 turned to the new four-valve engine that had

Among the greats . . . the World Champions troupe that toured Australia and New Zealand.
Back row, left to right: Ivan Mauger, Ole Olsen, Scott Autrey, Barry Briggs, Egon Müller.
Front: John Louis, Ronnie Moore, Tommy and Anders Michanek.

been introduced on a limited basis in '75. The main man behind the revolutionary new motor was Australian international Neil Street (in association with Ivan Tighe), who also rode for Newport in the BL and became a good friend of Tommy's. They both came from families who lived for the sport 24/7. Neil Street was father-in-law to Aussie No.1 and 1975 World Finalist Phil Crump, whose son, Jason, would go on to win the 2004 World Championship Grand Prix series. Jason's grandfather helped introduce Tommy Jansson to the new four-valve era.

But before that Tommy was going to spend another four months in Australia and New Zealand, racing in 14 star-studded meetings for the Ivan Mauger-Barry Briggs World Champions troupe. For the third consecutive winter he travelled Down Under and enjoyed the warm climate instead of the long, cold Swedish winter. He started to feel like a globetrotter and after arriving in Oz this time, he went immediately to the beach to soak up four hours of sun.

He burned himself badly – so much for being a cool and experienced globetrotter, he thought – and in a letter to Lotta he described his pain and stupidity which left him red and sore for days.

What he didn't tell Lotta in that letter was his plans for the future – for the winter of 1976-77. He was thinking about skipping Australia for South Africa. Tommy had heard other World Series riders talk about their previous winter's trip to SA, about the tracks, the enthusiastic fans, the great weather - and the whole adventure of being in that part of the world.

Like when a bunch of riders went to the world famous Krugerpark to spot wildlife and Ronnie Moore decided to get out of the jeep to take a photo up close to the animals. He started walking beside the car, looking for a great photo opportunity . . . when a lion spotted him.

'Nice photo,' Ronnie thought, but the lion had other ideas and Ronnie had to run for his life and dive back into the jeep. Thankfully, the driver kept the engine running and they left the agitated and hungry lion at great speed!

The political climate in South Africa was not something the speedway riders had talked much about. Not officially anyway. The hosts had demanded of their guests that they had to stay away from coloured people and were even discouraged from signing autographs for the 'non-white, second class citizens' in the apartheid system of South Africa at the time.

But the riders ignored their hosts' wishes. They talked with and signed autographs for everybody they met – of all colours.

Tommy wanted to go to Africa, to see more of the world and experience other foreign cultures. But the longer he stayed in Australia and New Zealand that winter, and the more letters he wrote to Lotta at home in Eskilstuna, he realised that, for the first time in his life, he was a little homesick. He realised that he couldn't go to South Africa alone – Lotta had to come with him.

He looked forward to telling her about his plans but he wanted to do it face to face, not in a letter. He had to check out some details first. Ole Olsen and Ivan Mauger arrived in Australia around New Year, 1976 having come straight from South Africa.

"It was just great," said Ole, the newly-crowned South African Champion.

'I'm going to go to Africa, together with Lotta,' Tommy decided.

★★★★★★

'I love you' read the sentence on one line of the letter.

'The track was 550 meters long, the turns were different from each other and it was quite bumpy,' continued the next sentence of the same letter.

The romantic turned professional.

Lotta got to know as much about the standard of speedway tracks in Australia as she did Tommy's affectionate feelings for herself.

He always included the thoughtful words 'regards to your mother and her husband'. Tommy encouraged her when she complained about her tough schedule in school and all the difficult tests she had to take. 'Keep going, you're close to your goal,' he wrote.

He also wrote about how much he missed her and that it was not the same being in Australia this time, while she was thousands of miles away. He repeatedly wrote 'I love you.'

The young Swedish speedway star was so in love that he hardly noticed all the young girls swarming around him in Australia. Everything was the same in that regard – in fact, the fans loved him even more. But he didn't care about the women. He had Lotta. He was in Australia to race. That was it.

His colleagues intervened and went between Tommy and the fans, in the same way that Tommy's good friend and room-mate, Gavin Elms, handled all the phone calls to their apartment in Putney.

"Oh, you're looking for Tommy. No, he's not here," Gavin would say, while at the same time looking at Tommy sitting on the sofa just a few feet away from him.

"He's in Sweden."

In Australia other diversionary manoeuvres were sometimes necessary. Some riders literally stepped in and took Tommy's place among female fans who were happy enough to settle for a second grade replacement instead of their their preferred heart-throb.

The American rider, Scott Autrey, admitted later: "Sure, we were jealous of Tommy. It was him who all the girls wanted."

Scott and Tommy were room-mates during a World Champions Series tour of Australia and New Zealand. Exeter star Autrey had previously raced against Tommy in England and he'd been impressed.

"Tommy rode like an American. I thought he was raised on a small track like Wimbledon, not a big track like they have in Eskilstuna. Tommy was so loose on the bike, even though he was quite tall for a speedway rider. He shifted his weight, rode very smoothly, never having to reduce speed. It was the California-style of racing."

In a swimming pool at one of the hotels where they were staying during the tour, Scott and Tommy were on their own. Ivan, Briggo and the older superstars were out of earshot.

"Tommy, one day those old guys are gonna be gone from the top. It's going to be you and me fighting to win the World Final."

Tommy looked at Scott, who was a trailblazer for the American influx to British speedway that would develop much more in the late 70s, as if he was mad.

Tommy wasn't going to say publicly what he was thinking but he liked how Scott's view of the future sounded. He shared the same thoughts as the Californian, except he was going to keep his thoughts to himself.

Scott's respect and admiration for Tommy would grow stronger during that winter. That Tommy said 'no thanks' to beers and parties in order to work on his bike was not something that bothered Scott. On the contrary, it impressed and inspired him.

The second World Champions troupe series in Australia and New Zealand featured another array of international names, who became like a touring rock 'n' roll band or a travelling circus. They had a lot of fun together, at speedway meetings as well as the barbecues and parties that followed. As well as the big two, Scott and Tommy, the all-star cast also included John Louis, Egon Müller, Jiri Stancl, Edward Jancarz, Anders Michanek and Ray Wilson.

They all had fun together – except one.

Ole Olsen wouldn't even stay at the same hotel as the others.

"Come on, Ole, join us for some water-skiing today," Anders Michanek said.

"No, I'll skip that," Ole said.

"Why don't you stay with us at the same hotel?"

"I can't do that, because then I'll become too friendly with the rest of you guys and then I can't race against you in the same way I normallly would."

Wheel to wheel with Ivan Mauger during the 1975 Internationale classic at Wimbledon.

★★★★★★

Two of Tommy's best results during his time on the other side of the globe included victories in races against World Champion Olsen. He had finished second to the Great Dane in one of the three World Series meetings held at Christchurch and saw off Olsen again in the semi-final at Melbourne before losing that final to Phil Crump. Tommy had also reached the final at Invercargill (beaten by Mauger), Newcastle (last behind Mauger, Olsen and Autrey) and Christchurch (third behind Mauger and Olsen). Tommy's only final win on that Australia-New Zealand tour of 1975-76 came at Auckland, where he led home Briggs, Olsen and England's John Louis.

The tour had seen Tommy produce consistently excellent form to earn him third place overall in the Australasian part of the series (the next leg of the tour, in the USA, was cancelled at the last minute) but it ended painfully for him.

At Bundaberg, near Brisbane in northern Queensland, it was close between Tommy and Olsen yet again. Those two were in a heat against Ivan and Edward Jancarz when Tommy clipped Ole's back wheel and crashed to the ground, badly damaging his shoulder.

"How are you doing," Ole asked as Tommy sat in the ambulance.

"It hurts like hell," Tommy said.

"After a crash, you always have to call home and tell your family that you're okay, so they don't have to hear about the accident from somebody else and get worried," Ole advised him.

Tommy did as Ole suggested and then travelled home to Sweden a little earlier than planned, boarding a flight to Europe that included stopovers in Hawaii and USA. His right arm was bandaged and he also had a dislocated shoulder and a broken collarbone.

It was the first time he'd been badly hurt on the track. It was early February and he was back home in winterland. Depressing?

No, not when he had Lotta.

He liked spending time with Lotta and her family. Tommy loved his own family too, but to spend time in an environment where nobody talked about speedway was a nice break from the everyday routine he normally loved more than anything else in life.

Lotta made him think a little bit more and he admitted to her that he felt he wasn't as knowledgeable as he wanted to be about the world outside of speedway. He wanted to know and learn more than just how to get a speedway bike to go as fast as possible.

She wondered how he felt after his crash and if he was worried about the upcoming season.

"No, I'll be fine. My time in plaster won't ruin my season. I'll miss a month of training but I'll make up for it in no time," he assured her.

He told her about his goals for the 1976 season – to reach the World Final again, to ride in the World Pairs Final scheduled for Eskilstuna in June and to win the Swedish Championship with Smederna again.

He waited for delivery of his first four valve-machine, having to travel by car from Eskilstuna to pick it up at a garage in Denmark, where a tuner had been preparing it for him. He borrowed his father's Mercedes and took Lotta along.

They had a great time and for the first time in his life he spent hours in a car not talking about speedway at all.

They had a picnic basket with them and made a few stops on the way before boarding the ferry between Helsingborg and Helsingor.

On the way home they were delayed in customs when Joel's car was searched. The customs officers suspected the young couple had been on a drugs-run from Amsterdam with a car containing marijuana.

Tommy was furious – Lotta had never seen him so angry.

The only thing they talked about during the trip that was speedway-related was the design of Tommy's new leathers. He had designed them himself and Lotta had some opinions about his ideas that he wanted to hear.

He wanted to look good on the track – only the best was good enough for him.

18
Home again

"When I saw that Tommy didn't put his left foot to the ground in the turns, like all the other riders did, that's when I understood that he was something special – why he was so much better than most of the other riders."

Eva-Lotta Lindh, after attending her first speedway meeting in England

"**H**i Tommy, this is Cyril. Bad news. We haven't been able to reach an agreement with Christer Lofqvist. He's not coming to Wimbledon."

"Too bad. Who's going to ride for us instead?"

"Don't know yet. I've made some contacts. We'll see," added Maido.

"How's Bosse been doing?" asked Tommy.

Bosse Jansson had been in England during the spring of 1976 for some practice rides, mainly because he wanted to gain the experience to be able to race in England, and also to sample the tougher competition of the world's most competitive league – not because he felt ready to ride professionally just yet

"Bosse's been riding very well," Cyril said.

"Use him, then," Tommy suggested.

A few days later the phone rang at Bosse's apartment in Eskilstuna. It was Cyril.

"No, I'm not looking for Tommy, I want to talk to you. How would you feel about coming back over here for a few meetings?"

"Sure, I'd love to."

All of a sudden a Jansson was at Plough Lane again.

Bosse was in England to make his debut as a professional speedway rider – something he didn't understand until he read the match programme for the night of Thursday, March 18 and it was there, in black and white: Number 3 – Bo Jansson.

"What, I'm supposed to race already?" he asked in amazement.

"Yes," confirmed Maido.

It could have been an easier start for him. Wimbledon's challenge match opponents were Reading Racers, spearheaded by experienced world class riders Bengt Jansson, Dave Jessup and John Davis. Wimbledon were granted a guest facility for the absent Lofqvist, who had fallen out with the Dons' London rivals Hackney the

Oh brother! Tommy and Bosse together for Wimbledon early in the 1976 season.

previous season and was again in dispute over money.

"Hello, Bosse. Good luck," was pretty much all Bengt said before the match.

After that, nobody was nice to Bosse anymore.

In his first heat Bosse finished third, followed by a second place – behind Benga – before Bosse picked up another third place and ended up last in the rest of his heats. Reading crushed Wimbledon, 46-32, with Bosse contributing four (paid five) points.

A few days later Tommy arrived back in England and on March 24 it was time for the next match, on the north-west side of the River Thames, against new London-rivals White City whose 'Rebels' team had moved from Oxford to a large stadium in west London. This was the opening meeting at the big stadium that staged events in the 1948 Olympic Games.

Bosse tried hard to impress but this time he felt out of his depth. In his second professional match he learnt just how big speedway in England really was. This was not even a Spring Gold Cup match or a Gulf British League fixture – it was another low-key challenge before the start of the real season – and he was riding in front of a bigger crowd than he'd ever done before.

Bosse came last in the fourth heat of the evening but Tommy won the fifth race to cut Dons' deficit to 13-17. The visiting Wimbledon riders felt good about themselves.

In heat six White City tracked Dag Lovaas and Trevor Geer against New Zealander Larry Ross and Bosse. Although too slow from the gate, Bosse wasn't far behind the rest going through the second turn, close enough to go for a small gap between the two home riders. But Ross saw the same opening too and went for the space himself. Ross, not caring at all about his Swedish team-mate, made the smart move

Bosse ready for his Dons debut.

while Bosse had to back off and ended the race way behind the other three.

Back in the pits, Bosse was upset. "Larry Ross – what kind of a f*****g loser is he? He put himself before me. I had to hold back and then I didn't have a chance in hell of getting anywhere.

"What kind of team-mate is that?"

Tommy looked angry as well. He was upset . . . with Bosse.

"Shut up. Here, you are on your own. If you're slow at the gate, nobody is going to help you. Then you're done, all on your own. If you are at the front and have a chance to go for the win, then do it without thinking at all about your team-mate."

"I see," Bosse muttered.

"This is England," Tommy emphasised.

Bosse rode in just one more heat – he trailed in fourth again – and Wimbledon lost the challenge match by two points.

The day after, Bosse learnt two important lessons.

Firstly, he wasn't ready to compete with the best in England – even if he did collect four points in Wimbledon's first Spring Gold Cup win of the season, 46-32 at home against Poole Pirates the night after the White City operner.

Secondly, that man from New Zealand was Larry Ross, an accomplished international rider.

When Bosse called home and told people in Eskilstuna about his adventures in England, he talked mostly about Tommy's success. Sure, he'd been aware of Tommy's popularity and stardom in England, but to experience it first-hand was a totally different matter.

The fans celebrated Tommy night after night – he always spent a long time after each meeting signing autographs and photos and posing for yet more pictures. The Swedish superstar didn't want to let anybody down. He treated all the fans with respect and took his time with them.

Many of the female fans particularly liked to get Tommy to sign photos taken of him with his shirt off. Tommy had not been too keen about posing for those photos, but a paper had been pushing for it and Tommy also understood the PR value to his club. It was good marketing.

He was a pin-up boy in London, which seemed totally insane for a working class boy from Eskilstuna. This was in 1976, long before another Swedish sports star would have the same fan appeal in London. No, Arsenal and Swedish international footballer Fredrik Ljungberg was certainly not the first super-Swede to become a big favourite in the English capital.

Always in demand . . . always helpful and polite.

"Don't you find it a little embarrassing?" Bosse asked his brother.

"No, I can't think that way – the fans like it."

"But don't you get tired of all the attention occasionally – all the autographs. Don't you just want to go straight home sometimes?"

"No, it's the fans who pay my salary," Tommy pointed out.

Bosse smiled and he knew it was partly true, but Bosse also knew that Tommy loved the attention and being in the spotlight.

Bosse reflected on what Joel had told his sons when they started racing – that racing speedway was 'like being an actor on stage.' Some people tried to hide from the spotlight, while others thrived on it.

Many fans also wanted to shake Bosse's hand and ask him for his autograph. He found that the English fans were more straightforward than those back home in Eskilstuna. They were thrilled to meet 'Tommy's brother.'

But when all the riders were introduced to the crowd on the centre green after a meeting at Plough Lane and Bosse was presented as 'Tommy's brother,' he became irritated. He took the microphone himself and said: "Sorry, but my name is Bo Jansson."

His new team-mates liked him immediately. Bosse never said no to a pint at the pub after a meeting, while Tommy preferred to go home. Bosse loved to talk and was more outgoing than his brother. He loved to have fun – and made sure he did. He was in England, racing with Tommy – nothing could beat this.

A little more experience and he could make a statement himself on the track. He felt good about himself.

Next stop . . . Exeter, March 29.

The most feared track in Britain, home of Ivan Mauger and the Exeter Falcons.

The track was heavily banked, more than any other track in Britain, and this was a place where ending up on your backside on a dog track was not the worst thing that could happen. Far from it. Losing control here could mean serious injury or worse – the fence around the track was made of solid steel. If you crash at Exeter, you'll hurt yourself.

On the way to Exeter, Tommy warned his brother: "This is the most dangerous track I've ever ridden. Consider it a practice session. Be careful."

In the pits beforehand, Bosse also learned that not everybody was treated equally in England. The stars were a level above everybody else and nobody was higher up the pecking order than Mauger. While everybody else knelt down in the dirt to work on their bikes, the four times World Champion was settled on the only spot in the pits with asphalt under his feet.

And on the track, inside that unforgiving steel fence, Ivan ruled.

He always wanted to make sure he intimidated his opponents' best riders as soon as possible. He wanted to show who was boss – but this time he was too eager from the start and got excluded from the opening heat. Tommy won the re-start.

In the fourth race, Bosse was out for the first time. He had the chance to choose gate positions and eagerly selected the inside, thinking it was the best, as it usually was at most tracks. But choosing gate one at Exeter was a beginner's mistake.

Bosse was fastest from the start, moved in tight in the first turn and felt the engine sound disappear behind him. 'I'm first, I'll win this, I'm way before the others,' he told himself.

What he didn't know was that the other riders had moved out close to the fence – due to the steep banking, they almost rode downhill – and all three of them just thundered past a shocked Bosse.

Bosse managed to register only one single point (plus bonus) in the match, and that was a gift third place after another rider had suffered engine failure.

Bosse was not a man who scared easily but Exeter's unique County Ground track freaked him out a little bit – although once again he was extremely impressed by his brother. Tommy scored another maximum as Wimbledon won the Spring Gold Cup match, 41-36.

Three days later, on April 1, the teams squared up again, this time in south-west London and Wimbledon won by an identical 41-36 margin. Tommy romped to a maximum for the third match in a row.

Bosse ended that home match with a zero in his points column and that was it for him in England – for the time being. He thanked all of his team-mates, even Larry Ross, who had turned out to be a very decent man and not a selfish egomaniac.

Bosse also thanked the management and the supporters who, in return, thanked him and many said that they wished to see him back in England again pretty soon.

As usual, Tommy stayed behind in the Wimbledon Stadium car park for a long time after the meeting, signing autographs. He was in good spirits, very friendly and making small talk with the fans. He was no longer the shy kid who had travelled to London in 1972 with his brother's Swedish/English phrase book in his bag.

'It's unbelievable that he's so polite to everybody,' Bosse thought, standing there

Home from home . . . The superbly appointed Wimbledon Stadium (above) and in the shadow of the pinetrees at the Motorstadion, Eskilstuna (below), where it all began for Tommy.

waiting for Tommy. Not even the most pushy fans made Tommy feel uneasy. Bosse had seen many riders become annoyed and turn their back on fans who got too close in those situations, but Bosse had never seen Tommy irritated by any fans, ever.

★★★★★★

Lotta was far away, while Bosse had gone back home to Sweden.

But was Tommy lonely? Hardly. London was starting to become as much home to him as Eskilstuna. In an interview with an English paper, he said that he wasn't looking forward to the start of the '76 season in Sweden and a resumption of all the mundane travelling between England and his homeland. Although when he saw the story in print he felt ashamed – it sounded like he didn't care about Smederna and the season ahead in Sweden.

He usually took all the newspaper clippings back home to his parents so that Inga-Lill could update her scrapbooks. But this particular story, mentioning his complaints about all the travelling to and from Sweden, he left behind in England.

Tommy enjoyed living with flat-mate Gavin Elms, who became one of his best friends. Ron Slade and Lisbeth Brusse, from South Africa, who also shared their apartment in the brick-built Millbrooke Court in Putney, occasionally joined them at speedway meetings. Gavin never missed a meeting – home or away.

He also took care of Tommy's gear and leathers, washed and cleaned them for him. And, when needed, he continued to be a perfect English language teacher.

Gavin had complimented Tommy on his postcards from Australia, that he had written all of them without any grammatic errors. Tommy had sent a whole bunch of them to their London apartment. It was obvious to all Tommy's new friends how much he loved to travel and explore the world.

London was still an adventure far removed from his real home – but it still felt like home to Tommy. He liked the nice life away from the track, spending time with friends, just sitting back in front of the TV and enjoying the privilege of being able to select from more than two channels. He loved hanging out at his favourite restaurant in the neighbourhood, the Chinese called Bayee House.

That lifestyle was in huge contrast to the speedway life he knew at Plough Lane.

The stadium that he also called home was a real stadium, so far different in size, structure and status from his local track in Eskilstuna. It even had a plush, carpeted restaurant at the top of the main stand, which had greatly impressed him when he first saw it on signing for the Dons. Nothing like that existed anywhere in Sweden.

The pits at Plough Lane were tucked away beneath the main stand, at the opposite end to the restaurant, or at least the home riders' section was. When the riders warmed up their bikes before the meeting, the noise from the engines would threaten the eardrums, while the heavy fumes drifting in the air and caused the riders to cover their faces with scarve to protect themselves.

Tommy was the star man who had his own regular position closest to the tunnel, leading out onto the track. There was an upward incline leading from the mouth of the pits to the pits gate on the first turn. Overhead was the roof covering part of the main stand, with the first bend terracing to the right as the riders entered the track.

There was cover all the way round – yes, Wimbledon Speedway was a great British speedway venue and a very special place.

The fans could get close to all the riders, poking their arms through the railings to touch them whenever they emerged from the pits entrance to watch the racing. The Dons fans, clad in red and yellow anoraks, hats and scarves, cheered their favourites, although they could also jeer Wimbledon's opponents – all in the name of fun and supporting the Dons, of course. The terraced area just to the right of the pits was the place where the most hardcore fans congregated, the ones who made the most noise.

Shannon Ruane was always among the fans in that section. Once she was able to lean forward and touch Tommy's leathers after a race. She put the dirt that came off in her hand onto a pink piece of paper and then added it to her Tommy scrapbook,

After settling his pay deal for '76, Tommy was soon back in action . . and on the front of the Dons' programme.

where she added the words: 'Tommy's dirt from his leathers.'

Tommy loved the short walk from the pits to the track, through the brick-built tunnel leading past the most excitable fans and out under the bright floodlights. In those moments Tommy could only agree with Olle Nygren who once said: "Speedway is supposed to be raced at night. When it's dark everywhere except on the track, in those moments it's truly exciting for both the fans and the riders."

★★★★★★

Cyril Maidment had not been impressed when Tommy was forced to miss the start of the season as a result of his shoulder injury sustained in Australia.

He had not been too happy about wage negotiations either. Tommy had become a really tough negotiator and demanded a high salary, backed up by his great friend Gavin Elms who wrote a letter to the club's management on Tommy's behalf.

Tommy wanted a signing-on bonus of £3,000. Wimbledon came back with a counter-offer. The club no longer wished to pay for Tommy's numerous flights between England and Sweden, so the No.1 lowered his signing-on fee demands and the club, in turn, agreed to pay his travel expenses.

Gavin would forever remember one of the Wimbledon's arguments for not paying Tommy such a large upfront signing-on fee.

"What if you get hurt racing in Sweden?" they argued.

Neither Tommy nor Gavin had even considered that possibility.

During the years in which Gavin followed Tommy around in England, he never saw him crash badly. Tommy might have deliberately laid his bike down a few times in order to minimise trouble or to avoid a fallen rider immediately in front of him, but nothing worse than that.

A question Tommy often asked Gavin was: "What's my average now?"

Immediately after every match Tommy wanted to know his CMA so that he could compare himself to the other top riders in the BL. He was always eager to know his position among the other stars of the biggest league in the world.

Gavin and the others at the apartment block in Putney had joked with Tommy many times about his sex appeal and were convinced that it was only a question of time before he met somebody he wanted to be with all the time. Tommy had just laughed and said they were stupid – and wrong. He had to concentrate on his racing and his career, nothing else.

"But if only you meet the right person . . . " they said many times.

"No way. It won't happen," he answered.

Now he was happier than ever . . . but he missed Lotta.

Nobody was more surprised about that than Tommy himself.

★★★★★★

Tommy was expectant and happy as he went to meet Lotta at Gatwick airport when she arrived on her break from school over the Easter period of 1976.

Almost instantly he took her to Watford, Hertfordshire, handily placed not far from the M1 and London's North Circular road (before the M25 was built).

"It's in this area where we're going to find our own place to stay," he said.

A few days later she could see, first-hand, that all the talk about Tommy and Bernt Persson not being friends wasn't really true. Tommy was going to race for the Golden Helmet at Cradley Heath, a decider against Swindon No.1 and match-race championship holder Martin Ashby, who'd hit the headlines as his country's World Team Cup hero at Norden, Germany the previous season. Tommy had claimed the first leg at Wimbledon, 2-0, but Ashby won both races in the return clash at Blunsdon two nights later, so a deciding third leg on a neutral track was required.

Tommy and Lotta stayed over at Persson's place in the West Midlands. Bernt was still a huge star at Cradley and also a great host for his guests from Eskilstuna.

When Tommy's bike didn't arrive at the Dudley Wood track in time on April 15, Bernt allowed Tommy to use his bike, powered by the new Swedish ERM four-valve motor. Tommy won and went back to London with the Golden Helmet.

But the most memorable moment for Lotta was her first visit to Plough Lane, when she was given one of the best seats in the house for the individual Daily Express Spring Classic meeting. Suddenly, meeting announcer Ken Tozer said: "Tonight we have a special guest here . . . we want to welcome Tommy Jansson's girlfriend, Eva-Lotta Lindh from Sweden!"

Some of the teenage girls in the stands felt like they'd been struck by a bolt of lightning. 'What the hell? A girlfriend?' Who was the girl who'd stolen their Tommy away?

The home favourite finished second in the ITV-televised meeting that evening, a point behind Reading and England's Dave Jessup. After losing to John Louis in heat 10, Tommy saw his title hopes disappear when he missed the gate off the outside grid (usually the best gate at Wimbledon) in heat 15 and trailed in behind Jessup and Phil Crump. It was the race that effectively decided the coveted title worth £500, which was some of the biggest prize money on offer at the time, when big name sponsors and TV coverage in England was still buoyant.

Although very impressive, Tommy still wasn't quite the finished article at top level. Reporting for Speedway Star, Philip Rising wrote: "Tommy is still prone to little errors or a slice of misfortune on big nights such as this."

Tommy would soon avenge that defeat by DJ – twice in quick succession on his home track – but how prophetic was Rising's view that the Wimbledon skipper was "prone to a slice of misfortune?'

Lotta seldom saw Tommy put his left foot to the ground while racing against many of the world's best riders, including World Champion Ole Olsen, John Louis, Phil Crump, Anders Michanek, Peter Collins, Malcolm Simmons, Scott Autrey, Martin Ashby and a very promising 16-year-old English sensation called Michael Lee. It was something Tommy had learned when Joel had forced him to practice without his steel shoe in younger years and it helped him to find the perfect balance.

After scoring 12 points and picking up a cheque for £200 in the Spring Classic, Tommy signed his usual raft of autographs, even if all the girls around him on this particular night were a little more subdued than usual. After all, they'd just found out that their beloved Tommy had a girlfriend. On the other hand, as soon as he smiled at them, all their resentment just melted away.

Luckily, Lotta wasn't the jealous type.

At home in the apartment in Putney, Tommy had displayed some souvenirs on the window ledge. Gifts from fans – everything from love letters to the popular aftershave, Brut. He felt stupid when Lotta saw all the stuff he'd been given and repeated over and over again that she was the only one for him.

Lotta trusted him.

She also noticed how considerate he was. When Lotta's mother and stepfather made dinner for them once, they served a very popular wine at the time called Adom Attic. Next time Tommy was invited to dinner, he brought a bottle of the same brand with him.

When Lotta celebrated her 22nd birthday he gave her an opal he'd bought at the airport in Hawaii on a stopover during his last flight from Australia.

"Don't you know what an opal means?" she asked him. "Bad luck!"

"I don't believe in stuff like that," he answered.

★★★★★★

On May 13, 1976 Tommy Jansson put on a brilliant show of class at Plough Lane.

The fans' favourite successfully defended his Golden Helmet title against Dave Jessup, winning the second leg 2-1 after having won the first leg at Reading three days earlier by the same margin. With the match-race crown safely in the bag, Tommy then pipped Jessup to victory in the individual Marlboro Southern Riders' Championship qualifying round with a fine 15-point maximum – one ahead of DJ, whose success in the Daily Express Spring Classic at Plough Lane a month earlier had quickly been forgotten by the Wimbledon faithful.

Jansson and Jessup dominated the early weeks of the '76 British season, Tommy's fourth maximum of the new season having come a fortnight earlier when he romped to a full 15 points in the home KO Cup battering of Birmingham.

The significance of his brilliant performances in both legs of the cup-ties against the Brummies was that they were Tommy's first aboad his new Neil Street-Jawa

Tommy and Dave Jessup about to toss for gate positions before their Golden Helmet clash at Reading.

four-valve conversion, the chain-driven, overhead camshaft engine he'd first enthused about with 'Streetie' in Australia the previous winter. Tommy had experienced mixed results with his first new Street engine in previous British meetings in '76 – and he was still having trouble with one back home in Sweden – but his first five-ride maximu of the campaign signalled a big uplift.

With this super-quick, four-valve power unit undernerath him, to match the speed of the new English Weslake engine that home-based riders like Malcolm Simmons, Peter Collins and John Louis were winning so many races on, who knows what Tommy could achieve in the coming months?

But it had been another tough start for the Dons, whose only major signing was that of Mick Hines from all-conquering Ipswich – he was controversially allocated to Wimbledon by the Rider Control Commitee that was meant to balance team strengths in the interests of competition. Hines' first double figure score of 11 coincided with the team's first BL win in four matches, 48-30 at home to Halifax on May 6. There was still no sign of Christer Lofqvist, who had also been allocated (but never showed up), so Wimbledon struggled on with guest replacements.

★★★★★★

Two more good friends of Tommy's were Dave and Sandra Dixson. It was Dave who had designed Tommy's personalised racejacket emblazoned with the Wimbledon 'star', Smederna's blacksmith logo and the Swedish national flag that was often worn in international and individual events.

Dave worked in the pits, while Sandra stood and cheered with other members of

Tommy's fast-expanding fan club.

He celebrated his triumph in the Southern Riders' qualifier that night with dinner at Bayee House – "you could never go wrong with chinese food," Tommy would say.

But he gave away part of his first prize from the Marlboro-sponsored qualifier. Tommy had no use for a box of cigarettes – he never smoked – although he kept the red-and-white anorak and t-shirt bearing the tobacco company's logo, plus the £25 he received for first place.

Gavin had been really pleased with Tommy's win in the SRCQ and was convinced his flat-mate was heading for the very top of his profession.

Sandra and Tessa Clements, who helped her to run the fan club after Lyn Styles quit to take up a full-time job, realised that demand for more Tommy Jansson merchandise and souvenirs was going to out-strip supply and that they also needed to expand the range. Photographs of Tommy sold very quickly and his adoring fans were always eager for more.

What none of his friends or supporters could have imagined on the night of Thursday, June 13 was that Tommy, who'd been immaculate all night, had just raced at Plough Lane for the last time. His last-ever appearance for the Dons came two nights later, in their eight-point BL defeat at Halifax.

★★★★★★

The season in Sweden had started for Smederna with a defeat against Anders Michanek's Getingarna and a victory against Lejonen.

On Wednesday, May 19, 1976, Smederna beat Dackarna 49-29. As usual, the chairman of Smederna's supporters' club, Gunnar Arnold, took a lot of new orders for souvenirs. A fresh batch of merchandise arrived at Motorstadion before every meeting and it was a job to keep up with demand.

Tommy was responsible – firstly, because he was so successful on the track; and secondly, because of all the good ideas he gave Gunnar. England were market leaders when it came to speedway souvenirs and, thanks to Tommy, Smederna also started selling a lot of colourful items that were not otherwise very common in Sweden at the time, such as plastic programme boards, stickers and different sets of metal badges.

The match against Dackarna was not a good night for Tommy. He collected only six points and had engine failure twice while leading. He cursed over his four-valve machine although, at the same time, he was very supportive of his team-mates.

Two lesser known Smederna riders did particularly well that night – Ake Dovhed, 39-years-old, who collected nine points, and young Tommy Mannby, 19, who ended the night with seven.

"I'm lucky that my failures didn't matter tonight. I'm really proud of my team-mates," Tommy said.

'With this team, we'll win the championship again,' manager Joel Jansson thought.

'The sale of souvenirs will certainly increase,' Gunnar Arnold mused.

The fans and the media were impressed that Smederna managed to win so impressively, even though Tommy had a rare off night and with both Bengt Jansson and Bosse Jansson missing from the line-up. When the best riders couldn't do it, the

Scorers: T. Jansson 15, D. Jessup 14, R. Johns 13, B. Thomas 11, M. Hines 11, B. Humphreys 11, E. Stangeland 8, D. Lovaas 7, I. Turner 7, K. Holden 6, L. Ross 5, P. Smith 5, D. Kennett 3, P. Gachet 3, B. Crowson 1, B. Shilleto (res) 0, I. Williams (res) 0.

Ht   1: Thomas, Ross, Lovaas, Kennett, 61.9.
Ht   2: Jansson, Humphreys, Gachet, Crowson, 61.9.
Ht   3: Jessup, Johns, Hines, Holden, 61.7.
Ht   4: Stangeland, Turner, Smith, Shilleto, 63.1.
Ht   5: Jansson, Hines, Ross, Williams, 62.2.
Ht   6: Stangeland, Holden, Kennett, Crowson, 63.2.
Ht   7: Johns, Smith, Lovaas, Gachet, 62.7.
Ht   8: Jessup, Humphreys, Thomas, Turner, 61.7.
Ht   9: Johns, Turner, Ross, Crowson (ef), 62.5.
Ht 10: Jansson, Jessup, Smith, Kennett, 62.0.
Ht 11: Hines, Humphreys, Lovaas, Stangeland (ef),
Ht 12: Thomas, Holden, Gachet, Shilleto, 62.8.
Ht 13: Jessup, Stangeland, Gachet, Ross (f.exc), 6
Ht 14: Johns, Humphreys, Kennett, Williams, 63.
Ht 15: Jansson, Lovaas, Turner, Holden, 63.3.
Ht 16: Thomas, Hines, Smith, Crowson, 63.4.
Ht 17: Humphreys, Holden, Ross, Smith, 63.3.
Ht 18: Hines, Turner, Kennett, Gachet, 63.5.
Ht 19: Jessup, Lovaas, Crowson, Shilleto, 62.5.
Ht 20: Jansson, Johns, Thomas, Stangeland, 63

Golden Helmet:
Ht   1: Jessup, Jansson (ef), 62.1.
Ht   2: Jansson, Jessup, 61.1.
Ht   3: Jansson, Jessup, 61.3.

Above: The scorers and heat details from Tommy's last-ever meeting at Wimbledon – the Southern Riders' Championship qualifier and Golden Helmet match-race, as they appeared in *Speedway Star*.

Right: Details from the same magazine, showing Tommy's final appearance for Wimbledon.

HALIFAX

May 15 by Peter Hale

WIMBLEDON'S fast-gating enabled them to keep the Dukes under pressure on the wet track but the determination of Graham Plant and Chris Pusey ensured a home win.

Plant was unbeaten for the third time at the Shay this season and he twice beat Tommy Jansson. Pusey was in the best race of the night when he passed reserve Larry Ross on lap three of Heat 12.

HALIFAX 43, WIMBLEDON 35
(Gulf British League)

Halifax: G. Plant 15, C. Pusey 12, C. Monk 6, I. Cartwright 5, S. Finch 3, A. Cusworth 1, M. Lohmann 1.

Wimbledon: T. Jansson 12, L. Rose 9, M. Hines 6, E. Stangeland 5, B. Beaton 3, R. Johns 0, B. Crowson 0.

Ht   1: Jansson, Pusey, Cusworth, Johns, 66.6.
Ht   2: Ross, Cartwright, Finch, Crowson, 68.6.
Ht   3: Plant, Stangeland, Beaton, Lohmann, 70.0.
Ht   4: Hines, Monk, Finch, Crowson, 70.2.
Ht   5: Plant, Jansson, Lohmann, Johns, 69.4.
Ht   6: Pusey, Cartwright, Hines, Ross (ef), 70.8.
Ht   7: Monk, Stangeland, Beaton, Finch (f), 70.2.
Ht   8: Jansson, Pusey, Cartwright, Stangeland, 69.2.
Ht   9: Plant, Hines, Ross, Lohmann, 70.4.
Ht 10: Plant, Pussey, Stangeland, Beaton, 70.6.
Ht 11: Ross, Jansson, Monk, Cartwright, 69.8.
Ht 12: Pusey, Ross, Finch, Hines, 69.2.
Ht 13: Plant, Jansson, Beaton, Cartwright, 70.8.

reserves saved the match – the exact ingredient that separates great teams from good ones.

This, according to most observers, was going to be Smederna's year. It was time to bring the championship home to Eskilstuna again.

Borje Carlsson, sports columnist in the local Folket newspaper, was critical of the local football team, IFK Eskilstuna, who lost the same night and he wrote: "...not even the most optimistic football fans can have any hopes left that IFK can come back this season. It doesn't matter that they have Kent Karlsson from the World Cup team of 1974. No, IFK Eskilstuna lack the team spirit that Smederna have."

He ended his story by adding: ". . . 3,800 spectators is going to become a lot more. because Smederna really do good things right now."

What nobody knew at the time was that the match against Dackarna was going to be Tommy's last ever in Eskilstuna.

He had less than 24 hours left to live.

Just seven days before he died, the final picture of Tommy at Wimbledon – on the night he retained his Golden Helmet after victory over Dave Jessup. The BSPA later gave the famous Helmet to the Jansson family to keep.

19
The End

"Everything happened so fast. We got tangled up together and one thought went through my mind – we're gonna crash, this is it."

**Lars Jansson, who crashed with Tommy
on May 20, 1976**

The day after the match against Dackarna, Tommy was in a bad mood. Partly because of the fact that his engine had worked so badly that he planned to travel early to Stockholm that night for the Swedish World Championship round to be able work on his bike on site. And partly because of his low number of points and the feeling that he was letting the fans down.

He felt that 3,800 fans had not shown up at the track to see him collect only six points – they came out to see him win all his heats.

Besides that, he was also going to miss Smederna's next match after the Swedish speedway federation had decided to move a previously postponed meeting to the following Tuesday – the same day Wimbledon were scheduled to visit Leicester for a British League fixture. According to his contract, Tommy had to race in England, that was his obligation.

"I have to race for Wimbledon that day, the schedule was set a long time ago. There is nothing I can do about that," he told disappointed fans in Sweden.

Deep down inside, he was angry with SVEMO – he wanted to race as often as he could for both Wimbledon and Smederna. He wanted to become a Swedish League champion with his home-town team again.

Joel was furious with the authorities and he had threatened them with a walk-over. He felt that SVEMO should respect the fixture programme in England, not ignore it completely.

On the morning of May 20, 1976 Tommy flicked through his small, black diary. During that month he'd already travelled between England and Sweden eight times. Before May was out, he was scheduled to compete in another eight meetings in the space of just 11 days, in three countries – Sweden, England and Finland.

He was a little tired of all the travelling, which only felt worse when he didn't reach his potential and a dreadful night like last night didn't help.

He was also tired from all the hard work he'd been doing on the bikes, which had

Tommy pictured just minutes before his fatal race in Stockholm.

recently led him to appoint Phil Pratt as his new engine tuner in England.

Misbehaving engines, many long trips, only a few off nights . . . but all that didn't matter much when he could spend time with Lotta. In her company he could easily forget all the hassles. She made him smile and when he spent time with her he felt happy and convinced that his future would be with her.

In her mother's beautiful garden, filled with a strong scent of flowers and in the shadow of cherry trees, he felt it was time to talk about South Africa. "Next winter I plan to go not to Australia, but to South Africa instead. Would you consider accompanying me?"

She smiled and thought to herself that if he'd have asked her to follow him to the moon, she would have said yes.

"Of course I want to join you on that trip!" she said.

"Great."

Tommy laughed and made jokes about how smart Lotta's mother's husband had made his leathers look – he had taken care of them after last night's meeting. His race suit was hung outside to dry and Tommy remarked that Lotta would be seeing a lot more of this cleaning up operation in the future.

Tommy and Lotta were sitting there together in the sun, dreaming about moving in together in a house in England.

"But, Lotta, you know . . . hmm . . . going to South Africa without being married . . . well, that might look odd. You know, it's different over there and . . . "

Tommy didn't have the courage at that moment to push the conversation any further forward than that.

He changed the subject.

Lotta complained about all the weeks she still had left to work in school. She liked the time she spent as an intern at a nursing home in the village of Flen, were she was working at the time and where she was going that same night.

They were both looking forward to England and a life together. Lotta couldn't wait, while Tommy had even written it up in his diary. His entry for June 4, 1976 read: 'Lotta finishes in school.'

Lotta was sitting in the backyard of her mother's house and felt a happiness she had never felt in her whole life. When Tommy had said goodbye she ran in to her mother and yelled excitedly to her about Tommy's words about going to South Africa and them not being married.

"What do you think he meant by saying that . . . do you think he wants to marry me?"

★★★★★★

During his whole speedway career Lars Jansson was famous for nothing more than being Bengt's brother – just as Bosse was widely known as 'Tommy Jansson's brother'.

Benga's brother was two years younger than him, not as skilled on the track and nowhere near as successful as the Swedish star and former World No.2 who remains a legend among supporters of Hackney Hawks.

Lars, 32-years-old, was riding for the Valsarna team from Hagfors, in the Swedish second division. At that level he was one of the stars and on his good days he could challenge the very best.

It was an uncle of the Jansson brothers who had got Bengt and Lars interested in speedway to begin with, when he'd taken the boys with him to meetings in Stockholm.

Lars liked to work with the bikes as much as the racing itself. Bengt showed early on that he was the best rider of the two of them and, from 1963 onwards, Bengt was always in a different class to his younger brother.

Lars' best result was fourth place in a Swedish Final. Every time he raced he did so with one thing in mind – to show that he was more than just 'Bengt's brother.'

The 1976 season had started brilliantly for him when he won a qualifying round of the World Championship in Malilla with a maximum 15 points. He had beaten many world class riders that night, including Bo Wirebrand and World Finalist Tommy Johansson. King's Lynn newcomer Richard Hellsen and a young Jan Andersson, who'd made his BL debut for Swindon Robins the previous season, were also in the line-up.

Now it was time for the next stage of qualification en route to the World Final – in Lars' home city of Stockholm. The Gubbangen track was very familiar to Lars, who was going to have brother Bengt for company on track.

Lars felt that this was a perfect opportunity for him to show what he was made of.

'I have everything to win, nothing to lose,' he thought during his trip to Stockholm.

★★★★★★

"How the hell are we going to make it without Tommy?"

Cyril Maidment was worried. Tonight's BL match at Sheffield Tigers was not an easy one, especially without their top rider. Cyril had strongly opposed the ban on commuting foreigners two years earlier and he praised his Swedish import every chance he got.

Many times, when critics and fans had doubted the practicalities and loyalty of riders dividing their league commitments between two countries at the same time, he reminded them that Tommy "always showed 100 percent commitment to both Wimbledon and Smederna."

The most important argument for Tommy and the other imports, according to Cyril, was that their presence – even though they were expensive due to their travel bills – made the English riders better. Just the chance of competing against the best riders in the world, week in and week out, made the young British riders develop faster. Cyril never wavered from that opinion.

But now he had other things on his mind.

Sheffield Tigers away. Without Tommy.

In desperation, the Dons' team boss had hunted high and low for a guest rider replacement before finally getting Hackney No.1 Dave Morton to fill Tommy's place at Owlerton – one of Mort's favourite tracks and relatively close to his Manchester base.

When Morton agreed, Cyril felt relieved and said: "This might turn out to be a great night after all."

★★★★★★

Anders Michanek and Bernt Persson had started to acknowledge each other again.

Bernt would never accept Anders' apologies for the crash in the Swedish Final of 1973 but, as time went by, Bernt had to get back to being normal towards his former best friend. Time had to heal all wounds, he decided.

Injuries and all the travelling had taken its toll on Bernt, who was also falling out of love with his beloved Cradley Heath. A few weeks before the individual round at Gubbangen Bernt had cancelled his contract with Cradley and decided he was just going to race in Sweden from now on.

On his day, Bernt could still beat the best riders in the world – indeed, to get to Gubbangen he'd won the previous round in Kumla with a maximum.

Tommy had also qualified for Gubbangen with a maximum in Lindesberg on May 9, when he led Hans Holmqvist and Christer Sjosten onto the rostrum.

Anders Michanek could also beat the best when he produced his top form. But he was 33-years-old – three years older than Bernt. Not even Anders had the same consistency or hunger for success any more.

Of the 16 riders competing at Gubbangen, nine were going to reach the next stage – the Nordic Final at Norrkoping, Sweden on June 2.

Both Anders and Bernt counted on making it. If there was any rider the two veterans feared, it was Tommy Jansson. Bernt and Anders both agreed on one thing: "Tommy Jansson is a future World Champion."

★★★★★★

Inga-Lill Jansson was supposed to go with the rest of the family to Stockholm that night but, because she had to work late, she stayed at home.

When she returned home to the apartment she found all Tommy's bags in his room. He was booked to travel back to England the day after and he'd said that maybe he'd spend the night at Bengt Jansson's house, in Taby, outside of Stockholm, and catch the morning flight from there.

'Okay, this means that now he's coming home tonight instead,' Inga-Lill thought to herself.

The whole family was in Stockholm, except her.

Inga-Lill planned for a night on her own. She had ordered pizza and was going to watch the TV series, Heirs, that she had started to follow with interest.

★★★★★★

Bosse Jansson had started to establish himself as a top rider in Sweden. He had missed the last match against Dackarna because of a fracture to his right hand, an injury he'd tried to keep a secret from his father.

Bosse hurt himself when he'd played football for fun with some friends. The day before the match against Dackarna, he had made a doctor remove his plaster cast, but the doctor had ordered Bosse to sign a paper accepting full responsibility in case he became involved in another accident. Bosse was racing at his own risk.

"If my father calls you, tell him it's nothing serious, just a slight bruise," Bosse demanded.

Joel wasn't stupid, he found out the truth and forced Bosse to take part in a junior event instead of the main senior match.

"That's below my dignity," Bosse complained.

He was furious and close to leaving the track, but Inga-Lill made him stop and think before he acted. "If you leave now, you'll never race for Smederna again," she warned him.

Bosse realised it was in his best interests to listen to his parents, both of them. He had been in a lot of pain while racing, but he managed to win both his junior-heats in good race times – even faster than a few winners in the main match.

Bosse felt that he belonged with the best, that he had the ability to perform at top level. In his first qualifying meeting before Gubbangen he'd ended fourth overall in the round at Kumla behind Persson, Tommy Nilsson and Soren Sjosten. The Swedish Final at Gubbangen was going to be Bosse's first big step on the international scene and he too was aiming for a place in the Nordic Final.

'Even if I'm going to cry out in pain, I'm going to make it to the Nordic Final –

I want to ride against Tommy twice,' he thought.

Bosse liked racing at Gubbangen, where he'd won the Swedish Junior Championship the previous year. Of course, now his opponents were of a much higher calibre but both Joel and Tommy believed that Bosse had a great chance to make it to the next stage.

When Joel and Bosse arrived at the track, they met up with Tommy in the pits. He was in a great mood, having travelled to Stockholm early to tune his bike at the workshop run by Per-Lennart Ericsson – a well known super-tuner who had worked for Anders Michanek for many years. After Michanek won the World Final in 1974, he brought Per-Lennart up onto the rostrum to join in the celebrations and to acknowledge his role in his success.

Per-Lennart didn't help everybody – he said no to many riders, but not to Tommy.

"Now my engine is going to work great. Now I'm not going to go up on my back wheel all the time. I'm going to be so much better from the gate," Tommy said.

Joel was a little sceptical.

"Are you really sure it's the bike's fault that you're not better at the gate?"

"I promise. Now I'm going to go straight forward, not lose time on my back-wheel," Tommy insisted.

Beside Tommy in the pits, Joel noticed a couple of boxes from some of his son's sponsors – some motor-oil and engine parts.

Bosse felt a little lost in the pits.

"Where should I take my place?"

"Wherever you want," Tommy said.

Tommy's mechanic, Kenneth Swedin, made some final adjustments to Tommy's bike. It was time to start it up and Tommy went away for a quick test spin on the track.

When he came back, he looked concerned and annoyed. Joel, who was going to watch the meeting from the pits, understood why. He'd seen how riders went all over the place on the bumpy track.

"The track is in really bad shape. It reminds me of farmland," Tommy told Joel and Kenneth.

Anders Michanek had raced at Gubbangen for many years – it was home to his Swedish team Getingarna. But he had never liked the track and had repeatedly complained about the bumpy surface. He had even been close to changing teams in Sweden, because he was sick and tired of having to race there so often.

Another rider who also called Gubbangen home was Lars Jansson. He was also in a bad mood, because he'd never enjoyed racing their either. It was such a big track, where speed mattered most, and there was never any close speedway at Gubbangen. Bengt's brother preferred more technically demanding venues over the big, fast tracks where speed counted for everything.

Now that the track was also in much worse condition than usual, Lars didn't have a good feeling.

★★★★★★

Bosse was standing tall when the announcer introduced the riders to the fans prior to the meeting:

"Number 12, from Smederna in Eskilstuna . . . Bosse Jansson."

"Number 13, from Smederna in Eskilstuna . . . Tommy Jansson."

The schedule meant that Bosse was going to make his first start in the third heat of the night, with Tommy taking his opening ride in heat four.

Lars Jansson wore number 15.

Heat one brought the first crash of the evening – Per-Ake Gerhardsson and Tommy Johansson both went crashing into the solid, wooden fence.

The red flag went up and the heat was stopped. Per-Ake had to be taken to the Sodersjuhuset hospital by ambulance because medical staff at the track were worried that he might have badly injured his back.

Johansson also complained of pain in his back, although he had to wait for the ambulance to return to the track before he too could be taken to hospital for a precautionary check-up.

Nobody in the pits had been surprised by the first race incident – not with the track as bumpy as it was on the night.

The vastly experienced Soren Sjosten was in heat two but when he came back to the pits after his first race, he was furious. "The track is so f*****g terrible," he fumed. "This is the worst track I've ever ridden and I'm not going to continue. This is it for me tonight, I'm not racing another heat."

Race three saw Bosse up against Bengt Jansson, Bosse Wirebrand and Christer Sjosten.

Tommy, aware of the abysmal track conditions, walked over to his big brother and said: "Be careful out there."

Bosse would never forget those words.

They were the last words Tommy ever said to him.

Out on the track, Bosse could just about suffer the pain in his damaged hand for one lap before he had to give up and cruise around for the rest of the heat. He reluctantly accepted that he wasn't fit enough to race again that night.

He told Joel that he'd had enough and that a reserve would have to take his place for the rest of the evening.

It was time for the fourth heat . . .

★★★★★★

Lars Jansson knew he was an outsider in the upcoming race. His opponents were: Tommy Jansson, Soren Karlsson (who had made his BL debut for Swindon just weeks earlier) and the vastly experienced Hans Holmqvist – all three having raced in the top division in Sweden and as professionals in England.

Normally Bengt's brother would not be expected to beat any of these riders, so he knew it was going to be very tough for him.

He had already been in a few battles with Holmqvist. In one race, Holmqvist had leaned so hard over Jansson in a turn – a tactic for which the former Wolverhampton and Oxford star was renowned – that his chain went right through Lars' boot and caused a nasty cut.

But the rider that Lars Jansson feared most in this race was Tommy Jansson. They had raced together with Young Sweden in England in the summer of '72. Lars had been impressed then by Tommy's willingness to learn and always improve. Tommy was so serious, on and off the track, that Lars was sure, like many others, that Tommy would one day become World Champion.

Lars didn't feel intimidated, though. He always managed to put aside thoughts of who he was up against and almost rode better when he was up against quality opposition. Under a lot of pressure, Lars could often raise his own game.

Like in another qualifier for the Swedish Final, when Lars was chased by his own brother in one heat. Bengt was in his favourite position – he was one of the best riders in the world when it came to sneaking up from behind – and he really tried very hard against Lars. But Lars remained strong and he made it over four laps. It was a great effort and afterwards Bengt couldn't help feeling happy for his brother.

Now Bengt was in the pits, wondering who he was going to cheer for. His own brother or his Smederna team-mate, Tommy? He just hoped that they were both going to make it through to the Nordic Final.

Tommy made a practice start, lifting on his back wheel as he did so. He made another start and, to his great dismay, the same thing happened again. Joel stood in the pits shaking his head. 'Is it really the bike that's the problem?' he asked himself.

Tommy was upset but his bike lifted again anyway. He was not supposed to start this way any more. Why didn't the bike respond to him like he wanted it to?

Even so, he still felt sure of winning the heat – without machine failure, he was the most talented racer in the field and he was going to win the meeting if only he performed to his normal high standard.

Tommy started off gate three.

When the tapes went up, Holmqvist roared ahead, while Karlsson and Lars Jansson also made decent starts.

Tommy's front wheel again lifted as he dropped the clutch – which is exactly what was not supposed to happen. He was angry, although he often performed at his best when he was fired up.

He started chasing the others.

He had four laps to make it and no-one doubted that he would.

It was in moments like these that had made him so popular. The spectacular chases from behind, the way he passed his opponents at will and thrilled the fans. This was also what made the sport so special.

It was time for some of that sheer brilliance again.

More than 3,000 spectators watched Tommy and they just knew he was not going to finish last in this heat, or any other that night. Among the crowd was Tommy's Smederna team-mate, Sven-Olof Lindh. Despite Tommy's bad start, Sven-Olof was also certain that Tommy would still win the race – he'd seen it happen so many times before.

Going into the third corner on the first lap, Tommy decided to ride around the outside, to pick up more speed and line himself up perfectly to pass Lars Jansson on the next straight.

Describing this race to me almost three decades later, Lars said he saw only Karlsson and Holmqvist in front of him. At the same time, Lars knew that Tommy

Last turn . . . a couple of seconds later, Tommy (left) crashed and died. Hans Holmqvist is on his inside.

would not be content to sit in fourth place. He was also aware that Tommy could be tough and ruthless on the track, although not at all dirty.

All the riders had to hold on to their bikes really tightly to avoid crashing on the bumpy circuit.

All of a sudden, Lars ended up in a big hole, lost control of his bike and careered towards the fence . . . at exactly the same moment that Tommy was about to pass him on the outside.

Their arms and handlebars became entangled. Lars felt they had got stuck together and at a speed of more than 60mph they were moving rapidly towards the solid, board fence.

A few thoughts raced through Lars' mind.

'We're going to crash.'

'This is it.'

'How am I going to hit the fence?'

Tommy, of course, must have had those same terrifying fears.

They couldn't shake themselves or their bikes loose. It was impossible to avoid what was going to happen next. They were going to crash very badly and there was no way of avoiding the inevitable.

★★★★★★

In the pits, Bosse heard somebody scream out loud: 'Oh, no. What a crash!'

By that time, Joel was already on his way over to where Tommy lay. Shocked fans had seen two riders slam, head-first, right in to the fence. Joel had seen the crash from the pits – as far away from the fourth corner, where it happened, as you could be. But he'd still been able to hear the sickening thud when the two riders thundered into the boards.

'This can never end well,' Joel thought to himself, as he ran across the football pitch inside the speedway track, towards the scene of the serious accident.

The track doctor had rushed to attend the two fallen riders and Joel was quickly on the scene too. The only thing he could think about was that Tommy needed air, so he removed his son's mask, goggles, helmet and also unbuttoned Tommy's No.13 racejacket.

The sight of the blood almost made him lurch backwards in shock, for he could clearly see that Tommy's beautiful face had been badly damaged.

The ambulance had returned from its second trip to the hospital and the crew ran over to Tommy. The doctor did her best to make Tommy breath again.

But he was gone.

Sven-Olof Lindh was in the stands with tears in his eyes.

When he saw his friend being carried away to the ambulance, he saw one of Tommy's legs fall to the side. It was at that moment that Sven-Olof knew it was over.

Bosse, who had also run across the football pitch and was standing by Joel's side, didn't want to comprehend the worst. The only thing he could think about was how Tommy´s beautiful face had been badly damaged. 'Poor, Tommy, he always looked so good,' a stunned Bosse remembers thinking.

Joel didn't want to understand either.

"Come on, drive!" he barked to the ambulance crew. "You're need to hurry – fast."

As the ambulance took off, Joel and Bosse went back to the pits together and found somebody to drive them to the hospital. Joel called the race director and told him: "I'm not sure how this is going to end, but don't race a single heat more before we know for sure how Tommy is doing."

Before joining his father on their way to hospital, Bosse momentarily sat down and Bernt Persson walked over to him.

"Can I have a cigarette?" Bosse asked.

They took one cigarette each.

Bernt was badly shaken up. He remembered the time when he'd been to Poland for pre-season training and he and the others had attended a Polish league match in which one Polish rider had died on the track in front of their eyes. After that tragedy, Bernt had been sick and lay in bed for days afterwards. He started shaking and developed a fever. It took him a while before he got over it.

Like all the other riders in the sport, he was aware of the risks involved in racing. A few times, when he had been cruising around to the starting gate before a race, he'd thought to himself: 'I might never get back to the pits again.'

Now he and Bosse finished their cigarettes, clinging to the hope that Tommy was going to make it all right. Bernt mumbled to himself: 'No, no, no – not Tommy. Not Joel's kid.'

Back out on the track, Bengt Jansson was by his brother's side. Lars was badly hurt, bleeding and in a lot of pain.

Bengt couldn't believe it. His own brother and one of his best friends, involved in the same crash. Both were in very bad shape.

"How are you?" Bengt asked Lars.

Lars never lost consciousness. His jaw and nose were broken but he knew he'd been lucky. He was in severe pain and he wasn't going to race again that night, but he was okay.

At least he was still alive.

Nobody told Lars about Tommy's condition.

Nobody in the car that took Joel and Bosse to the Sodersjukhuset hospital, in the southern part of central Stockholm, said anything during the drive there.

Joel had seen bad crashes before, of course. He had attended the funerals of two riders who had died on the track.

But for the sport to take his own son away from him . . . no, that just couldn't happen, he repeatedly told himself. Joel refused to give up hope and when they arrived at the hospital a glimmer of light emerged when a nurse told him and Bosse that Tommy had been taken for x-rays.

"That's good, he can make it. This is the capital of Sweden, they have all the resources they need here," Bosse said.

Back home in Eskilstuna, Inga-Lill was watching television, having just finished her pizza. In the background, she listened to the sports report on the radio but when the phone rang she turned the volume of the radio down. Luckily she did, because that's when they reported her son's horrific accident.

At least she received the terrible news direct from her husband.

"There's been an accident," Joel said.

Thoughts of all Bosse's crashes through the years immediately flashed through Inga-Lill's mind.

"Is it Bosse?" she asked him.

"No, it's Tommy. We're at Sodersjukhuset hospital. I don't know how this is going to end. I'll call you as soon as we hear anything," Joel told his wife.

Inga-Lill wanted to travel to Stockholm at once but, instead, she called a few people, including her mother, and they all promised to come over to comfort her.

Lotta was at a friend's place in Flenm before starting her shift as an intern at the nursery home at 9.30pm.

She had been telling her friend about her planned move to London and the trip she would be taking to South Africa with Tommy the following winter.

"I've never been this happy in my whole life," an excited Lotta told her.

Bosse, still wearing his speedway leathers and boots, and Joel were sitting by themselves in a waiting room at the hospital and desperate for news of Tommy's condition.

The door opened, a doctor walked in and Joel stood up.

"How is he doing?"

"Who are you?" the doctor asked.

"I'm Tommy's father."

"He is dead," the doctor said.

"What?"

"He was dead on arrival."

"What?"

Tommy had died of severe head injuries and a severed artery in his neck.

Joel didn't want to understand. He started crying. Bosse didn't know what to do. He asked a nurse for a cigarette and she gave him a packet.

Joel pulled himself together enough to call Inga-Lill. She grabbed the phone immediately.

Joel said: "We don't have a Tommy any more."

★★★★★★

Back in the pits at Gubbangen, mechanic Kenneth Swedin had collected all of Tommy's belongings together.

Anders Michanek had felt sick when he'd heard bells from a church nearby, announcing some evening ceremony. Anders suspected it was a very bad omen and he feared the worst.

Hans Holmqvist had already told all the other riders that whatever news they were going to hear from the hospital, they weren't going to continue the Swedish Final qualifying round that night.

"Everybody who wants to stop racing for the night, raise your hand," Hans asked.

Everybody raised their hands.

Bengt Jansson talked to a reporter from the Expressen newspaper, saying: "Tommy and me have been racing together in Smederna since 1973. We have been racing against each other for years in England. Tommy is the best young rider we have. He is a future World Champion."

A moment later the sad news came over the speakers.

"The meeting is postponed. Tommy Jansson has died."

Bengt Jansson broke down and started crying.

Kenneth Swedin sat down among all of Tommy's equipment while many riders started crying. A boy in the stands passed out. Kenneth looked at his blue t-shirt with the words 'Tommy Jansson Speedway' printed on it. He removed the shirt, turned it inside out and then put it back on again. He didn't want to talk to anybody – not about Tommy.

He knew this was it for him, he was going to leave the sport forever.

Bengt Jansson stood still, like he'd been struck by lightning.

"It's unbelievable. He was so great. He was the best."

Benga started crying again.

★★★★★★

When Tommy's grandmother, Maja, arrived at Inga-Lill's place, she wanted to calm her daughter and showed her some towels she had made for Tommy. They were for her grandson to take to England, to his new house where he was going to live with Lotta.

"Tommy is dead," Inga-Lill said.

"Why? Why?" Maja screamed as she collapsed to the floor.

The radio reported the tragic news again.

In Flen, Lotta was still at her friend's house, unaware of what had happened, when her friend's boyfriend came over. Lotta told him about her and Tommy's plans but the boyfriend acted very strangely at the mention of his name.

Lotta left quickly to go to work and couldn't help thinking about the boyfriend's strange behaviour. He then told his girlfriend about the awful news he'd heard on the radio – the news he'd been unable to mention to Lotta just seconds before she'd left them to go to work.

At the same time, the evening sports news on TV began with a report of the speedway tragedy at Gubbangen.

At home in Falun, Gote Nordin was sitting in front of the television when he suddenly screamed out. "Noooooo."

★★★★★★

Lotta arrived at work, a nursing home for mentally retarded patients. One of the patients greeted her at the door and said. "There has been an accident . . . a guy has died . . . they said so on TV."

Lotta didn't understand what the patient was talking about. Then her boss emerged from the TV room and confirmed the devastating truth: "Lotta, they just said on television that Tommy has died in an accident."

At that monment, the front door opened and Lotta's friend and her boyfriend came in. They took care of Lotta, who was so shocked that she hardly knew what was happening around her.

"It must be a mistake, it can't be true. It must be a misunderstanding," she cried.

When they arrived in Eskilstuna, Lotta's mother and her husband were waiting anxiously for her outside the door to their house.

That's the moment when reality struck Lotta.

Tommy was never going to come back to her again.

★★★★★★

A 39-39 draw away against Sheffield Tigers, where Wimbledon's guest rider Dave Morton had collected a maximum 15 points. He had achieved the impossible, or he had done what Tommy usually did.

Cyril Maidment was suitably happy.

Next Tuesday the Dons had an away match against Leicester Lions and were looking forward to welcoming Tommy back into their line-up, even though Cyril knew that Wimbledon's superstar was not happy about missing a league fixture for Smederna.

But he also knew how loyal Tommy was towards Wimbledon. The march up the standings had just started – and on the way back home to London Cyril called home.

That's when he heard the news.

"I just can't believe it's true," he said.

He had been involved in speedway for more than 30 years and had seen people die on the track. He had seen some complete nutcases flirting with disaster.

How *Speedway Star* reported the tragedy as its page 3 lead (left) and (right) how
the *Daily Mirror* broke the story the morning after it happened.

But most of them escaped in one piece.

Tommy was in a class by himself. In many ways, Cyril had looked at the young Swede as a perfectionist, a rider who was never dirty and never took any stupid risks.

Something like this just couldn't happen.

Not to Tommy.

★★★★★★

On the way out from the hospital, Bosse and Joel met the parents of Per-Ake Gerhardsson, who still didn't know how badly injured their son was after his crash in the first heat, which seemed to have happened an eternity ago.

It was when Bosse saw the Gerhardssons that he broke down. He sat down on the roadside and cried, while Joel tried to comfort him.

Together with Kenneth Swedin and Smederna supporters' club secretary Gunnar Arnold, Bosse and Joel sat in a car for the hour-and-a-half long ride back to Eskilstuna.

Nobody said anything. Not a single word.

Back in the apartment at Tornerosgatan, Inga-Lill was waiting anxiously together with Bosse's wife Vivianne, other relatives and friends.

The phone was ringing off the hook. Bosse, still wearing his leathers and boots from the fateful meeting, walked in to Tommy's room. He promised his parents he'd stay there overnight, but the only clothes he could borrow were Tommy's.

Bosse laid down and tried to sleep in his brother's bed – but, not surprisingly, he didn't sleep a wink that night.

20
City in mourning

"We're thankful for the short but rich years that we were allowed to have Tommy here with us. Today, we have to say farewell. Tommy is gone. But he will live in our hearts."

The priest Orjan Blom during Tommy's funeral.

Ivan Mauger was deeply saddened by Tommy Jansson's fatal accident. In Tommy, the great Mauger felt he had seen the future of the sport. What he had liked most about him was his riding style. Ivan had never heard any riders complain about Tommy being dirty out on the track. He was intelligent on a bike and overpowered others by smart overtaking manoeuvres. He was tough, but always fair.

When Ivan and Barry Briggs brought Tommy along on their winter tours of Australia and New Zealand, it was because the Kiwi veterans felt that Tommy had all it took to be a World Champion – he had the looks, personality, talent and, most importantly of all, he had the ability to fully maximise his talent.

After the news of Tommy's death, Ivan considered all those great qualities in his good friend, and he said: "In the end, there was only one thing that Tommy lacked – and that was luck."

The two weekly English speedway trade publications, Speedway Star and Speedway Mail, which Tommy read avidly, reported the horrific news to their stunned readers. The Star revealed later that Tommy was about to become a regular, new star writer for their monthly sister publication, Speedway Express. In fact, Tommy had written his first article before returning to Sweden, which was prepared for printing until the awful news reached their east London offices and his column was 'pulled' just 24 hours before the press deadline. As The Star wrote in its tribute, nobody had a bad word to say about the popular, polite personality who had the speedway world at his feet.

For a while, Smederna seriously considered postponing the rest of their season and pulling out of the Swedish League. They decided to let the Jansson family make the final decision and after five postponed matches, Bosse – on behalf of the family – arrived for a meeting to discuss the immediate future with riders, management and others involved in the club at a restaurant in town.

Bosse said: "We have to continue in Tommy's spirit. We can't close out the season, we have to start racing again. That's what my brother would have wanted."

Ake Dovhed was one of the first riders to speak up, saying: "Okay, let's race on for Tommy."

Others found it difficult just to go on. Mechanic Kenneth Swedin never returned to the sport. Joel had originally believed that Kenneth was going to return but he felt unable to and left speedway altogether.

Sven-Olof Lindh, who had won so many heats by 5-1 in partnership with Tommy, retired. "No, I can't continue to race. Nowadays I'm scared out there on the track," he admitted.

"She just has to come along."

Shannon Ruane's mother called Cyril Maidment and pleaded with him that the delegation from Wimbledon Speedway would have to take her young girl with them to Sweden for Tommy's funeral in Eskilstuna.

"She won't be able to continue her life otherwise. She is devastated," Shannon's mother told Maido.

Another young female fan in London had passed out when she heard the news of Tommy's death.

The only problem for Shannon's mother was finding the cash for the plane ticket to Stockholm. The family managed on a tight budget and the trip to Sweden was very expensive.

"I have to say goodbye to Tommy," Shannon pleaded.

Shannon's mother sold their television and used the money to buy a return air ticket for her daughter.

TOMMY JANSSON

* 2 oktober 1952
† 20 maj 1976

Priest Orjan Blom had never seen so many people in the Klosters kyrka church. He had never seen so many flowers, nor this number of sad faces in one place at the same time.

Before the funeral service began they had to close the heavy doors to the church, while outside police officers had to control the large crowd and re-direct traffic around the building. Thousands of people lined the street outside the church that spring day of Saturday, June 5, 1976.

Because of his faith, Orjan Blom found the strength he needed to complete the service but he was clearly shaken up. He remembered his first meetings with Tommy very well, when he'd been in a class reading for Tommy's confirmation.

Tommy had been shy and quiet, but he had

After his confirmation, a young Tommy and father Joel in church – the same church in Eskilstuna where Tommy's funeral was held.

still made an impression on Orjan, who recognised a fire burning in the young man. He sensed that this was a youngster who was going to make sure he accomplished what he wanted to do in his life.

Exactly nine years after his confirmation there, Tommy's ashes were buried in the grounds of the same church.

Orjan started: "Jesus said: See, I'm with you to the end of the day.

"This quote from the Bible was given to Tommy during his confirmation in this church, nine years ago to the day. Today, the same words from the Bible have to speak to those of us who are gathered here for Tommy's funeral. We all feel a sadness that can't be described with words."

Anders Michanek was sitting alongside his then wife, Margaretha, in the church and had to fight back tears. He was sad and angry. Very angry, because of the sheer injustice that a young man like Tommy was gone forever.

The day after the accident, Anders had seriously thought about retiring as a rider. He felt he'd had enough of the sport that took the life of one of his best friends.

"I give up, I don't care any more. It's not worth it," he said.

Margaretha tried to comfort him and said that "life goes on." The same day Anders travelled south for a meeting in Germany, and he had a car and a trailer without brakes. The trailer was all over the place behind him. He was driving like a madman, making one stupid overtaking move after another. He didn't care about anything, including himself.

A police car finally stopped him and before the officers even said anything to Anders, he gave them his driver's licence.

"Here, take my driving license. If you don't, I'm just going to continue to

Inside the church during the funeral service. Thousands of mourners had to wait outside.

drive like this."

One of the officers looked closely at Anders and said: "Listen, we know what happened yesterday. Just take it easy from here on, okay?"

They allowed him to continue, despite his reckless driving. Anders decided that despite everything, he was not going to quit racing.

Margaretha was right – life does goes on.

Anders was sitting quietly in the church trying desperately to come to terms with Tommy's death and the unjust, dark side of speedway. Riders had died before Tommy and riders were going to die after him.

That was the sad truth.

But stop racing? No, he was a speedway rider, that's what he was, and he was going to continue to be one.

Bengt Jansson had been thinking similar thoughts to Anders. He had decided not go back to England and race immediately after the accident but, after some further time spent mulling it over, he was back in business for, even though he skipped some meetings for Reading here and there. But he admits he had a problem recapturing the joy of racing again.

He missed his team-mate Tommy and, of course, Bengt was also very sad for his brother's sake.

Lars Jansson never raced again after the accident. He suffered from depression for a long time after the crash and it took him years to exorcise his feelings of guilt.

He'd ask himself: 'Could I have done anything to have avoided the crash?'. Why am I allowed to live my life and not Tommy?'

Lars knew that it could easily have been him who died in that horrific crash.

Orjan Blom kept taking about the grief they all felt.

"A family mourns their son, a brother, a loved member of their family. Eskilstuna mourns one of the city's finest athletes of all time. Many people, here and all over the world, mourn their friend, and many thousands of people in our country and abroad mourn their idol."

Then Orjan turned to the delegation from England and said a few words to them in English.

Cyril Maidment was finding it increasingly tough to come to terms with Tommy's death. Not only was Tommy 'Mr Wimbledon Spoeedway', he was also a very good friend of Cyril's. Tommy had been like a son to the Dons promoter, who was finding it very difficult to accept that his No.1 star rider had suddenly gone.

Cyril had been part of Tommy's life – watched him mature from a skinny kid who could hardly speak a word of Engliush into an eloquent man, an international star and genuine World Championship contender . . . even if he did only drink orange juice down the pub.

Wimbledon had planned to postpone all meetings for a few weeks after the accident, but then the club decided that they would go ahead much as planned. Not for financial reasons, not because the sport was going to cast aside its feelings at the loss of a top rider. No, Cyril made his decision based on one notion – this is how Tommy would've wanted it. Maido was absolutely sure about that.

In 1976, Tommy had ridden just 14 official league and cup matches, plus that challenge fixture involving his brother at White City. Five days after he perished in Stockholm, the Dons returned to action, losing 35-43 in the BL at Leicester, where King's Lynn favourite Terry Betts scored 10 as the guest replacement for Tommy. Indeed, Wimbledon were granted the use of guests for the rest of a very emotionally draining season in which they would slump to 16th place in the final table.

But some of Tommy's spirit lived on in the '76 Dons. In the first home meeting after his loss, on June 3, their pre-season signing from all-conquering Ipswich, Mick Hines, played a true captain's role by scoring a maximum, with Larry Ross paid for the lot, as the Dons demolished Leicester, 54-24, in the return league encounter. There was obviously a sombre mood hanging over Plough Lane in the weeks and months that followed – and as former England and Ipswich boss John Berry observed in his poignant tribute that appeared in the British retro Backtrack magazine in July 2006, "As with Cyril Maidment, I don't think the place ever recovered from Tommy's loss. The spark just never returned. The magic that was Wimbledon had

Farewell Tommy . . . .the funeral on June 5, 1976.

Riders Mick Hines and Stefan Salomonsson lay flowers at the grave of their former team-mate and skipper. Just visible in the left of the picture are Wimbledon riders Edward Jancarz, Roger Johns and Rob Jones.

Cyril Maidment standing by as Tommy makes a point to the referee on the pits phone at Wimbledon. Tommy was like a son to Maido.

disappeared forever."

In fact, Berry's Ipswich Witches – destined for a second consecutive BL crown that sizzlingly hot English summer – were the visitors to Wimbledon on July 15, 1976, when the Dons put up another stirring show before the special VIP guests that night – Joel, Inga-Lill, Bosse Jansson, Lotta and Bosse's wife, Vivianne. Mr and Mrs Jansson and their son were introduced to both teams and presented flowers to the riders before heat one of the Spring Gold Cup Final.

It was a particularly emotional night for another Swede at Plough Lane that night – Stefan Salomonsson, a former team-mate of Tommy's at Smederna, was making one of his first appearances for the Dons following his recent arrival in Britain.

A sombre and emotional night at Wimbledon, as Cyril Maidment (left) greets Joel, Inga-Lill and Bosse Jansson before the Dons gave a very spirited Spring Gold Cup Final performance against Ipswich.

Berry recalls the occasion: "As a Cup Final, this meeting was selected to become a special tribute to their lost young star. Tommy's family were there and the second half was peppered with special guests (in addition to Wimbledon and Ipswich riders, the supporting event also featured Barry Briggs, Dave Jessup, Martin Ashby, Gordon Kennett, Bengt Jansson and Barry Thomas).

"I remember the evening well. It was not a happy time. Cyril Maidment was barely coping. The Dons had chosen Tommy's guest carefully. Martin Ashby (Swindon) was paid for 13 points from five rides, while Mick Hines and Edgar Stangeland rode their hearts out.

"Ipswich were without the injured John Louis. Sad though the evening was, we were not about to give anything but our professional best. However, I couldn't help feeling the result was fitting. Wimbledon won 40-38 on the night (though Witches won the trophy with a narrow aggregate success over the two legs).

"Despite the victory, far from being an exciting night with a cup final atmosphere, the mood was sad and sombre. Maidment was a real character. Normally he was brilliant company, with a wicked, laid-back wit and a refusal to let things get him down.

"That night there was no flicker in Cyril's eyes. In fact, to my mind, he was never the same man again. It was as if he had lost his own son."

Cyril Maidment, the former England, Belle Vue and Wimbledon rider, and manager of the Dons, later emigrated to the sunshine isle of Tenerife, where he died on his 75th birthday, January 31, 2004.

A collection held during the interval of the SGC final raised £780 for the Tommy Jansson memorial fund – obviously, no money could possibly come close to compensating for the loss of their son, but the family were nevertheless touched by the warmth and sincerity of their hosts and the British supporters, who contributed money in collections held the length and breadth of the UK.

Tommy would not have wanted everybody to stop doing what they normally did. He wouldn't have wanted silence to rule at Plough Lane, Motorstadion in Eskilstuna or any other speedway track in the world.

The sound was never going to die. The sound that Tommy had loved so much.

The sound of speedway bikes.

Cyril looked around him in the church. He saw Anders Michanek with his blank expression and tears in his eyes. Cyril saw Tommy's parents and brother Bosse. He saw all the flowers at the coffin. On each side of the coffin was one person holding a flag – to one side Smederna's banner and on the other side the red and yellow colours of Wimbledon Dons.

Closest to Cyril in the church were his riders from Wimbledon – and Shannon Ruane. After the accident Shannon had been so sad, she hadn't been able to attend school. She was heartbroken, totally convinced that she was never going to feel happy or laugh again.

She remembered Tommy's smile and all the times he had said: "Hello, Curly Head," and thanked her for her corny poems.

Now he was gone.

Why? Why?

Orjan Blom continued: "Tommy's life was not long but during his short years in the sport he loved so much he experienced successes and victories few others even come close to. Despite his youth Tommy was among the elite in his sport, a sport that demands great skill and talent."

Anders Michanek looked at the coffin, remembered his and Tommy's two triumphs in the World Pairs Final and Anders couldn't help thinking what he'd never said out loud. 'There would have come a day when Tommy would have out-fought me and become better than me. If he had lived he would have become the champion of the world.'

He was not the only one in church thinking just that.

Joel Jansson was thinking the same thing. Not because he had wished it for his own sake – he was never the type of man who liked to step in the spotlight because of his son. But Joel knew how much Tommy had wanted to be successful.

What Joel had admired most in Tommy was his youngest son's stubbornness and determination. The fact that Tommy never took anything for granted, that he never expected any free rides or easy solutions. Tommy never expected anybody else to do the hard work for him.

Joel knew what Tommy had wanted more than anything else – the chance to be as good as he could be. And as good as he could be was, yes, the best in the world.

Now that chance was gone. Tommy was never going to be able to fulfil his dreams and just the thought that his son had been robbed of that golden opportunity made Joel feel a terrible pain.

There is nothing in life a parent wants more than the best for his or her children. Tommy had it in his hands, which made the end of his life all the sadder.

Many years later Gote Nordin would say: "If Tommy had lived, he could have become as great as Tony Rickardsson."

Orjan Blom continued: "But when we are gathered here today to say farewell to Tommy, we don't only look at him as a star in his sport. Today we also want to remember Tommy's rich personality. The reason for Tommy's popularity and why he became an idol for so many, young and old, was not only because of his racing ability."

Lotta was one of few people in church that day who didn't think about speedway at all. She was thinking about the man she had come to know and love and it was a different person to the one most other people knew, especially all those thousands of fans outside the church for whom Tommy was only a speedway star.

She was thinking about a 23-year-old man who had written 'I love you' in all his letters to her from Australia, remembering how he'd written that sentence up and down and at all levels on the writing paper. She was thinking about the young man who wished he knew about more things in life than speedway, who felt a little embarrassed at his ignorance of other things. The man who often said that there was so much more he wanted to learn.

The man who had given her an opal – the stone that was said to signify bad luck.

She was also thinking about the move to England they had both planned, the trip to South Africa the following winter and Tommy's talk about marriage.

At the coffin, Lennart Rytterstrom was holding Smederna's blacksmiths banner and he focused on a point between two bricks in the church wall in order to avoid fainting. He was scared that he was going to fall down, cry or whatever. Then Lennart found a spot on the wall where he could fix his gaze, and he never moved his eyes during the rest of the service.

Orjan Blom: "Tommy had a great personality and a style that made him so popular and loved. All of us who had the honour of knowing him during his successful career will agree that he never became conceited and full of himself. In the midst of all his success he remained the same mellow, almost shy, human being, that he'd always been. That's why we miss him so much, why we feel an emptiness both for a champion in his sport and for a rich personality."

American star Scott Autrey and Tommy never had the chance to become very close friends – the Aussie tour on which they got to know each other well ended pretty quickly afterwards. But, years later, Scott said: "I think it's great that a book is going to be written about Tommy's life. During all my years in speedway I met thousands of people, but Tommy was special.

"He was such a gentleman, so serious with a burning desire for the sport and he was a truly great person. You can't say that about many people and this is something I really want to say to his parents."

Anders Michanek remembered that he'd always considered Tommy to be a little boring when he'd rather work on his bike than follow the other guys to the pub. At the same time Anders had admired the young man because he was so dedicated and serious, when the opposite was so common among people who just talked a good game but rarely delivered.

Tommy had been the genuine article and he also had a wonderful sense of humour. He had made Anders laugh too – even in Poland, in times when there usually wasn't too much to laugh about.

Tommy's team-mates from Smederna and friends from his home town were inconsolable. They had all been so impressed by Tommy's ability to break free from the everyday life they all knew and experienced in Eskilstuna.

He had made it in the big world. In England, Australia – he had made it to the big arenas. To many of Tommy's friends, even Poland sounded very exotic and it was certainly a place they would never get to see.

Tommy had come out into the world and he had become a star. Not because his father had helped him or because of his good looks. It took a lot more than a pretty face and a lithe physique, which brought him an interesting offer to pose half-naked for a tabloid newspaper, to become a truly great speedway rider.

Tommy had never expected any favours of any kind and never leaned on his father for support. He had only put pressure on himself and he alone made the decision to become a star.

It was not because he wanted to be rich and famous that he went into speedway. It was because this was what he had decided to do in life . . . and whatever a person was going to do in his life, he was supposed to do it as well as he possibly could.

Orjan Blom: "Today, on this wonderful summer day, we celebrate Tommy's last time here on Earth. His life's race is over. Tommy has reached the finish line. For the rest of us, all we can do is say goodbye. All of us here in church today want to unite with Tommy's family in a thank you for all he has given us.

"We are thankful for the short but rich, rich years that we were allowed to have Tommy here with us. Today, we have to say farewell. Tommy is gone. But he will live in our hearts. Not even death can take away our wonderful memories."

Orjan Blom then asked the question everybody in church had asked themselves: "Why?"

People of faith may have an easier time dealing with grief at moments like these. The faith gives them strength to carry on with their lives and also hopes of reuniting with the deceased. Some people in church were praying that they would meet Tommy again and hoping that they were going to hang out with him and talk about speedway, just like the good, old days.

Others just felt an unbelievable sadness and found it hard to find a reason to keep on living.

Bosse felt hatred. He couldn't help it. He hated old people. He could become angry when he met old people out walking in town.

'How can you live, when my brother wasn't allowed to live?' Bosse would find himself thinking. He felt ashamed for his thoughts, and tried to fight them, but it wasn't easy.

Sometimes he also got the feeling that he saw Tommy. Bosse could be walking down the streets of Eskilstuna and all of a sudden, he'd stop in his tracks and stare at someone in the distance. 'Hey, that's Tommy,' he'd think wishfully.

Bosse wanted so badly for it to be true. He wanted everything to just be a horrible

Bosse lowering Tommy's ashes into the ground in Eskilstuna and the headstone shaped like a speedway racejacket showing the emblems of Tommy's only two clubs – Wimbledon and Smederna.

nightmare. He wanted to wake up again and see his brother standing there again in real life.

Inga-Lill still felt uncertain if she'd made the right decision not to see Tommy one a last time. She was given the opportunity to see his body, but was advised against it. Was that the right decision?

Maybe she should just have gone to the hospital for a final farewell – maybe she would just have been able to recognise her son's natural beauty once again.

At the same time, she understood that Tommy's forceful crash into the fence at Gubbangen had badly damaged his face.

She didn't want to see him like that.

She wanted to remember his beautiful face, his smile, his sparkling eyes. Inga-Lill felt a sadness that hurt. She was never ever going to see her son smile again. Never again hear him laugh. Never experience her youngest son raising a family, kids and settle down. He was never going to come home to her with her grandchildren eager to meet grandma and grandpa.

Orjan Blom was looking at the Jansson family when he said: "We are not alone in grief and feelings of loss. Jesus Christ suffers with us. He shares our grief and pain. It´s a comfort for all of us in grief to know that Christ is on our side: 'See, I'm with you to the end of the day.'

"That promise also means that Tommy is not alone in death. It's our belief and our hope that Jesus Christ is with Tommy when he takes the step over the border to the land were we can't follow him. Now Tommy rests in peace and quiet after a life that was short, but still, I'm sure, more full of experiences than most people get to experience."

Lotta had suffered physical as well as mental pain in her grief and she hadn't been able to do anything but stay in bed since the accident. All the letters that Tommy had sent to her, plus presents like the opal – even if the stone almost scared her, she wanted to keep it and treasure it forever.

Years later, Lotta met and married Lennart, with whom she has two daughters. With her husband's full approval, she continued to occasionally visit Tommy's grave and lay flowers in loving memory of the young man she lost.

Orjan Blom ended the funeral service with the words: "Death is not the last word. Death's power is broken down by Jesus Christ. That's why Tommy's funeral here today doesn't have to be only an occasion of darkness and despair. We can all hope for a reunion once upon a time in a world where all sadness, all suffering and all tears are just going to be a fading memory. When we now, here today, suffer our grief and miss Tommy dearly, we can hold tight to, and believe the promise of Jesus Christ, a promise that remains through life and death: 'See, I'm with you to the end of the day.' Amen."

Lotta had great difficulty believing in thoughts of a possible reunion. But in the midst of all the sadness, she found some solace in the fact that she had known and loved Tommy in the first place and she would cherish memories of their all too brief time together.

The laughs, the long conversations when night became day, all the memories – like the romantic trip to Denmark, when they picked up a speedway engine and then got stopped by customs.

The meeting at Plough Lane when the public address announcer had said that "Tommy Jansson's girlfriend" was there. All the wonderful memories.

Nobody could ever take those away from her.

In Lotta's heart, Tommy was going to live forever.

Above: Tommy's two-valve Jawa bike and his Swedish international racejacket were on display at the Eskilstuna track during the staging of the 2006 Speedway Grand Prix. These items are usually displayed at the city's main library.

Left: Smederna and Wimbledon both staged annual memorial meetings in honour of their former No.1 and captain.

21

Changing Wimbledon

"I can't stop liking speedway. I just can't."

Joel Jansson

At the main entrance to Wimbledon Stadium a lady sits at the gate collecting tickets. 'Maybe we'll get close on 1,000 spectators tonight,' she thinks, 'that would be nice.'

It's Weymouth Wildcats, the best team in the league, who are visiting. That should draw a crowd. On the other hand, this is the Conference League – as far away from Tony Rickardsson, Jason Crump and the other Grand Prix stars as you can possibly get.

Just inside the main entrance at Plough Lane there is a table set up with souvenirs of all kinds – t-shirts, scarves, pin badges, pencils, magazines and a book about the classic team entitled The Complete History of Wimbledon Speedway.

Behind the table there is a white wall. In many ways this wall symbolises the wonderful history of Wimbledon Speedway, or at least it used to. It was a wall of pride, a mural covered with elegant paintings of some of the track legends who have entertained the crowds at the old stadium through the years, among them Barry Briggs, Ronnie Moore and Tommy Jansson. Many of them had signed their autographs on the wall.

But, before the 2004 season, the enthusiastic group of people who ran Wimbledon Speedway arrived at the stadium – sadly, now used only for greyhound and stock car racing after the Dons were effectively forced out at the end of 2005 – and realised that all the speedway paintings had been covered over with white paint.

The explanation from the Greyhound Racing Association, who own and run the place, was: "We wanted to refresh and improve the stadium."

Greyhounds raced here in Tommy's days, but then the dogs played second fiddle to the crowds that were attracted to see the Dons in action on Thursday nights from March until October – with perhaps the exception of the one-off, annual Greyhound Derby meeting held there.

"No, we ain't gonna get a thousand fans in here tonight," says the woman at the gate, with an air of resigned sadness in her voice.

"How can anybody prefer to watch greyhound racing over speedway?

Unbelievable," she added.

Together with her good friend, Keith Yorke, the woman sponsors a young rider by the name of Mark Baseby, who had just got started in the sport.

"For young males with a lot of extra energy, speedway is the perfect sport. If you can help somebody to get to race speedway instead of hanging out on some street corner with nothing to do, you're definitely doing a good thing."

Suddenly, Bosse Jansson is asked to sign autographs.

It's Wednesday, April 20, 2005 and Bosse is back were his brother was a superstar and where Bosse himself got a chance to experience the life in what, at the time, was the best speedway league in the world.

"It's probably 20 years since somebody in Eskilstuna asked for my autograph," he smiles. "Now I've already signed a few and the match hasn't even started."

Bosse could easily echo the views of many who prefer to look back and claim that 'it was better in the past,' but he doesn't. He looks out over the empty stands and still considers the place to be sacred ground.

He feels that this place has a lot of history, despite the racing dogs, battered stock cars and all the white paint in the world.

"It was fantastic to be here when there were around 8,000 people in the stands – a magical atmosphere. But it's still a fabulous stadium," Bosse says.

When the match gets underway, Bosse quickly points out than none of the riders involved would be good enough to even claim a place in the Smederna team.

But this is the Conference League – the third tier of English racing – and times have changed. In the past, during Tommy Jansson's days, a rider with ambitions to win the world title just had to be racing in England, competing against the very best on a weekly basis.

In 2006, it's the other way around. A rider who wants to become World Champion has to ride regularly in Sweden and Poland. Weymouth Wildcat Lee Smart and the other riders in this meeting would do anything for a chance to race professionally in Sweden, in the most competitive league in the world and where most of the GP stars race every week of the season.

The woman from the main entrance takes her seat in the stands and after every heat she dutifully fill out her programme, detailing points scored and winning times and she speaks highly of the home team's veteran leader Mark Burrows. He beats most of the kids, except Lee Smart.

"Sure, it was more fun here in the past but I still love speedway. It's a wonderful sport," she says.

The woman is 43-years-old and she has two daughters. Her name is Shannon Ruane.

★★★★★★

If speedway was music, it would be punk rock.

A heat is like a punk rock song – short, aggressive, one hundred percent energy and a lot of heart.

The late Joe Strummer, the legendary front man of The Clash, was once on tour with his last band The Mescaleros, who were warming up for Offspring. During a

The Jansson family back at the 'new' Eskilstuna speedway track in 2005 – Joel Inga-Lill, Bosse and Bosse's son, Jimmy, who rides in the Swedish second division.

show in Munich, Strummer all of a sudden found himself in front of a crowd who showed no respect for history. The fans threw bottles and stones at Strummer and his band, so Strummer reacted and walked out among the crowd.

"I had to leave the stage and re-educate the fans. And no, I didn't have to raise a fist, not even a finger. Hey, I'm a big fan of new bands like Green Day and Offspring, but what the fans have to realise is that this music has a history. And to throw stones at us . . . no way was I going to accept that."

The young fans in Germany got a history lesson they needed and understood without the situation turning ugly.

When Smederna host the Indianerna team at the start of the 2005 season and Joel Jansson takes his seat in the stands, it's easy to start thinking about Joe Strummer. With all due respect to today's superstars in Smederna – former world champions like Billy Hamill and Nicki Pedersen, a Grand Prix rider like GB captain Scott Nicholls and a young talent like Morten Risager . . . none of these guys would be here today, at the new stadium in Eskilstuna, if it wasn't for one man.

Joel Jansson.

Without him neither the club nor the stadium would have existed.

He won the fans over to begin with as a brave rider and later on he was the manager who led the team to its first league championship. He also helped made world stars of two young men named Tommy Jansson and Bernt Persson.

Many fans at the new Smedstadion, now an established GP venue, recognised Joel during the match against Indianerna. Some say 'hello' to him, some just look at him, while other people stare and whisper to their friends: 'Look, it's Joel Jansson over there.'

Joel doesn't have to do it the Joe Strummer way and re-educate anybody. Not any more.

For a few years in the 80s he had a falling out with the new promoters at Smederna. He said what he felt, stepped on some toes and all of a sudden he wasn't welcomed at the stadium any more.

On the other hand, during that time the sport was in decline in Sweden and at Eskilstuna. Many fans left after Tommy died, believing that the sport had gone with him.

Smederna managed to regain the league title the year after Tommy's death. That's when Bernt Persson finally came back to town and led a team that also included Bengt Jansson, Stefan Salomonsson, Bosse Jansson and Ake Dovhed.

That was the last time a team from Eskilstuna – in any sport – became champions of Sweden. True, it was close when Smederna went to the finals in 2003 but lost the decisive match at Smedstadion, in front of almost 8,000 fans.

Eskilstuna is a speedway town once again. The local football-teams have struggled big time, and the only other elite sports outfit is a handball team called GUIF.

The 2005 version of Smederna is a team that includes a few world class riders, even if the team's aims for the season are modest, they dream of finishing in the top four and no more.

Joel doesn't go to meetings very often these days. He left the sport as a manager and team leader immediately after Tommy's accident.

Bosse continued as a rider until 1979, when he crashed badly. He broke six ribs, his right arm, left wrist, tore a muscle in his left leg and damaged his hip. The next day, Joel came up to his son at the hospital and said: "God damnmit. Now that's enough."

Bosse never raced again.

Just as Joel and Tommy had done before him, Bosse did get to experience the thrill of winning the Swedish League championship. Just like the other men in the family, he could still call himself a champion.

Bosse's son, Jimmy, has tried to follow in the Jansson family speedway tradition and has ridden in the Swedish Elite League, although the 25-year-old is currently racing in the second division for Bysarna. He hasn't been able to live up to other people's high expectations of him. Speedway is a very tough sport, where talent alone is not enough.

Joel and Bosse at Eskilstuna for the 2006 Grand Prix, where Tommy is still remembered.

After seven heats between Smederna and Indianerna, the scores were tied at 21-21. Many riders have got into trouble, including the veteran Magnus Zetterstrom, the man they call 'Zorro' who has been racing like an amateur.

If a rider goes into a meeting in the wrong frame of mind, if he starts thinking too much and suffers unexpected problems with his bike, then even the best can look like a novice.

The talented, young Dane, Morten Risager, is doing everything wrong in this match and is withdrawn from his third ride.

Nicki Pedersen is too over-zealous in one race and forgets to use his brain. He knocks into another rider – something he did a lot when he was younger – and finds himself excluded from the heat.

Maybe it's a tough call by the referee and Nicki loses out because of his reputation. If his name had been Leigh Adams, it might have been a different story . . .

But this is an important part of speedway.

Nicki is unlucky, but you often get the luck you deserve. You get the respect you deserve – including from referees.

Joel can't help saying "it was better in the past" and he is referring to the speed. He thinks the riders are going too fast today and points out that the one who moves fastest from the gate usually wins the race. There are too few passes and too few tight, exciting races.

Every time somebody manages to make a pass, Joel is impressed. And he really likes Danish No.1 Pedersen. "Nicki is in a class of his own."

Then it's time for a re-start of the ninth heat. Nicki has been excluded by the referee and the home team's Eric Andersson is standing alone at the gate surrounded by two 'Indians'. Andersson is 21-years-old and he hasn't been able to secure a spot in either Tony Rickardsson's Masarna team or Greg Hancock's Rospiggarna.

Smederna is Eric's last chance to make it in the big league.

Eric is slow at the gate but still riding extremely well and manages to get by both of his opponents. He makes a couple of brave, smart moves and the fans cheer wildly when he suddenly hits the front.

But the celebrations are premature. Eric slides down on the third lap and still receives a standing ovation from the fans.

Joel smiles knowingly: "He rode too fast for his ability."

His smile doesn't fade.

Joel looks exactly the same as he did an hour earlier when he walked around the pits and all the bikes started up. Joel shouted over the noise: ". . . this sound . . . it's wonderful."

When the match is over, and Smederna have won 54-41, Joel considers who has impressed him the most. Nicki Pedersen collected the most points, David Howe won three of his four races, Scott Nicholls had 11 points. The old 'Indian' Kaj Laukkanen ended the night with 12.

"Eric Andersson impressed me the most," Joel says.

Eric scored one point in his first heat, then crashed and had to rest for the remainder of the night. Eleven riders ended the evening with more points than him.

"Eric showed a great attitude and an impressive willingness to win. It went a little too fast for him this time, but when he has full control over himself and his bike – and if he keeps going for it – something big can happen for him."

Joel smiles again.

"Eric's racing in the ninth heat? Oh yeah, that was great to watch."

When he says this it's easy to remember one evening at home in Tornerosgatan. Joel had been sitting there talking about the good, old days for hours. He had talked about Tommy, the record crowds, the championship years. He had laughed a lot.

But when he talked about the evening of May 20, 1976 Joel had tears in his eyes.

Then, suddenly, in the middle of another conversation, he says: "I can't stop liking speedway. I just can't."

The memory of Tommy Jansson was honoured with memorial meetings for many years, in both Sweden and in England.

Even if nobody had to answer for the safety and poor condition of the Gubbangen track that fateful May evening in 1976, the accident provoked a wide and positive debate about safety issues. Nowadays, many of the fences surrounding tracks in both Sweden and England are so much better than they were in Tommy's day.

If only an air-fence had been in place at Gubbangen when Tommy crashed there. Had that been the case, he would have got up on his feet, brushed the dirt off his black and white leathers and joined the re-start of heat four of the Swedish Final qualifier in Stockholm.

The phrase 'what if' constantly comes back to Joel and Inga-Lill and that is what has made them suffer since their son died doing what he loved more than anything else. Only those who have lost their own child can even begin to imagine the full horror of the Jansson family's nightmare experience.

What if Tommy had been first out of the gate that fateful night?

What if Lars Jansson hadn't lost control of his bike on the rough track?

What if Tommy hadn't tried to pass Lars at exactly that moment, and had done so instead just a second or so earlier or later?

Joel and Inga-Lill treasures all the memories from the years in which their youngest son lived. Sometimes they think that Tommy lived a short life but he still experienced more things in his 23 years than most people do even if they live to be a hundred.

But often they'll return to the same phrase.

What if...?

What if...?

And ever since the accident that took her son's life, Inga-Lill can't bear to watch a single race without thinking again how dangerous the sport is. It doesn't matter who's in the race or how exciting it is.

The only thing Inga-Lill feels is worry for the riders competing.

Shannon Ruane have been offered £400 for her scrapbooks in which she keeps her photos of Tommy, along with autographs, newspaper cuttings and the pink piece of paper preserving the dirt from Tommy's leathers.

"Of course I feel a little stupid looking at this stuff today but I was a young girl at the time. I was crazy about him," she smiles.

These days Shannon works at a nursing home. She lives in Kent with her partner, Steve, and has a good relationship with her two adult daughters.

For Shannon it was not better in the past.

When she grew up as Shannon Laurence in the rough area of Wye Street, Battersea, SW11, it was with a mother who was poor – Shannon's father had left home for good when his daughter was very young. Her mother met a new man, but he became a nightmare for both Shannon and her mother, and life wasn't comfortable for them until he was out of the picture.

For Shannon growing up, happiness in life meant speedway. The best moments of her teenage years were when she could get away from home, escape the rough reality and an abusive stepfather.

The golden moments at Plough Lane meant a chance for her to feel real joy, and to laugh and celebrate. Just have fun and feel the thrill when her idol recognised her and said: "Hello, Curly Head."

Shannon doesn't hesitate when she says: "I had some tough years growing up. If it hadn't been for speedway and Tommy, things would have gone bad for me."

When Tommy died it was as if Shannon had lost a member of her own family. She still recalls with horror the morning paper and the headline Speed Ace Killed – and that day she had to be sent home from school because she cried so much.

But the fact that she had so many great memories thanks to the sport made her strong and kept her going in life. Later on she lost interest in speedway but it was rekindled a few years ago and in 2005 she helped out with a bit of rider sponsorship.

"Speedway gave me so much joy when I grew up," she says. "Now I want to give back to the sport any way I can. Maybe you can say it's like going full circle. What's so great about the sport is how much joy it gives people."

Shannon never had a son. "If I had, I would have immediately named him Tommy," she admits.

She knows at least two Wimbledon supporters who have named their sons Tommy, after the Dons' Swedish legend and one of the most popular riders to ever wear the famous yellow star.

Shannon has two daughters, Emma and Sophie. Emma has Inga as her middle name – after Tommy's mother. Shannon explains: "I think Inga is a beautiful name, and I also gave it to my daughter to honour Tommy's memory."

Shannon can talk for hours about Tommy Jansson and the golden years of the early 70s at Plough Lane.

"Those of us who got the opportunity to experience Tommy's time at Wimbledon are very lucky.

"And we will never forget him."

Index

More publications from Retro Speedway

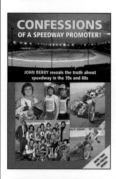
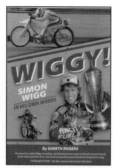
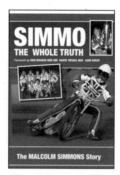
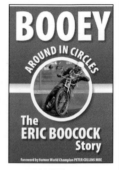